Rural Arab Demography
and
Early Jewish Settlement
in Palestine

Rural Arab Demography
and
Early Jewish Settlement
in Palestine

*Distribution and Population Density during
the Late Ottoman and Early Mandate Periods*

David Grossman

Translated by Marcia Grossman

Routledge
Taylor & Francis Group

LONDON AND NEW YORK

This edition is published by arrangement with The Hebrew University Magnes Press Ltd., Jerusalem
with the assistance of The James Amzalak Fund for Research in Historical Geography
In the series ISRAEL STUDIES IN HISTORICAL GEOGRAPHY
Edited by Yehoshua Ben-Arieh and Ruth Kark

First published 2011 by Transaction Publishers

2 Park Square, Milton Park, Abingdon, Oxfordshire OX14 4RN
711 Third Avenue, New York, NY 10017

Routledge is an imprint of the Taylor & Francis Group, an informa business

First issued in paperback 2017

Library of Congress Catalog Number: 2010027867

Library of Congress Cataloging-in-Publication Data

Grossman, David, 1934-
    [Ha-Ukhlusiyah ha-'Arvit veha-ma'ahaz ha-Yehudi. English]
    Rural Arab demography and early Jewish settlement in Palestine : distribution and population density during the late Ottoman and Mandate periods / David Grossman ; translated by Marcia Grossman.
        p. cm.
    Includes bibliographical references and index.
    ISBN 978-1-4128-1466-9 (alk. paper)
        1. Land settlement--Palestine--History--19th century. 2. Land settlement--Palestine--History--20th century. 3. Jews--Palestine--Population. 4. Arabs--Palestine--Population. 5. Palestine--Population--History. 6. Palestine--History--1799-1917. 7. Palestine--History--1917-1948. I. Title.

HD1516.P18G7813 2010
304.6095694'09041--dc22

2010027867

ISBN 13: 978-1-4128-1466-9 (hbk)
ISBN 13: 978-1-138-51430-0 (pbk)

IN MEMORY OF

My sister, Sara Grossman Wacksztok

and

my niece, Rachel Grossman Toyber

Contents

List of Illustrations

Chapter 1

Figures

Fig. 1.1: *Fallah's* home
Note the three levels: Bottom – Animals; Center – Human dwelling (and sleeping area); Top – Storage area.
Source: Wilson, C.W., *The Land of Judea & The Jerusalem Environs,* Republished by Ely Schiller, 1976, p. 9. Courtesy of Mr. Ely Schiller, the publication rights holder.

Fig. 1.2: Head portage by women
Source: Manning, S.*, Those Holy Fields: Palestine Illustrated by Pen and Pencil*. Republished by Ely Schiller, 1976, p. 24. Courtesy of Mr. Ely Schiller, the publication rights holder.

Fig. 1.3: Boat owners and sailors in Jaffa Port
Note the rocks and the two sailing ships in the distant background. Because of the risky passage, passengers were transferred from the ship to the port by boats.
Source: Jacob Landau, *Eretz Israel in the days of Abdul Hamid,* Jerusalem: Carta, 1979 (Hebrew), p. 142. Courtesy of Professor Jacob Landau, who holds publication rights over this book.

Fig. 1.4: Activities on the threshing floor
Note the use of oxen for the threshing work.
Source: Wilson, C.W., *The Land of Judea & The Jerusalem Environs,* Republished by Ely Schiller, 1976, p. 107. Courtesy of Mr. Ely Schiller, the publication rights holder.

Fig. 1.5: Plowing hilly land near Jerusalem
Source: Manning, S., *Those Holy Fields: Palestine Illustrated*

by Pen and Pencil. Republished by Mr Ely Schiller, 1976, p. 17. Courtesy of Mr. Ely Schiller, the publication rights holder.

Chapter 2

Figures

Fig. 2.1: Ibrahim Pasha's military camp near Jaffa, 1836
   Source: W.H., Bartlett, *Jerusalem Revisited,* 1855. Reprinted in R. Kark, *Jaffa, A City in Evolution, 1799-1917,* Jerusalem: Ariel Publishig House, 2003,1976 p. 16 (Hebrew). By courtesy of Professor Ruth Kark and Mr. Ely Schiller, the publication rights holders.

Fig. 2.2: Egyptian cameo found in Jaffa
   Source: Found in Jaffa. Courtesy of Professor Ruth Kark who holds the copyrights of its publication.

Fig. 2.3: Ruins of a watermill in Mir
   Note the ruins located near the copious fountains of the Yarkon. Mir was settled by former Egyptian mill workers.
   Source: Professsor Shmuel Avitzur, *On the Banks of the Yarkon River, 1947,* Tel Aviv: Dvir, 1980 (Hebrew), p. 91. Courtesy of Ms Nili Keinan, heir of the late Professor Shmuel Avitzur, who holds the publication rights of this book.

Fig. 2.4: Two types of *Antilyas*
   Note the camels that operate both types.
   Source: Professsor Shmuel Avitzur, *Man and His Labor, Atlas of the History of Work Tools and Production Equipments in Eretz Israel*, Jerusalem Carta, 1976 (Hebrew), p. 63. Courtesy of Ms Nili Keinan, heir of the late Professor Shmuel Avitzur, who holds publication rights of this book.

Fig. 2.5: The Bosnian village inside ruins of Caesarea
   Source: Zvi Ilan, "Turkmen, Circassians and Bosnians in the northern Sharon," David Grossman, Avi Degani and Avshalom Shmueli (eds.), Hasharon Between Yarkon and Carmel, Tel Aviv: Eretz and Ministry of Defense, 1990 (Hebrew), p. 285. Courtesy of Professor Avi Degani, Editor of Eretz Series, who holds the rights of publication of this book.

Fig. 2.6: The house of the former Bosnian *Bek* of the *nahiya* of Caesare
   Source: Zvi Ilan, "Turkmen, Circassians and Bosnians in the northern Sharon," David Grossman, Avi Degani and Avshalom Shmueli (eds.), *Hasharon Between Yarkon and Carmel*, Tel Aviv: Eretz and Ministry of Defense 1990 (Hebrew), p. 281. Courtesy of Avi Degani,

Editor of Eretz Series, who holds the rights of publication of this book.

Maps

Map 2.1: Egyptians in the coastal plain
  Source: Drawn by David Grossman.

Map 2.2: Jaffa's *saknat* (detached neighborhoods),
  Source: Palestine Exploration Fund, Sheet 13 of 26 sheets, 1878, modified by David Grossman

Map 2.3: Saknat Abu Kabir and the surrounding citrus groves
  Source: Professor Ruth Kark, "Jaffa, from village to town, changes in urban structure," David Grossman (ed.), *Between Yarkon and Ayalon, Studies on the Dan zone and the Lod Valley,* Ramat-Gan: Bar-Ilan University Press, 1983 (Hebrew), p 114. Courtesy of Professor Ruth Kark who holds the copyrights of its publication.

Map 2.4: Egyptian families in Samaria
  Source: Drawn by David Grossman.

Map 2.5: Egyptian dispersal and settlement process in Palestine
  Source: Drawn by David Grossman

Map 2.6: Jewish settlement distribution in the period 1918-1948
  Source: *New Israel Atlas*, Tel Aviv: Survey of Israel, 1995 (Hebrew), p. 46. Courtesy of Survey of Israel. All rights reserved by the Survey of Israel © 2010.

Map 2.7: Algerian settlements: Distribution pattern
  Source: Drawn by David Grossman.

Map 2.8: Distributions of Circassians and Bosnians in Palestine
  Source: Drawn by David Grossman.

Map 2.9: Plan of Bosnian village in Caesarea, drawn by G. Schumacher
  Source: Zvi Ilan, Turkmen, "Circassians and Bosnians in the northern Sharon," David Grossman, Avi Degani and Avshalom Shmueli (eds.), Hasharon Between Yarkon and Carmel, Tel Aviv: Eretz and Ministry of Defense, 1990 (Hebrew), p. 282. Courtesy of Professor Avi Degani, Editor of Eretz Series, who holds the rights of publication of this book.

Chapter 3

Figure

Fig. 3.1: A page from the Syrian H 1288 Yearbook (1871/2)
  Source: Salname (Yearbook) of Vilayet Suriye, Hijra year 1288 (1871/2).

Chapter 4

Chapter 5

Note that a major part of the basin is flooded.

Source: Photographed by David Grossman in the early 1990s.

Fig. 5.6: Part of Beit Netofa basin, summer season

Note that practically all the land is under cultivation.

Source: Photographed by David Grossman in the early 1990s.

Fig. 5.7: Cave dwelling in S. Hebron

Note: Some of the caves are (still) occupied by *fallaheen* (pl. of *fallah)* and their flocks in the winter season. During the rest of the year the *fallaheen* lived in their permanent houses or wandered in the area in search of pasture for their herds.

Source: Photographed by D. Grossman c. 1980.

Maps

Map 5.1: Swamps in Palestine, 1925

Source: The map was prepared for the annual report of the Mandate government to the League of Nations.

Chapter 6

Figures

Fig. 6.1: Intensive irrigation close to Bethlehem, in an area of copious water springs

Source: Photographed by David Grossman, January 1985.

Fig. 6.2: Plowing rough land, probably near Nablus (near ancient Shechem)

Source: Jacob Landau, *Eretz Israel in the days of Abdul Hamid,* Jerusalem: Carta, 1979 (Hebrew), p. 91. Courtesy of Professor Jacob Landau, who holds publication rights of this book.

Fig. 6.3: Irrigated fruit trees and other crops in a wide basin in Fari'a Valley, east of Nablus

Source: Photographed by David Grossman in the late 1970s.

Fig. 6.4: Low grade soils on a rocky hill in southern Shefar'am {Shafa'amar}sub-*nahiya*

Source: Photographed by David Grossman, December 1990.

Charts

Chart 6.1: Adjusted hectares of agricultural land per person: Jerusalem District. *Nahiyas* or Their Parts, 1871/2-1945

Chart 6.2: Adjusted hectares of agricultural land per person: Acre Rural Zones 1871/2,-1945. *Nahiyas* or their part.

Chart 6.3: Adjusted hectares of agricultural land per person: Nablus Rural Zones 1871/2-1945

Chart 6.4: Jewish and Arab adjusted hectares of agricultural land per

Preface

This book covers the late Ottoman period (mainly 1870-1917), but since agrarian subjects are still a major politically-charged issue, it also draws largely on data from the British Mandate period (1917-1948). The earlier part of the book focuses, however, on demographic topics, specifically on migrations, size, density, population growth and the pattern of distribution in rural Palestine before the inception of the Jewish rural settlement (1882). The discussion devotes a full chapter to tracing the little-known Muslim ethnic groups in Palestine's rural areas. The largest group consisted of Egyptians, but Algerians, Bosnians and Circassians also settled in rural areas of the country. Their settlement zones coincided with those that eventually became the Jewish core areas and the present State of Israel. The direct factors behind the migratory waves were political and socio-economic ones, but natural resource instability also played a significant role. The Arabs arriving in Palestine in earlier centuries were more widely distributed. Their core rural zones were in the central mountain axis, but also in the coastal plains of Gaza and in the Galilee.

The findings are based on a critical evaluation of Ottoman data. My regional approach and personal field work facilitated the evaluation of both quantitative and descriptive data on the impact of Arab and Jewish settlement processes and patterns as well as on the effects of both groups on agricultural resources. Some of the main conclusions are:

- The density of the rural Arab population in the zones occupied by the Jews, after 1882, was about one third of that the Arab core zones.
- Between 1870 and 1945 in the decline in the rural Arab per capita farmland was mainly due to population growth. The impact of Jewish land purchases was much lower.
- The spatial pattern of the Egyptian and other Muslim migrant groups was similar to that of the Jews. Their destinations were mostly in sparsely settled areas.

These and other basic facts could have provided a rational basis for Arab-Jewish cooperation which might have resulted in mutual benefit, but emotions, incitement and fears were stronger than simple reasoning. The same attitude prevails even in the twenty-first century, after almost a hundred and thirty years. Will it continue to last for a similar length of time in the future as well?

Purpose, Subjects, and Research Contribution

This volume explores the distribution of the rural population in Palestine at the onset of the last third of the nineteenth century (about 1870). But the need for background information necessitated the moving of the starting date earlier. Because of the scarcity of agrarian data, it was also necessary to extend the discussion towards the end of the British Mandate period—1945, when the last Village Statistics list was available. This was especially vital in chapter 6, which discussed concepts and issues dealing with the dwindling agricultural land reserves. This extension was also vital for assessing the impact of Jewish land acquisitions on the availability of agricultural land for Arab farmers. My search for explanations for the rural population distribution according to the official zones also required the extension of the time-scale to events that took place both before 1870 and beyond the end of the Ottoman period (1917).

This volume is the translation, but also a partly updated, shortened, and revised version of the Hebrew book which was published in 2004 by Magnes Press. This English volume is more suitable for laymen than the original, but like the earlier text, it is mainly targeted for (English-speaking) academic communities of geographers, demographers, and historians who are interested in the subject matter, but are not necessarily familiar with the spatial and political structure of Palestine. I expect that a number of the findings will arouse controversy among some readers. This should be considered a welcome result, testifying to the achievement of the book's contribution to an exchange of information and ideas concerning controversial issues.

The findings of this volume confirm that during the formative period of the rural Jewish settlement process, the new villages were established mostly in sparsely settled zones. This is not totally new, but the method that I used to tackle this question is an innovative regional approach that facilitated the identification of Jewish settlement regions more effectively and precisely than previous studies. My efforts to delineate the Jewish settlement zones were based largely on modifications of the Ottoman 1871/2 administrative boundaries; that is, by subdividing the latter, where necessary, by grouping village territories. This regional-based method necessitated keeping the territorial boundaries constant for about a half century, from the early 1870s to 1922. The latter date marked the first British census which provided a comparative data-base that I consulted for validating and verifying the Ottoman data of c. 1870. The bottom line of my conclusion is that the early generation of Zionist settlers differed from many members of the post-1967 generation, who targeted for settlement the densely settled Arab lands rather than the low-density areas that the pioneers favored.

I do not intend to detail here the methodological problems encountered. I moved much of this material to the notes to avoid bothering the reader with cumbersome details. Some of the issues, however, especially the problem of calculating the population size when the official lists contain households only, are discussed in the text. I also encountered incorrect arithmetic calculations and a lack of adequate maps.

In addition to the basic data sources mentioned above, which were drawn from the Provincial Syrian Yearbook for the *hijra* year 1288 (1871/2), I was aided by the findings of numerous research studies on the Arab rural scene and on records of the events that shaped the timing of the demographic fluctuations. I have also been assisted by my own field research, including oral interviews with village heads that were carried out over the past thirty years. Comparing this information with written references enabled me to judge the validity of the field data. On the basis of these sources I concluded that the official 1871/2 data are reasonably acceptable, even though they are not absolutely accurate.

I believe that the contribution of this book extends beyond the limited specific case that it discusses in detail. The first chapter deals with the major factors that affected population size and distribution. The discussion of non-Jewish migrations and settlement (chapter 2), particularly the large Egyptian one, reduced the land reserves available for later migratory waves. The book's core chapters are 3 through 6. They review earlier findings, present additional sources and discuss the regional system adopted for the analysis of the data. They also contain, where necessary, concepts and theories that help to explain the data.

The study culminated in the sixth chapter, which deals with agricultural density (the amount of farmland per person). My estimates were based on three sets of data that extend over three-quarters of a century (1871/2, 1922, 1945). Generally, land scarcity was a serious problem in the Arab core zones (where Jewish settlement was minimal) by 1945 because agricultural land reserves were not adequate for sustaining the growing population rate (2.5 percent).

The seventh chapter is devoted to general conclusions. It contains a discussion of the Jewish settlement process in relation to land quality and dwindling land supply plus a section devoted to the Bedouin population which was not enumerated either in the1871/2 publication or in the British census of 1922.

Some of the main conclusions of this study are:

- The size of the rural Arab population in the zones occupied by Jews after 1882 was about one tenth of that which occupied the Arab core zones.
- Most Egyptian settlement areas coincided with those of the Jewish zones.
- Between 1870 and 1945, the decline of Arab per capita farmland was mainly due to Arab population growth rather than Jewish land acquisitions.
- Most of the migrants' (Jewish and Muslim) settlement zones were "leftovers" characterized by some form of resource "disability."

Acknowledgments

At this point I would like to express my gratitude to the many people who aided me in this project. A great number of them are not even known to me by name. Some are the people who were interviewed in this study, but my concern is that I will not be able to properly thank those whose names I do know.

Let me start by mentioning those who are no longer with us. Shim'on Ben-Shemesh, the late chairperson of the Jewish National Fund Institute of Land Use and Land Policy Research, and his colleague, Alexander Posnanski, were instrumental in initiating and supporting the study on which this book is based. They also made many useful comments on its first Hebrew draft. I also wish to mention Professor David H.K. Amiran, an Israel Prize Laureate, who died shortly before my Hebrew version was published. His teaching and advice were instrumental in laying the foundation for the geographical approach that I have adopted in the present volume.

I am happy to be able to express my gratitude to my living teachers and colleagues, Professors Moshe Brawer and Yehoshua Ben-Arieh, both of whom contributed to the fruition of this project, and assisted me during the long years of our shared interest in the historical and rural geography of Palestine. Professor Ben-Arieh has been instrumental in advising me throughout my present and previous research publications. He and Professor Ruth Kark accepted my request to include the present English volume in the series Israel Studies in Historical Geography. Ruth Kark has collaborated with me on a number of previous publications which are related to the present work, and I have greatly benefited from her knowledge and scientific approach. I am also indebted to Professor Nahum Gross who read the original Hebrew manuscript and made useful comments. My colleagues, Professors Gideon Biger and Yossi Ben-Artzi also read and commented on parts of the earlier version. I am grateful for their constructive critical comments and suggestions. Of course, none of the persons mentioned above is responsible for errors that may still exist in any part of this book.

I would also like to express my appreciation for the assistance that I received from the staff of my publishers, Magnes Press. Dan Benovici, the former director, and Hai Tzabar, the present director, who both took an active part in shaping this volume and encouraged me to improve its contents and style. Tali Amir contributed to the improvement of the original Hebrew version and Joan Hooper edited the English version.

I am grateful to my assistant, Netanel Halabi, who was especially helpful in translating and transliterating Arabic words. Dr. David Sivan also deserves my deep gratitude for obtaining data on the population of the Israeli Bedouin tribes and recording them. I am also obliged to Shawki Hon, the manager of the Rehaniya Circassian Museum for filling in gaps in my knowledge. I am indebted also to the staff of the Cartography and Remote Sensing Laboratory of the Department of Geography and Environment of Bar-Ilan University. Moises (Moy) Zonana and Efrat Morag were indispensable in drawing the maps and contributing to the translation of the illustrations for the present English version, and to our former students, Yafit Cohen, Orli Hayami, and Lev Kornibad, who contributed to the Hebrew edition and indirectly to the present volume. The meticulous requirements of Magnes Press placed a great burden on them, but they successfully faced the challenge.

I owe heartfelt gratitude to my friend, Professor Martin Glassner of Southern Connecticut State University, who hosted me in his department for my 1993/4 sabbatical year. His assistance enabled me to spend 1993/4 in New Haven, consulting the rich library of Yale University. He has also provided helpful comments on a late version of the present manuscript.

I am also indebted to Professors Michael P. Conzen and Marvin Mikesell of the Committee on Geographical Studies, the University of Chicago. The months I spent with them and at the University libraries enabled me to enrich my archival sources, especially of the Ottoman Yearbooks. The staffs of both universities were more than helpful in granting my every need.

The academic foundations and institutions which enabled this research project include: the Commission for the Encouragement of Research at Bar-Ilan University, the Schnitzer Foundation for Research in Social and Economic Policy in Israel at Bar-Ilan University and the Littaure Foundation. I am indebted to Bar-Ilan University's previous rector, Professor Hanokh Lavi, and to the present rector, Professor Yossi Manes, for their assistance in the publication and translation of this book.

Finally, I must also mention the help given me by my family. My children repeatedly rescued me from computer problems that seem so "elementary" to their generation. My wife Marcia (Michal) Grossman served as the main translator from the Hebrew version of this book into English. She also proofread both manuscripts and gave intelligent advice on many parts of the text. Two other persons who contributed to the translation work are Shulamit Berman and Helene Landau. I thank both of them for their meticulous and thorough work.

1

Economic, Social, and Political Background

Introduction

The road leading from Gaza to the north was only a summer track suitable for transport by camels and carts…. In the rainy season it was impassable.

In the villages on both sides of the track … no orange groves, orchards or vineyards were to be seen until one reached Yabna Village. Trees generally were a rare sight in these villages…. Nor were there any vegetable gardens to be seen in any of these villages except at Jora on the sea (Asqalan). In the Hawakir around the villages—small plots fenced around by cactus hedge—one could find in the winter green onions and in the summer cucumbers and water melons.

In all the villages … between Gaza and Jaffa there was only one well in the village and in the smaller villages there were no wells at all…. Not in a single village in all this area was water used for irrigation. Water was scantily used for drinking purposes by man and beast.

Houses were all of mud. No windows were anywhere to be seen. The roofs were of caked mud. Every house was divided in two parts—one part slightly elevated above the other. The family lived in the elevated part while in the lower part the cattle were housed. The cattle were small and poor. So were the chickens [see figure 1.1].

The fields were sown with wheat, barley, kursena and lentils in the winter and with dura and sesame in the summer. Fields used for summer crops one year were sown with winter crops the next year, and so in rotation. The ploughs used were of wood…. Not a village could boast of a cart. Sowing was done by hand; harvesting by the scythe and threshing by animals. Fields were never manured.

The lands were all held in *musha'a* ownership. Every second year the fields were measured by stick and rope and distributed among the cultivators. Division of land always led to strife and bloodshed.

The yields were very poor. Wheat yield never exceeded 60 kgs per dunum and barley about 100 kgs per dunum. The wheat yield went to the government in payment of the tithe and to the *effendi* in payment of interest on loans. The *fallah* himself made his bread from dura.

The sanitary conditions in the villages were horrible. Schools did not exist and the younger generation rolled about in the mud of the streets. The rate of infant mortality was very high. There was no medical service in any of the villages distant from a Jewish settlement. In passing a village one noticed a large number of blind, or half-blind persons. Malaria was rampant.[1]

Fig. 1.1
Fallah's home

Source: Wilson, C.W., *The Land of Judea & The Jerusalem Environs,* Republished by Ely Schiller, 1976, p. 9. Courtesy of Mr. Ely Schiller, the publication rights holder.

This 1913 description which, according to the Royal Commission's report, was written by a Jewish traveler (whose name was not disclosed) reveals that even as late as the second decade of the twentieth century, the condition of the rural Arab population was unsatisfactory. Agricultural tools, the system of cultivation, and, most importantly, human welfare had hardly started to improve as a result of the economic and technological benefits of the modern system.

The purpose of this book is to discuss the subjects that were either directly or indirectly related to demographic change or were likely to have shaped the population of Palestine growth rate and its socio-economic transformation. This introductory chapter is devoted to a discussion of the topics that this 1913 citation has highlighted and the circumstances that account for the poverty and the misery that emerge from this succinct, but nevertheless quite detailed, account. My treatise focuses on some of the natural and man-made factors that were known to have had a significant impact on the use of resources and on other economic factors. It focuses, however, primarily on demographic issues.

Timing the Inception of Modern Economic Development

During the second half of the nineteenth century, Palestine played an important economic role in the Ottoman Empire. It entered this era in a very poor state, but the Crimean War of 1853-1856 brought a significant political change. The involvement of European powers, and their contribution to the eventual victory of the Ottomans over the Russians, raised foreign involvement in the country's political and economic affairs. The war generated demand for food and raw materials that were the major export goods of the empire. The end of the Crimean War (1856) was, according to many experts, a major economic turning point because of the decisive European impact on the successful campaign. The war caused, however, several undesired economic results, the worst of which was the large debt that the Ottomans accumulated as a result of it. They never managed to repay these debts, and one consequence was that by 1873 there was a severe financial crisis that forced the Ottoman administration to submit to an international debt management program.[2]

Whatever the impact of the war on the Empire, there is some disagreement about the Crimean War's role in shaping economic development and the demographic change that accompanied it in Palestine. Most historians agree that there was some success during the second half of the nineteenth century, but do not agree about the exact time of its occurrence. The dating of the inception of change varies partly with ideological or other biases, but it is also affected by the perception of the relative importance of various forces that account for modernization and development.

Many Jewish researchers tend to consider the First *Aliyah* (Jewish migration into Palestine), that was directed mostly to rural areas after 1882, as the starting point of Palestinian economic development. This event accounted, according to its promoters, for long-term development, which was more important than that of any other occurrence. This is the position taken by economic historian Nahum Gross[3] who emphasizes the decisive impact of Jewish capital investment by Baron Edmond de Rothschild and other Jewish investors in the Palestinian economy. The rise of the Hovevey Zion movement (The Lovers of Zion that preceded the 1897 founding of the Zionist Movement) was, according to him, vital for creating the necessary conditions for lasting economic progress.

Other scholars took a different position. They admitted that European migrants and commercial interests that followed the Crimean War played a significant role in shaping the modern sector, but they emphasized the important role of internal forces that took place mainly after 1865, when most of the negative impacts of the war were no longer felt. They believed that it was the rising economic involvement of local communities (including local Jews and Christian inhabitants), and particularly their investments in manufacturing and crafts, that triggered the onset of development.[4]

The 1831 conquest of Palestine by Muhammad Ali was also a major turning point that strongly affected Palestine. But it did not last long, because the Egyptian army was forced to retreat in 1840. The next decade was among the most chaotic of the century. The year of the publication of *hatt-i-sherif* (an Honorable Decree), 1839, that opened the period of the *tanzimat* (reforms) and continued on through the early 1870s, was a significant socio-economic take-off, but its impact on Palestine was hardly felt, because of the chaotic conditions that accompanied the retreat of Muhammad Ali's army in 1840. The eruption of the Crimean War worsened the already deteriorated security, because most of the military forces were diverted to the front and, consequently, the local forces were thinned out.

The internal conflicts of the 1840s and 1850s were partly the result of settling of blood revenges and other forms of lawlessness, which were partly "postponed" from the 1830s because the Egyptian governor, Ibrahim Pasha (Muhammad Ali's son), managed to establish security by means of harsh punishment for local infighting and other forms of violence (see additional details in chapter 2).[5]

Among modern Palestinian historians there is an additional theory pertaining to the onset of the development process. It is based partly on events of the Muhammad Ali era, but its main argument is based on the assumption that the onset of development preceded the mid-nineteenth century. In fact, this school of thought argues that the Western Powers were responsible for the collapse of the development process, rather than for its promotion. Bashara Doumani, who is a leading representative of this Palestinian-centered school, claimed that the city of Nablus sowed the seeds of the regional development. Even though its industry was based mainly on the production of soap (a byproduct of olive oil presses), the central location had a highly effective network of commercial relations that dealt in cotton, olive oil, and various grain products. Therefore, it had the potential to develop into the economic and political center of southern Syria. The intervention of the Western Powers and the expulsion of the Egyptian army dealt a severe blow to Nablus's progress, because it shifted the pole of development from Nablus to Jerusalem and the coastal cities.[6]

Advancing the onset of development to the early decades of the century, or even to an earlier date, contradicts the accepted opinion of most scholars that modern development roots were not a result of Nablus's early traditional crafts and industries. The changes initiated during the *tanzimat* period (1839-1870) laid the legal foundation for many basic economic principles that had an impact on the process of development. Among the fundamental secular laws that were enacted were the 1858 Land Code whose significance will be treated in some detail below and the Local Government Reform of 1864. Even if these laws had no immediate effect, they laid the basic infrastructure for modern economic development. Doumani's hypothesis, which is based on the assumption that *tanzimat* did more harm than good, also ignores the impact of the post-1876 period, the year of Sultan Abdul Hamid II's accession to the throne that is widely considered as the resumption of central authority that stimulated economic development.[7] In fact, it coincided roughly with the onset of the Jewish immigration and with those of German Templers (whose earliest colony was established in Haifa in 1868) and other European ethnic and religious groups.

Furthermore one may doubt that Nablus had a real chance to compete with the emerging coastal towns. The relative decline of Nablus and its environs was indeed related to the transfer of the economic core from the inland town to coastal areas, but this can hardly be blamed on the central government. Furthermore, even Jerusalem, which was the administrative capital and was clearly favored by the British administration, was unable to surpass Haifa, Jaffa, and, later, Tel Aviv in economic importance.

An even more outstanding example is Haleb (Aleppo), whose location gave it, when camel transportation was the norm, a prominent position on the main road between Syria and Iraq. It was, in fact, the third most important economic center in the Ottoman Empire (after Istanbul and Cairo).[8] This position was lost when coastal trade replaced inland commerce. It is unlikely, thus, that the government could have prevented this change even if it had desired to do so. The phenomenon of the transfer of economic activity from interior parts of country to coastal areas was indeed worldwide. It occurred because of far-reaching changes in transportation and commerce. In the Middle East, dependency on camel caravans was gradually displaced by steamship transportation during the nineteenth century because water routes were cheaper and also because of a basic change in the direction of commerce.

This transformation hurt interior cities and sped up the development of the coastal areas of Palestine. The attempt to relate these changes to the government's direct policy decisions has no basis. In fact, the few industries in Nablus also benefited from the progress in the emerging coastal trade.[9] The question "What would have happened if there had been no new economic-technological development?" is interesting, but clearly irrelevant.

There were many reasons for the widening economic gap between the internal towns and those of the plains. The gradual transition to modernity brought about structural changes in building materials, in technology, in organization, and in class status. Neither local nor central Ottoman governments had the means to arrest these changes or to modify them and adjust them to a more desired spatial orientation. In fact, only towards the end of the nineteenth century did the central government begin to adopt a policy of economic investment: increased expenditures on infrastructure, fiscal policies intended to encourage investors, industrial growth, and the creation of an agricultural bank. But the enactment of legal reforms did not always bring about the desired results, because they were not accompanied by a parallel change in administrative efficiency. These policies would have been more effective if the new legal progress had been accompanied by a proper implementation system, which would have made the new developments accessible to the poor *fallaheen* (peasants; plural of *fallah*). Unfortunately, this was usually not done.

The Physical Infrastructure

Infrastructure is vital for human survival and its improper functioning is a prime stumbling block to economic development. Without adequate transportation facilities, emergency services or first aid installments are ineffective and places located far from adequate roads may even be exposed to death in emergency cases. Infrastructure is, therefore, a main demographic factor. Peripheral locations and other areas of inadequate accessibility lagged behind urban areas, not only in purely economic terms, but also in demographic growth. Their death rates were still high even during the later nineteenth century when the core regions were already experiencing a reduction of death rates. The poor state of the roads was a major impediment even after the invention of the automobile and the end of the Ottoman era. In fact, it took about two decades after the onset of British rule to complete the construction of a paved road that connected Jaffa and Tel Aviv with Haifa.

Poor accessibility of the rural areas impaired an additional essential vital "resource" for development: human interaction (aside from the most immediate local level). Without it, not only commerce and industry, but also the possibility of exchanging ideas, the transmission of information and the diffusion of inventions were badly affected. The obstacles to the flow of information thus completed the vicious cycle of a poor economy that led to the lowering of the possibilities for improving economic production and prevented the elimination of poverty. In rural areas the main means of transportation consisting of animal power and head portage was fairly widespread. It was prevalent particularly among women (figure 1.2).

It is not surprising that the poor physical condition of the Palestinian infrastructure was repeatedly mentioned in consular reports of the Western powers. An example is an American document dealing with the commercial potential of Palestinian agriculture. It contained a long discussion of the problems associated with marketing the grains of the Hauran area, considered to be the bread basket of Syria and Palestine.[10] Even though large amounts of grain grew in the area, the distance to the Mediterranean seashore and the poor roads connecting them made the ports totally dependent on transportation by camel caravans. This substantially raised the shipping costs, and when world grain prices dropped, export was no longer profitable.[11] This was the case during the 1870s. The crops were of good quality, but the high price of hauling them to the port compared negatively with the relatively low prices of grains in Europe after the completion of the American railroad system (in the

Fig. 1.2
Head portage by women

Source: Manning, S., *Those Holy Fields: Palestine Illustrated by Pen and Pencil*.
Republished by Ely Schiller, 1976, p. 24. Courtesy of Mr. Ely Schiller, the publication
rights holder.

1860s). The outcome was the loss of the Hauran's former comparative
advantage in the world market. The impact of American agricultural
mechanization and other technological developments in the American
farm sector made it increasingly difficult to export grains, even for the
more accessible coastal plain producers.

The first railway tracks in the Ottoman Empire were laid only in 1869, mainly in order to connect the European provinces with the capital. A rail line had been planned to connect Istanbul with Anatolia and other remote places, but the British company that was responsible for the project delayed its completion for a long period and the rail tracks to Ankara were finally laid down only several years later. This delay provides an unusual insight into the vital importance of communication. During 1874 there was a drought that resulted in a severe famine that lasted into the next year. The most hard-hit area was Anatolia. The government provided some help, but because of the absence of effective means of transportation, its assistance failed to reach many of the worst affected areas. In January 1875 Ottoman officials complained to the British ambassador, Sir Henry Elliot, that "if the railway had been extended to Ankara as [the British] had intended the devastating famine of 1874-75 would not have occurred."[12] The severe financial collapse of the Empire, that reached a climax during 1875, aggravated the effects of the natural disaster. The blow to the farm sector erased the last hope of the administration to avert the financial crisis.[13]

The primary purpose of the Ottoman rail lines was actually to improve the administrative link between the center and the provinces, rather than to generate commercial and industrial development.[14] Much of the vast Turkish interior was obviously far from the railroad line, and the transportation that was introduced had, therefore, less economic impact than was expected. The effectiveness of transportation was less effective for reducing the poverty and deprivation. The most deprived were the inhabitants of the poorly accessible peripheries who could not afford to travel to the nearest towns for medical assistance or schooling. The results were high illiteracy, high infant mortality, and low life expectancy. The inefficient and corrupt bureaucracy discouraged investments by local and foreign businessmen in these areas.

In rural Palestine the plight of the periphery was fairly similar. The rudimentary infrastructure impaired access to social and economic services. Suggestions to improve the infrastructure, mainly for linking the main economic and political centers, were not totally absent, but very few were implemented. By the 1870s, according to one of the sources, the government was presented with a plan to rebuild the hazardous Jaffa port (see figure 1.3) and construct a rail line connecting it and Jerusalem, but, apparently for political reasons, the idea was rejected by the authorities. Foreign businessmen and politicians were also responsible for the inaction, partly because they doubted that the rail line project

Fig. 1.3
Boat owners and sailors in Jaffa Port

Source: Jacob Landau, *Eretz Israel in the days of Abdul Hamid,* Jerusalem: Carta, 1979
(Hebrew), p. 142. Courtesy of Professor Jacob Landau, who holds publication rights
over this book.

would be profitable. The British consul complained that Jerusalem had
no commerce and no real industry and, therefore, foreign investors were
not enthusiastic about projects to improve transportation facilities.[15]

The principal considerations of the British government appear to have
been essentially politically and religiously motivated. They were concerned that a railway line would increase the influence of the Russians
and the French, since the main beneficiaries would be Russian-Orthodox
and Catholic pilgrims, and even Jews. The French Catholics were, in
fact, those who showed the greatest interest in the rail line project. But
the policy of the Ottoman officials was more similar to that of the British, since they too were worried that the train would increase foreign
involvement and decrease their own control over the region.[16] The Jaffa-
Jerusalem rail line was eventually completed only in 1892.

The laying of tracks to places of religious importance, like Mecca
and Medina, was a different matter. The line from Haifa to Dar'a, in
the Hauran, which was completed in 1905 and linked with the Damas-
cus-Hijaz railroad, was, therefore, an achievement that was acclaimed
without reservation. Furthermore, the work on the Hijaz line, unlike other
rail projects in the Ottoman Empire, was carried out by the Ottoman

administration itself, and was paid for by taxation and contributions of wealthy Muslims.[17]

Because Haifa was the last terminal on the line, it played a dominant role in the Hauranian grain trade. The development resulted in reducing the dependence on camel caravans, and became an important harbinger of economic development to a number of sites on the line. The Jezre'el Valley (Plain of Esdraelon), that provided the most suitable level land for laying the tracks, received a major benefit. Its easternmost end, the then hamlet of Beisan (Beit She'an) enjoyed a surge of development as did Jisr al-Mujami'a, where the line crossed the old bridge on the Jordan River. Haifa, the Mediterranean terminal, was clearly the major beneficiary. The line's narrow gauge was, however, a handicap. It prevented the connection with the (future) Cairo-Beirut line and the Jaffa-Jerusalem rail lines, both of which used standard gauge.

The expansion of major road networks was also influenced by political factors, but governmental indifference and bureaucracy were added handicaps. According to a report of 1878, the only Jaffa-Jerusalem road that was fitted for wheeled vehicles for the occasion of the visit of the Austrian emperor and his son in 1869 was already out of service (i.e., less than nine years later).[18] The road was eventually repaved only in 1881. It was, in fact, the first Palestinian road that was fit for the use of wheeled wagons.[19]

Intensive road building began only in the 1880s. The work was carried out by recruiting all suitable males from adjoining areas. Summaries of the work force enabled an estimation of the population of the Jerusalem and Acre districts (see chapters 3 and 4 for added details). The Templers also pioneered the first regular transportation services in the country, by connecting their Haifa colony (which was founded in 1868) and Nazareth by a regular wagon service. Later they also established a similar horse-carriage line that ran from Jaffa to Jerusalem.[20]

The impact of the negligent Ottoman bureaucracy is repeatedly mentioned in European accounts that deal with the poor physical condition of the infrastructure. A British consular officer complained that it was difficult to obtain information about the commercial accounts of the port of Jaffa because the Ottoman customs officials refused to provide any data pertaining to customs income. American reports from the same period agree. Conditions at Gaza port were even worse. The port was situated several kilometers from the city and was not easily accessible. Consequently, the consular officers stationed in the town were unable to obtain any statistical data about port activities.[21] The poor access played a part in the deteriorating economic performance of Gaza and in widening the economic gap between it and Jaffa. Gaza was the prime economic core of the country before the nineteenth century, but since then it lost its economic status mainly because of the declining importance of its role as the "camel port" for Egyptian commercial traffic.

Its downfall was halted, to some extent, by the rising Scottish demand for barley, which was needed for whisky and beer manufacturing. Gaza's adjacent northern Negev area was a major supply source of this drought tolerant product. This development gave rise to the growing steamship traffic and an agricultural expansion that was accompanied by the establishment of permanent settlements by local and Egyptian *fallaheen* (see chapter 2) who migrated into the area hitherto utilized almost entirely by Bedouin nomads.

In spite of the complaints about the poor trade records, there is a fairly large amount of statistical data on the Palestinian foreign trade. The data suggest that Ottoman inefficiency and faulty infrastructure were not the only impediments to international trade. The Palestinian producers suffered from climatic fluctuations as well as other natural hazards and frequent price fluctuations. Other constrictions were the inadequate security conditions that accompanied the political instability.[22]

The developing infrastructure of Palestine did not keep pace with the more advanced developments that took place in other parts of the globe and even in one of its closest neighbors. The completion of the Suez Canal in 1869, that enabled the bypassing of the traditional land routes, had a mostly negative impact on external Palestinian trade. The cheap ocean transportation generated strong competition from countries whose products had previously been too expensive to enter Europe's markets. The most affected commodity was wheat. After 1869 it was imported from India to Europe through the Suez Canal at a price much lower than that of Palestinian wheat. As a result, the latter's market-share gradually declined and eventually completely ceased.[23]

As already noted, Palestine's agricultural trade was adversely affected by the improved United States infrastructure. Rising efficiency gave it a significant edge over its potential competitors. Scale economies that resulted primarily from its vast land resources also added to its relative advantage. Even Europe was affected by the rising American success. American wheat and other New World grain products were imported throughout Europe in vast quantities. By the 1880s British food imports (by value) from the United States exceeded British exports, but while the British could compensate for this trade imbalance with their rising industrial exports, the Palestinian farmers and traders had no alternative industrial sector to replace their deteriorating trade capabilities. Several large-scale Palestinian producers managed to stay in business for a while, but they too were eventually broken financially.

World War I aggravated the Palestinian situation. Another negative impact was the 1910 invention of artificial silk (rayon). This revolutionary development was particularly devastating for the rich Lebanese landlords whose family fortunes were acquired by raising mulberry trees for the silk worm. An example is the Sursouk family whose fortunes were based on natural silk production. It owned extensive mulberry estates in Lebanon and Syria, but eventually expanded into Palestine, where it owned vast territories in the Jezre'el and Beisan Valleys and the adjacent Galilee zones.[24] The Sursouks and other absentee landlords covered their losses by selling their large Palestinian properties to the Zionist land purchasing organizations. (The implications of these real estate deals are discussed later in this chapter. See below for further discussion of Sursouk's Palestinian estates.)

The obvious conclusion is that the failure to develop its infrastructure and to find adequate responses to the growing challenges posed by the modern industrial and agricultural development outside Palestine resulted in the worsening of Palestine's position in world markets. However, this might not have affected the *fallah* whose participation in international commercial agriculture was still minimal. International trade was of little concern to his family's welfare as long as he could provide for his family's subsistence. His scant surplus was usually sold in local towns rather than abroad. His difficulties arose when he faced conditions that left him with little or no surplus, or when his surplus had to be spent on interest charges and other impositions. The fact that the taxes were paid in kind enabled him to disregard the vagaries of the international markets when conditions were favorable. It was the tax collectors and the merchants who bought the crop from the *fallaheen* who felt the gradual erosion of their income. The end result was that they sold most of their properties to those who were most interested in purchasing it—the Jewish organizations.

Taxation and Military Draft Policies

Government policies had a profound impact on the *fallah*'s economy. Their influence affected practically all aspects of his daily life. The main contact was via the tax policy that siphoned off practically all the surpluses that the *fallah* had managed to produce. The extent of this practice is evident in the imperial budget of 1872-73, whose major income originated in taxes that were imposed on the rural population, while the benefits of this sector accounted for a small portion of the public expenditures. More specifically, the rural sector accounted for 85 percent of the population and submitted over 52 percent of all revenues from taxes (most of this in property taxes), while its share of government services accounted for only 46 percent of the direct and indirect government expenditures. Their share of the commercial and health spending was especially low.[25]

The disproportionate burden of the rural sector was aggravated by the deeply imbedded system of tax collection that was based on tax farming (*iltizam*) system. The system was common in ancient times and is still practiced in some developing countries. It was very suitable to the Ottoman administration because of the chronic shortage of trained officials. Theoretically, the tax farmers received their concession by bidding the amount the government would receive from the sum they were able to collect. They could, then, keep for themselves the extra sum they collected above the predetermined bid. In fact, many were appointed without a tender. They did, of course, take upon themselves the risk of losing their expected income if they failed to collect the fixed sum. Natural disasters or other unforeseen events lowered the ability of the taxed persons to pay, thus depriving the tax farmers of the expected profit. In order to ensure themselves against such incidents, the tax farmers (*multazmin*) used to apply pressure on the communities under their control. Although this was not the system's intention, it encouraged the tax farmer to raise the burden especially during hard times.

One of the first attempts to alter the system in Palestine and Syria was made by Ibrahim Pasha in the early 1830s. But the effort failed. In 1839, the tax farming system was officially abolished for the entire Ottoman Empire under an Imperial decree (*hatt-i-sherif*, see above), but the *multazmin* continued the practice. An additional effort to abolish it was made in 1856, but this too did not succeed. Taxes were farmed out in Palestine and Syria until at least the 1890s and in most places even during the early twentieth century. They were completely abolished in Palestine only during the British Mandate administration. However, during the *tanzimat* (reforms) period, the Ottoman government established special boards of officials in each region, charged with supervising the system. Additional information on this reform is provided in chapter 6.[26]

The tax rate on the crops was supposed to be 10 percent (tithe), but usually it was much higher.[27] In addition to this tax, various impositions were usually charged, adding up to 450 *grush* (piasters) to the land tax, when the annual wage for a day laborer was 1,000 to 1,500 *grush*. But the tax burden was lowered after 1840 and during the following thirty years no household paid more than forty *grush* a year.[28]

These impositions reflected the tax farmer's evaluation of the *fallah*'s absorptive capacity. In the Gaza Sub-District, the total sum amounted to one half of the entire income of the *fallah* even though the official rate was only 10 percent.[29] This was probably a sort of progressive tax based on the evaluation that Gaza's productive capacity in a region having high-grade agricultural resources. During the decade of the Egyptian administration (1831-1840), taxation was especially high, even though the governor, Ibrahim Pasha (Muhammad Ali's son), who was appointed governor of Syria, had promised, when he took office, to ease the tax burden. The imposition of the new head tax was one of the causes for the 1834 uprising.[30]

The land tax was usually paid in-kind. The evaluation of the produce took place on the threshing floor, and was accompanied by long negotiations between the farmer and the officials (figure 1.4). The name of the farmer was written down in the tax *daftar* (notebook) alongside of the amount due. Only after this procedure was completed was the *fallah* allowed to remove his grain sheaves from the field.[31]

There were, however, several institutions that were exempt from the tax or paid a lower rate. The tax on produce from land which was donated to Islamic institutions (*waqf*) was lower than the rate imposed on private owners. The prevailing custom was to limit the donations to the *waqf* to a period of three years, but it could then be extended to another similar number of years. In many cases the agreement was renewed for successive multiples of three years (*'aqad*s; e.g., twenty-one years equaled seven *'aqad*s). But despite the limitations, abuses of *waqf* were prevalent and the donations frequently acted as a tax haven.[32]

Several changes were made in Ottoman tax policies during the reform (*tanzimat*) period, but, as already noted, the system of tax farming survived despite repeated attempts to replace it by a more progressive system. The most important rural tax was still the tithe (*'ushr*) which was charged on agricultural produce. It contributed at least 40 percent of the Ottoman treasury's income. Another important tax was the *voryo* (*virko* or *virgo*) which was a property tax levied on buildings and other real estate properties.[33]

In 1886 a fundamental fiscal reform was decreed. Its main purpose was to prevent the widespread abuses that added various local imposi-

Fig. 1.4
Activities on the threshing floor

Source: Wilson, C.W., *The Land of Judea & The Jerusalem Environs,* Republished by Ely Schiller, 1976, p. 107. Courtesy of Mr. Ely Schiller, the publication rights holder.

tions to the official tax. The land tax was still the tithe, but between 1897 and 1900 several sums were added on top of it. These additions were intended to finance special outlays (e.g., public education, an agricultural bank and military expenses), bringing the land tax to 12.63 percent. Several additional changes were later introduced and while some of the taxes were raised, religious and welfare institutions were totally removed from the tax roll. In spite of some shortcomings, this policy reflected a shift to Western standards. The system was retained, with no change, by the Mandate administration until 1925. A few changes were introduced during the next decade, but the tithe system based on taxing the crop was still retained. Only in 1935 was it drastically altered.

The new impositions were charged on farm plots. The criterion was the land's productive potential rather than the volume of the crops actually harvested (see chapter 6 for added details).

An issue closely related to the welfare of the rural population was the draft policy. By lowering the amount of manpower available for farm work, the military draft further reduced the already scant, after-tax, subsistence resources of the *fallaheen*. The recruits were, of course, the young, most able bodied work force, and their removal resulted in a deep dent in the family's economic welfare.

The military recruitment policy was even more resented than the tax hikes. In 1834 a rebellion against Ibrahim Pasha was ignited mainly by the obligatory draft, although the promulgation of the head tax was also greatly resented. Ibrahim Pasha's development policy of extending cultivation in the peripheral areas, as well as his schemes for raising farm production and planting new crops, clearly contradicted his own draft policy.

Conflicting purposes of this kind are not unique. The preference for a military option was dictated most probably by Muhammad Ali, Ibrahim's father. But the preference for "guns over butter" has been the choice of rulers throughout history. Only the means and their relative harshness differed. They are dictated by technology and, not least, by personality. The latter is treated below.

The Demographic Impacts of the Fiscal and Military Draft Policies

The merciless massacre of certain northern Negev Bedouin tribes who participated in the 1834 rebellion caused a great population reshuffling that produced a chain reaction that reached as far as the Sharon Plain. This was but one of the cases that revealed the harsh outcome of the military draft policy. The Bedouin were almost totally obliterated from the poorly drained zone southeast of Ramla. This area was offered for sale and in 1839 a group of Jerusalem Jews showed interest in buying it, but the attempt failed and the area was eventually settled by Egyptian deserters of the retreating army. The demographic impacts of Muhammad Ali's military campaigns were thus positive and negative.

The draft policies had some dire consequences even before the hostilities began. Contemporary reports on the reaction of the Palestinian population to recruitment for the Crimean War of 1853-1856 include descriptions of the violent reactions by potential draftees. There were many cases of people who mutilated themselves or their children to avoid conscription. The drafting raids were usually conducted during the night.

They were accompanied by loud screams and by people fleeing through the windows of their homes. Many of the villagers fled to the Bedouin who managed to escape the draft (and any other obligations).

The consequences of the draft were more severe in the rural areas than in the urban zones, because the *fallaheen* lacked financial means to pay (either by legal ransom or by various illegal means) for their own or their children's release from military service as the affluent city dwellers could. The burden of the military service, just as the burden of taxation, fell heavily on the *fallaheen*.[34]

The demographic significance of the taxation system and the military draft was not uniform. Kamal Karpat stated that the "conscription system introduced by Mahmut II in 1838, and then the general conscription in 1855" never applied to Christians.[35] Only Muslims were recruited.

The Muslims were again recruited to fight in the Balkan wars of the late 1870s, in which they suffered heavy losses. Schölch quoted a contemporary source (Yusuf al-Khalidi) who said that as many as 10,000 Palestinian soldiers perished in these wars.[36] The result was that their numbers were reduced, while the Christian population grew.

The draft was associated with additional, indirect, demographic effects. As already noted, many Muslim males spent their most productive years away from home. They had no opportunity to marry and develop their economic potential or their property. Many ex-servicemen never returned to their original homes. There were other reasons, however, for the Muslim demographic stagnation. Even though they were considered to be the elite class, they fell behind the non-Muslims in their level of education and were less exposed to preventive medicine and modern sanitation. However, their higher death rate was only partly due to the conscription policy, although it must have had a great impact on the demographic growth rate.

Despite the disruption of the wars, the eruption of a cholera epidemic during the late 1860s and the widespread famines of the 1870s, Palestine showed some demographic improvement during the later part of the century. The introduction of modern medicine, the economic development that followed the Crimean War and, not least, the relatively longer periods of peace, brought a gradual demographic turnaround, but the more remote rural places, whose populated was predominantly Muslim, were still least affected by these improvements. The impact of the military draft continued to affect mainly the poor rural Muslim population that was unable to amass the payment necessary for escaping conscription.[37]

Urban/Rural Relationships: Notables, Tax Farmers, Officials, and Merchants

It might have been possible to ease the pressure of the government's fiscal policies if they had been imposed equitably and efficiently. But because of the scarcity of trained personnel to enforce them, and because of the dependency on an officialdom over which there was little or no control, it was difficult for the people of the weaker sectors to ensure their legal rights and withstand arbitrary actions. Local governments were in the hands of a well established class of notables (collectively known as *a'iyan*), some of whom were almost permanently engaged in mutual rivalries that occasionally turned into spells of open violence.

In order to retain their special positions, these notables had to establish reciprocal ties with the local government officials. These connections depended on the payment of bribes and on a network of entwining relationships that was often outside the formal legal system. All public figures were included in this aristocracy: religious leaders, judges, tax farmers and commercial functionaries—merchants, industrialists, and other capitalists. The members of the *a'iyan* class were interested in retaining stability in order to guarantee a steady supply of raw materials and services that they acquired in the rural hinterland. The *fallah*'s welfare was only of marginal concern to the *a'iyan*, but it was not in their interest that he be dissatisfied. They made sure, therefore, that a fair (though low) subsistence level was maintained in the rural area. This traditional paternal nature of the *fallah/ a'iyan* ties was thus of mutual interest to both classes. It guaranteed a stable economic subsistence and assurance of support during harsh times.

The *fallaheen*'s relations with the political authorities were more problematic. They were completely baffled when faced with government officials who had no direct economic interests in their welfare. Therefore, it is likely that certain rural areas were badly hurt when the status of their traditional benefactors declined. Their welfare depended on the local rural/urban ties. The difference between Nablus and Jerusalem provides a useful example of the varying roles played by localities. The reciprocal rural/urban relationships were strong in the Nablus hinterland but not in the Jerusalem one. In the latter case there were fewer mutual economic interests between the city's *a'iyan* class and its hinterland, partly as a result of the city's religious diversity and the strong outward orientation resulting from the role played by tourism and pilgrimage. The rural areas were relatively free of the *a'iyan*, but they also reaped some benefits from the international status of Jerusalem.[38]

Agriculture and Land Tenure

The unstable condition of the *fallah*'s economy was largely the result of his struggle to accumulate surpluses in good years for coping with harvest failure or other crises. Many farmers had great difficulty in amassing enough reserves to buy means of production such as draft animals or vital tools. Cultivators who had their own means of production were able to maintain an acceptable lifestyle, but the *fallaheen* who were forced to work as sharecroppers usually received one fourth, or even less, of their crops and did not have the means to purchase vital inputs. Consequently, they had no way of escaping from the vicious cycle of poverty. Even the owners of one draft animal were unable to plow all the land that was at their disposal during the six-week plowing season (figure 1.5). Shortage

Fig. 1.5
Plowing hilly land near Jerusalem

Source: Manning, S., *Those Holy Fields: Palestine Illustrated by Pen and Pencil.* Republished by Mr Ely Schiller, 1976, p. 17. Courtesy of Mr. Ely Schiller, the publication rights holder.

of capital prevented the acquisition of prime land or even the purchase of simple agricultural tools. The unrelenting human-generated economic pressure harmed the *fallah* no less than did recurrent droughts or other natural disasters.

There was also a shortage of manpower—the most important production factor in pre-industrial times. One of the reasons for this was the low-density of population. Another cause was, as already noted, the military draft which targeted the same age groups as the farm-worker population did. Human labor rather than the amount of land was the limiting factor since the *fallaheen* did not suffer from a lack of areas that could be put to cultivation. Agriculturalists who faced land shortages could, at least theoretically, farm peripheral fields taken from the *mawat* ("dead" land considered unfit for farming because of its distance from the village, or because it was too rocky or swampy). Land classified as *mawat* could be revived. Legally, this involved official permission and, according to the 1858 Land Code, it was available for a nominal fee and was free from tax payment for ten years. But since in many places there was no effective supervision of the *mawat* use, many squatted on such areas. Before the Land Code went into effect, this category was even more easily available. The Islamic *Shari'a* laws and the local political administration actually welcomed its cultivation. Somewhat similar legal rules applied also to abandoned lands, that is, land that was either uncultivated after three full years or left unused because its owners migrated elsewhere or died without any heirs. Such lands were declared *mahlul* and reverted to the government, which was the legal owner of most agricultural land. It was only in the late 1860s that the Ottoman administration conducted surveys to find out the extent of unused land. The findings revealed that there were many villages that had vast tracts of vacant land and a fairly large number of villages that were totally deserted. The use-right of many of these areas was later publicly auctioned and transferred to rich merchants or declared *jiftlik* (estate; in Palestine the term refers to estates of the Sultan).

The original purpose of these land laws was to encourage cultivation and increase the administration's income from taxes by reviving marginal land and transferring it to a new user. In fact, the vacant lands found their way to absentee landlords, who let them out to sharecroppers. Only in areas where there were no sufficient land reserves were villagers obliged to become sharecroppers.[39] But toward the end of the nineteenth century the ranks of the landless farmers had grown, partly because the available unused areas had been transferred to *effendi*s (title of Turkish dignitaries) rather than to villagers. The alternative to sharecropping was not very appealing. The use of the swamps involved health hazards, and squatting on rocky State Domain was also not very attractive. Labor demands were high and the *fallah*'s simple tools could only work around the rocks, but were not able to remove them. The returns from these alternatives were even more meager than those that were obtained from farming absentee landowners' fields under the sharecropping system.

It is common to consider these absentee landowners (*effendis*) as exploiters because of their unrelenting exploitation of their poor farmers. But one must take into consideration the fact that they took on various risks that occasionally left them bankrupt. A well-documented example was the blow to the silk industry caused by the competition of Asian producers by World War I and by the invention of artificial silk. As already noted, the Beirut-based Sursouk family was hard hit by these events. Such crises resulted in selling parts or all of the vast estates to Jewish land purchasing organizations.[40]

The absentee landowner considered his real estate as exchangeable property. His sharecropper's function was, accordingly, to generate as much income as possible for the owner. But the low income due to the cultivator (no more than a quarter of the yield) was insufficient for feeding his family. To improve his family's subsistence he needed more land, that is, the land's "carrying capacity" (for a discussion of this concept see chapter 6) had been lowered. The *fallaheen* poverty was attributed therefore to the landholding system and, more specifically, towards the oppression of the sharecroppers. However, the absentee landholding system was largely the result, though not exclusively so, of the 1858 Land Law. There was sharecropping even earlier, but it was not dominated by urban-based absentee landowners, who were completely detached from the rural peasantry. The *effendis* were not part of the traditional economy, and they cannot be held responsible for the demographic conditions of the country during most of the nineteenth century.

The contribution of the Land Code to the emergence of the absentee landowner class was the direct result of the formal registration requirement. The *fallah* was often unable to obtain the modest sums required for the registration of his use rights, while the *effendi* was willing to pay, in addition to the official price, various handouts. A related, more serious problem was the *fallah*'s worry that registration was intended to prepare the ground for the imposition of additional taxes. Many merchants, moneylenders and other town-based people exploited the ignorance of the peasants and their unfounded suspicions and offered to register the land for them. Some officials also took advantage of their position to compel the *fallaheen* to register their properties in their (the officials') names. In exchange they offered to release the *fallah*'s sons from military service or granted them various other benefits.

The enforcement of the new law, which was never complete, was associated with additional land alienation practices. As noted, neglected land was legally declared state property. Land was also confiscated from tax evaders who were unable to pay the required sums. The people who fared worst were the Bedouin. They had been accustomed to collect a form of "protection money" called *hawwa* (brotherhood) and regularly disregarded civil obligations. In addition, they had little awareness of the value of the land.[41] They also believed, on the basis of previous experience, that the new policy would not be imposed effectively. In fact, however, much of the territory they possessed in the Negev was classified as *mawat*, which was practically, even if not legally, free. Much of the tribal territories of the Jordan plains and parts of the Galilee were actually defined as the private estate (*jiftlik;* see above) of the Sultan.

There is no general agreement about the Ottoman purpose for issuing the Land Code. A widely held explanation is that its purpose was to raise funds. Still another was that the intention was to modernize the economy by removing what was widely considered to be an obstacle to agricultural development, the traditional *musha'* system. This interpretation is shared by most scholars. It rests mainly on the fact that the 1858 law did not recognize group ownership. But this is also suggested by the role played by the British, who had completed a full century of Parliamentary Enclosures, that is, privatization of holdings, when the Ottoman Land Code was formulated.

The *musha'* was the most common land holding practice, though it was not the only one. Its rules and regulations were based on unwritten traditions and were not legally documented. It is, therefore, difficult to find any reference to it in the laws of the *Shari'a* or in any other source. It was, most probably, a custom which developed under the accepted system of land management.[42]

Legally, *musha'* land was part of the *miri* (originally Emiri – the land of the Emir). It refers to land whose ultimate owner was the State, which delegated the right of possession to approved persons. The *fallaheen* and other taxpayers were entitled to use it. In fact, most of the land under Ottoman rule was included (and is still included) in this category.

The *musha'* was practiced even by absentee landowners, who preferred it over paid laborers, as a means to save expenses on administration and supervision. The *musha'*, more strictly, *musha' al-balad,* refers to the common land of a village or a town. It was not a land owning system but, rather, a communally based land management system. Under this method the land belonging to the villagers (the shareholders) was periodically rotated among them, but the details of the system varied among regions or among villages in a certain region. The duration of the inter-rotation time might have originally depended on the length of the cultivation cycle, which depended, in turn, on soil conditions. But judging from the available data that were scribbled on the fiscal maps of the British Mandate period, the correlation between the agro-technical time needed for land recuperation and the traditional length of the seasons between re-allocations was low, because there were other, non-agro-technical factors that defined the specific re-allocation dates. Farmland was distributed in a prescribed manner to the clan or family heads. The common practice was the use of lots. This was usually performed by calling on children to pick out marked stones from leather bags or other containers.

The main objection of the Ottoman government, and later also of the British Mandate administration (and the French in their Syrian Mandate) was that the shareholders had no incentive to improve land that they would have to abandon after the end of their short-term tenancy. Graham-Brown noted, however, that this issue was purely "academic" and had no practical implications, since the *fallah* lacked any surpluses or investment capital for improving the farm.[43]

Several other recent researchers expressed quite similar opinions. One of them stated that the "British officials argued [that] the *musha'* was an archaic system, an obstacle to investment that blocked any chance of development."[44] There are several ways to explain the function of this "archaic" communal system, but it is not intended to fully cover this issue. It is evident, however, that there was some advantage to pooling resources for tackling either natural hazards or manmade ones.[45]

The Agrarian Structure: Its Implications for Rural People

The agricultural sector supplied mostly subsistence crops. Among the questions that we have to ask are the following:

- To what extent was there any process of change in Palestine during the four centuries of Ottoman administration?
- And if there was any, was the process sufficient to satisfy the growing population during the last phase of Ottoman rule?

- Did it help raise the *fallah*'s standard of living by introducing new crops?

The answers are not clear cut. There is, however, evidence that new strains of food crops were developed and introduced into the Middle East during the Ottoman period, but agricultural techniques did not change substantially, and there is little evidence that the Arab peasants' condition was improved.

The introduction of cotton to the Empire, probably before the sixteenth century, testifies to the existence of cash crops once their economic advantage was revealed. Raw cotton was apparently brought to the Middle East from India. In Palestine its cultivation was concentrated mainly in the Galilee coastal plain and the Jezre'el Plain. It was produced also in the fertile coastal plain north of Gaza and in the Jaffa area. In the eighteenth century it was shipped mainly to France.[46] Its cultivation contributed to the development of some textile manufacturing, though it was of minor importance. In the early Ottoman era Safad was a major textile manufacturing center, but it relied on imported raw materials, mainly imported wool. Another textile center was reported in the late eighteenth century in Majdal, north of Gaza where, according to Volney, "they spin the finest cottons in Palestine, which, however, are very clumsy."[47] For a considerable period cotton was Palestine's principal export to Europe and other regions of the Ottoman Empire, even though it was considered to be of inferior quality.[48]

The introduction of cotton was not a unique phenomenon. Throughout the Ottoman era new crops were grown that had originally been discovered in America. Although it is difficult to pinpoint exactly when these and other innovations were introduced and how they spread, there is no doubt that they engendered changes in the way that agricultural land was utilized, especially in regions with access to trade routes.

The most important of the "new" crops were maize, tomatoes, potatoes, tobacco, and sorghum. At the end of the eighteenth century haricot beans (*lubia ifranjia*) were successfully cultivated in Aleppo (Haleb) and were soon in great demand, spreading rapidly to the rest of the Middle East. Another agricultural innovation was the adoption of cochineal, a cactus used for dye production that was brought to Tripoli (Lebanon) by Ibrahim Pasha during the 1830s. Although potato crops were successfully introduced in Europe, especially in Ireland and Russia, they never took root in the East apparently because the climatic conditions of the Mediterranean region enabled the cultivation of a wide range of edible carbohydrate-rich foods. Thus potatoes were not as vital as they were in regions with severely limited agricultural options. Another reason was that the severe summer heat spoiled the potatoes and prevented their storage for the next planting season. It was not until World War II that the Mandate government built refrigeration plants that overcame this problem.[49]

Although these developments also improved the cultivation of traditional crops by improving agro-technical methods, the chief innovation was the expansion of arable land by using methods that surmounted the difficulties of working the soil during the summer dry season. Plants introduced during the Ottoman period were summer crops that enabled the use of the land more than one season per year. This is evident particularly in the southern coastal plain of Palestine, where summer crops like melons and watermelons could benefit from the summer dews of the local sandy soils.[50] This facilitated the transition from a two-year cycle to a triennial field system that mostly included two consecutive years of tilling. This innovation contributed to the intensification of agricultural production and the extension of arable land.

In many places the production of food crops (especially winter wheat) became more efficient. The progress was measured by the yield to seed ratio. In the Hauran Plain the ratio in good years reached 21:1. The barley ratio was even higher. The quantity of seed needed for a given area in the nineteenth century was thus smaller than that required in the sixteenth century.[51] Compared to European countries, however, the standard yield in Palestine was low. Measured by yield per hectare the amount of seed required was 24,000 liter per hectare, while in Europe it was as low as 10,000 to 20,000 liter.[52]

The 1858 Land Code and its impacts have already been discussed. Here I will add a few comments on their regional and ethnic results. The most outstanding was the loss of the Bedouin claims to most of their traditional grazing areas. Parts of the Jordan Valley (Jericho, Beisan, the shores of the Sea of Galilee), the Jezre'el Valley and most of the coastal plains were converted to agricultural production. Their owners were either rich land owners or small owner cultivators. But the Bedouin were not necessarily evicted. The land just changed owners. Laurence Oliphant described the transformation of Jezre'el Plain as land which "is divided between two great proprietors, the Sultan himself…and the Sursouks."[53] The latter obtained by public auction 21,000 hectares in this wide valley (called by him and most Europeans Esdraelon).[54] Oliphant observed that in his time Palestine was enjoying security, agriculture development and material progress while the rest of the Ottoman Empire was in constant decline (see also chapter 5).

The *fallaheen* were usually not dispossessed, and even if the land was not registered as stated in the 1858 law, they could continue the use of the land that they held. The eviction of the *fallaheen* would have entailed a considerable social price, and the government was more interested in maintaining the farmer on cultivated lands than in collecting the legal registration fees. Inalcik and Quataert did not believe that the transfer of land to *effendis* affected a large number of small landholders, and stated that the execution of the law did not entail the eviction of *fallaheen*. Their opinion is based, however, on evidence from Turkey and Anatolia,[55] but it applies also to Palestine, where most of the smallholdings outside the coastal plains and the inland basins were not affected by the modifications. The usually low agricultural yields (see chapter 6) suggest that the *fallaheen* who continued to use traditional methods did not improve their economic conditions.

Natural Disasters and Their Outcomes: Selected Events, 1860-1902

The frequent fluctuations in agricultural production were caused by natural disasters rather than by human-derived events. But in some cases the damage was done by a combination of both. Severe droughts occurred frequently. In some cases, the disasters were multiplied when in addition to the droughts there were also severe locust ravages. This happened in the agricultural season of 1865-66 when most of the summer crops, including cotton and sesame, were hard hit.[56] Similar multiple calamities erupted again during 1870 when the recorded rain in Jerusalem (where recording started in 1847) was only 318 millimeters.[57] The locust damage of the same year was relatively light, but the late 1870s proved to be among the worst years. During 1877 there was a severe drought and most of the crops failed. The problem was multiplied again, but this time by damage that was caused by field mice. In 1878 the fruit, olives and summer crops were again subjected to a locust invasion, even though rainfall amounts reached an unprecedented peak. The local soap industry, based on olive oil, was also severely hit because of the losses sustained by the olive crop.[58]

The series of disasters that occurred in the 1870s was partly the result of the combined impact of natural and the man-made mishaps. The latter were caused by the Balkan wars that brought about economic hardships and food shortages. The villages located in the Jerusalem zone suffered from water scarcity. There is little information about their specific conditions, but judging from the records concerning a village located near Jerusalem, where the villagers had to buy water from the nearby village, even though they had some 60 cisterns in their own settlement, the situation was bad.[59] It is probable however that in some areas, where the population was lower, the problem was less serious.

Conditions in Jerusalem itself can also indicate the probable severity of this event and its impact on the surrounding villages. The town's water supply depended mostly on cisterns that were fed by rain water. By the end of the summer their contents were murky, and as the dry summer progressed the water became more heavily polluted. The worsening water supply aggravated the already poor sanitary conditions and, consequently, negatively affected the health of the population.[60]

Severe earthquakes also befell Palestine. The frequency of the occurrence of severe ones was not very great (only about one in 80-100 years), but their human toll and property damage could be devastating. Over three centuries there were three strong earthquakes: 1760, 1837, and 1927. All three had very harsh consequences, but while the first and the second hit hardest in Safad and Tiberias and the surrounding Galilee villages, the last one hit the Nablus zone of the Samaria region most severely. As with the drought, the earthquake disaster was accompanied by additional horrors. In the case of the Safad earthquake, the poor sanitation resulted in the eruption of a cholera epidemic that increased the earthquake toll. After the 1927 quake, however, the population was spared the horrors of major epidemics because of the better hygiene and the availability of far better medical services during the Mandate era.[61]

The impression gained from the available sources is that natural disasters (like a locust plague or epidemic) were accepted as a decree from heaven, even though there is some evidence of the attempts by certain officials or private citizens to take some pre-emptive action or to improve the post-occurrence situation. One rare example is that of Ibrahim Pasha. The British consul who was searching for him in 1836 finally found him east of Aleppo (Haleb), where he was busy with 10,000 of his soldiers in an attempt to eradicate the locusts that had devastated the agricultural crops.[62]

Pest Control and Health: Economic and Demographic Impact

The development of agriculture supplied means of livelihood that broadened the economic base and permitted the growth of the population. But population increase also depends on lowering the death rate. I will attempt to show that the centralization process was vital for the demographic transition that led to sustainable population growth. There was no real substitute for controlling health and disease or for providing sanitation control and disease preventive services. These and other services, especially those that were necessary to prevent contagious diseases and pests, could not be tackled effectively by a relatively small, decentralized authority under the conditions that existed in Palestine during the nineteenth century.

The plagues which broke out from time to time caused many deaths. But this was not the only harm they did. Directly or indirectly, they impaired agricultural production and other vital activities. They caused a shortage of working hands because the plague attacked a large number of young farmers. The quarantines that prevented population mobility also hampered various necessary activities in the agricultural sector and in other vital areas.

The epidemics originated in neighboring states, but even when it was possible to prevent their penetration into Palestine, nothing was done. For example, in 1883 there was an outbreak of cholera in Egypt, but in spite of measures taken, the disease was transmitted to Palestine.[63] There was a similar outbreak in 1902 in the center of Palestine and other areas, but it was only moderate. This incident, like many outbreaks of cholera before, was caused by the pilgrims on the way back from Mecca.[64]

The prevention method was to impose government control on international and inter-regional crossing points. These activities needed coordination and cooperation of many communities that the inadequate information networks were unable to provide. Admittedly, the process of stemming the spread of infections was slow, but one of the outstanding successes of the Ottoman government was its almost total stamping out of bubonic plague throughout most of the Empire. This effort began in the 1830s and was completed by the forties. Cholera, on the other hand, was not so fully controlled.

The process that brought the spread of bubonic plague to an end was thoroughly documented by Daniel Panzac, who studied its outbreaks throughout the Ottoman Empire from 1700. He showed that between 1800 and 1845 there were at least sixteen years that Palestine and Syria suffered from eruptions of plague, that is, an average of about one every three years. But most of these events were relatively moderate and short-lived. Each of them was different from the others in its intensity and did not spread evenly throughout the country.[65]

Plagues broke out frequently during periods of drought or other crises. The worst drought, which continued for two consecutive years, took place during 1836 and 1837. In 1837 there were also locust and cholera outbreaks. The natural disasters' causal relationship was unknown, but it seriously upset the resource balance and aggravated the sufferings of the country's inhabitants.

The threat of the bubonic plague, which drastically reduced the world's population during 1348-50, was stamped out in most of the West during the early part of the nineteenth century, but in the Ottoman Empire the results of governmental action were felt somewhat later. This achievement was brought about by improving the sanitary conditions through a series of activities initiated by the central government throughout the Empire. The outcome offered substantial proof that only a political body which controlled international entry boundaries and sea ports could prevent a renewed spread of plagues.

One of the most effective methods for preventing the spread of plagues was the quarantine. Quarantine quarters were set up in ports and border crossings. In order that this system succeed, strict and often even cruel enforcement practices were required. A notable example of this was the advice given to the Sultan by the British ambassador in January 1839. His advice was that the Ottoman guards should be granted the right to shoot anyone attempting to escape from quarantine.[66]

The process of suppressing the plague was a long one. It began in the early 1830s, but the most important step was taken only in 1838 when the Sultan appointed a Supreme Sanitation Commission and under it Provincial Commissions in provincial centers. They were instructed to establish quarantines and appoint guards. The results of establishing the quarantine were impressive. The last plague in Egypt was in 1844. The Jerusalem quarantine was operational only after 1848. There is no doubt that Palestine profited even earlier from the quarantine policy. It successfully prevented the spread of the plagues that erupted outside the country.[67]

It is difficult to evaluate the demographic impact of the quarantine policy. However, the success against the bubonic plague did not stop the outbreak of other diseases, and one must consider that there were other factors that influenced the number of deaths and the sustainability of the population. But the cessation of the spread of plagues was a major demographic event. It marked the transition from a static or declining population to the onset of sustained population growth.[68]

The significance of the Sanitation Commissions was also an important landmark. They led to the development of health services and the acceptance of modern medicine. They also introduced and spread the idea that disease should not only be cured but even completely prevented. This is not the proper place to go into a full treatise of the various aspects of this innovation, but it was clearly a major watershed in the medical history of Palestine. It can be stated that health and economic developments went hand-in-hand. The improvement was slow, but this short historical review seems to provide added proof that Palestine's demographic takeoff date was sometime around the mid-nineteenth century.

Despite the improvements recorded above, the state of public hospitals was still unsatisfactory throughout the Empire. The number of hospitals was too small and there were too few doctors and health personnel. The situation was especially inadequate in the rural areas where most Ottoman citizens lived. There was a high rate of infant mortality and a large number of deaths from infectious diseases, such as typhus and tuberculosis, even at the beginning of the twentieth century.[69] The health conditions in the cities of Palestine were not as harsh as in other districts because of the relatively large number of religious institutions, especially Christian and Jewish ones. This development was contingent on the existence of consuls or lower-rank representation of the Western powers. The situation stood out especially because of the large number of missionaries, but the spreading secular education also contributed to the demands for improved health facilities. The competition among the large number of Christian sects contributed to the growth and the increased geographical distribution of hospitals and other health institutions and services. The missionaries were forbidden to preach Christianity to Muslims, but there was no prohibition on providing medical help. In order to improve their medical and sanitary needs and counter the missionary influence, the Jews established their own hospitals and other medical clinics. Most of them were financed by European and American philanthropists. But they also founded several medical insurance cooperatives that were based on membership's fees.

The Significance of the Demographic Transition

Because of insufficient data on growth rates and other vital statistics, it is difficult to effectively demonstrate the extent of any given factor on demographic processes. However, despite some disagreement, there is a broad consensus about the positive demographic impact of the modernization process of the late nineteenth century.

McCarthy believed that the impact of the post-1882 Jewish migration on the growth of the Arab population was minimal. This conclusion stems from the absence of any correlation between the number of Jews and the number of Arabs in the various Palestinian zones.[70] The problem with such statistical deduction is that the official data refer only to Ottoman citizens, while most of the Jewish migrants were not citizens of the Empire. McCarthy also believed that the important changes which influenced the demographic situation were essentially economic and technological, rather than the health and sanitation conditions. Improved transportation, the development of commerce, the growth of local industries, and the improvement of personal and material security created new sources of income and encouraged the transfer of workers from the villages to the towns.[71]

As shown above, the improvement of health and sanitation could have also been a powerful factor. It is very likely that the combination of health and economic improvement generated the movement from rural areas to the growing towns, where accessibility to modern medicine and health services was more readily available. It encouraged the *fallaheen* to consult physicians, take prescriptions and use various other medical services. There is thus a strong, though complex, interrelationship among the various demographic factors.

Improved administration and security also affected the demographic transition. The successful submission of warlords who were involved in internecine disturbances until 1859 played an important part in the population growth in Palestine (see discussion of *Qais-Yaman* conflicts in chapter 5). The alternative narrative, that the pre-1850s prosperity was the major population growth force,[72] ignores the difficulties facing decentralized authorities, in planning and supervising projects like anti-plague policies, hospitals and a variety of other health facilities.

The opinion that the main constriction was the poor security condition and other man-made troubles adds another item to the complex list of factors. However, from the *fallah*'s point of view the natural hazards and their impact on man and resources were clearly of paramount importance. The reason for this is rooted in the unstable condition, and the absence of any form of protection or insurance against the vagaries of nature and especially the timing of disasters whose occurrence was known to crop up at unpredictable intervals. The farmer's unique perspective was usually absent from most of the macro-scale economic literature. The combination of living on the verge of subsistence, unstable political conditions and impending natural hazards creates a lifestyle of constant uncertainty that may lead to actual catastrophes. This complex combination, rather than any single one of them, is then the real culprit.

An example of the demographic effect of this lethal combination was the massive out-migration from villages around Acre during the rule of Ahmed el-Jazzar in the late eighteenth century. The immediate factor was an increase of the tax rate to finance his building projects. But, unfortunately, this policy coincided with a long drought period. To make things worse, the price of cotton, the main cash crop, was declining. These combined events led to the desertion of many villages and a consequent depopulation of the Acre rural hinterland.[73]

Extreme combinations of manmade disasters and natural ones frequently arose during periods of bloody local wars. An example of compounded disasters is the multi-stage Hauran rebellion. It started in 1879 and lasted into the twentieth century. Like other rural uprisings, it originated in a struggle against oppressive taxation, but it was aggravated by natural disasters.[74]

In Palestine there were also widespread disasters, but usually not as complex and durable as that of the Hauran. Hebron suffered from a severe drought from 1783 to 1788. Jerusalem had a similar situation in 1787. Tiberias and many Arab towns were hit even harder. The worst incident of this period was the severe famine that afflicted Egypt (1783-85). According to Volney, it lost about a sixth of its population. His usually trustworthy and carefully worded report suggests that the demographic decline was mainly due to massive out-migration from the country to Syria (mainly Acre and Sidon) and Palestine (the term referred by him to Gaza District). The disaster lasted over three successive years and was among the principal causes for one of the greatest migration waves of Egyptians into Syria and Palestine (see chapter 2).[75]

Development Progress between 1880 and the First World War

The Royal Commission's description of a traveler (published in 1913 and quoted on the first page of this chapter) suggests that the modernization processes had not reached the villages of southern Palestine by the early twentieth century. The *fallah*'s lifestyle remained unchanged and his exposure to technology was still minimal. In many villages no technical innovations could be seen, even though there is some proof that development processes had been initiated during the last thirty years of Ottoman reign. The present section is concerned with the development process that occurred after 1880 and its significance for rural areas. The *fallah* profited from some of the improvements that were introduced by the Ottoman administration, but the higher socio-economic sectors reaped the main benefits.

In the last decades of the nineteenth century the central government set up a few institutions whose purpose was to stimulate agricultural production throughout the Empire, but at the grassroots level few of these initiatives were felt. In 1888 an agricultural bank was set up to facilitate the farmers' accessibility to credit, and in 1893 the Ministry of Forests, Mines, and Agriculture was instituted.[76]

There was, however, considerable improvement in the sanitation services (waste removal) and in the communication infrastructure (the telegraph system). A system for controlling pests, which also took care of eradication of locust swarms, was instituted. Migrations from the farms to the main towns also increased, and a sort of urban proletariat took form. Urbanization was accompanied by a decline of the traditional rural sector and a gradual advancement of a modern economy.[77] The increase of imports (according to records of 1908) was accompanied by a negative balance of trade. But this suggests that consumption of quality products was increasing and that there was a general growth of the local market. There is also some evidence that the *fallaheen* increased the marketing of fresh crops to the expanding cities, as can be discerned from available data on the food supply that reached Jerusalem from the surrounding villages. The development process clearly benefited also from improved transportation facilities and road construction projects, and particularly from the completion of the Jaffa-Jerusalem rail line, that started operations in 1892.[78]

Summary and Conclusions

Even though the *fallah* absorbed some modern innovations, the rural sector, which was encountered by visitors to Palestine during the last phase of Ottoman rule, did not exhibit a noticeable degree of agricultural progress. Studies conducted by official commissions and other researchers confirmed that the Palestinian agricultural sector lagged considerably behind most equivalent Western ones and was still based on pre-industrial tools powered by human and animal muscle. Before the last quarter of the nineteenth century Palestine's industrial level lagged behind that of its neighboring countries. Syria and Lebanon had textile factories and the latter, in particular, had a highly specialized silk industry. For most of the nineteenth century, Palestine was, in fact, the periphery of the periphery, that is, the periphery of the Ottoman Empire which was part of the world periphery.[79]

Some progress was made during the last part of the century, but development was selective, and its influence hardly reached the *fallaheen*.

In fact, in some respects, progress even worsened their condition. The Ottoman Land Law of 1858 fostered the development of the absentee landlords (*effendis*). Most of them belonged to the city-based elite. A collateral result was the expansion of the number of sharecroppers who belonged to the very lowest stratum of the rural class. This and other reforms (the *tanzimat*) widened the gap between the *fallah* and the urban elite.

The development of trans-oceanic commerce benefited the peri-urban farmers and those who had access to the rising steamship transportation and even to the existing sailing ships. Citrus fruits, melons, watermelons, and cotton were exported by small sail ships or steamships. In the southern Gaza area, where most winter grain crops were excluded by the dry climate, there was a growing barley export trade. The citrus crop generated_more widespread and stable markets. Citrus exports grew steadily and gave rise to substantial profits to its growers and to the workers that they employed who lived in the poor *saknat* (neighborhoods) that arose around Jaffa after 1840. The latter's standard of living remained, however, low. The cotton industry was rather unstable and was associated with economic fluctuations that were strongly influenced by overseas competition and political conditions. Its decline after the American Civil War hurt many farmers who had previously benefited from high war-time prices. Similar short-lived war-time prosperity was associated with grain production during World War II, when demands for food raised the price of wheat above the pre-war level.

The factors that constricted the changeover from the traditional grain-based economy to a commercial system were varied, but two of them were paramount. The first one was external: the *fallah*'s inability to compete with the American grain producers and other New World breadbaskets. The second was internal: the rising family size and the consequent demographic growth. An expression of these factors was the continual decline of grain exports during the last decades of the nineteenth century, and the eventual transformation of Palestine from a grain exporting country to an importing one. Another aspect of the second factor was the increasing local demand for food by immigrants as well as by the rising number of city dwellers. This demographic change was beneficial to the farmers.[80] But while the imported wheat was preferred by many of the migrants over the locally produced grain, the farmers could still benefit from selling their locally-produced fruit and vegetables or their meat and dairy products in the growing urban markets.

The rising population pressure, the slowly changing agrarian systems and the rising urban living standard did not completely obliterate the subsistence economy. But the need to provide immediate food security to their families reduced the *fallaheen*'s ability to devote time and energy to activities such as education or improved health and sanitation. Thus, they were unable to free themselves from the vicious circle of poverty in which they were caught. The eventual result of this pressure was to encourage the younger generation to leave the village and migrate into towns.

The traditional industrial sector was also negatively affected by the change, but the main losers from the Industrial Revolution were the neighboring countries. Paradoxically, Palestine benefited, to some extent, from its peripheral economic position. Unlike Syria, Lebanon or Egypt, it had little to lose from it because, with few exceptions, industries were virtually non-existent. When the European low-cost textiles reached the Middle East, mostly after 1840, the traditional textile industries of the neighboring countries crumbled, while Palestine lost nothing.

Many Palestinian *fallaheen* did profit from the economic transitions that took place during the last two decades of Ottoman rule. It is more difficult, however, to specify and rate the contribution of each change. It may be easier to identify the major factors for the poverty and insufficient progress and find those responsible for it. Conventional wisdom holds that the government was the main culprit. An effective, stable and uncorrupt government would have been able to assist the poor and refrain from actions likely to harm their welfare.

To be fair, however, it has to be admitted that the Ottoman government was also caught in a vicious cycle of its own. Shortage of funds resulted in a poorly trained and poorly paid staff. This led to inefficiency and attempts to obtain supplementary income through *bakshish* (tips), bribes and other corrupt practices that, in turn, resulted in intensifying the plight of the poor who were unable to pay the bribes. Similar corrupt and inefficient practices are widespread in our own time in developing countries. The remedy is not simple, but a first step, that has already proved to be effective, is a policy of family planning. Likewise, proper investment in services such as education, health, family planning, or physical infrastructure in transportation and communications would have brought about a substantial improvement in the standard of living of the rural sector.

The legal merit of the Ottoman Land Law can be questioned. The main problem was the required registration. The rest was mostly based directly on the *Shari'a* (Islamic law). The central government was not monolithic, however. As early as the first third of the nineteenth century one could discern the budding of development and some non-conventional approaches to the granting of government services. This is clearly evident in the crusade or campaign against plagues and the establishment of sanitation services, but there were economic changes also. These governmental interventions did not always have immediate effects. Development was a gradual process, and certainly not always sufficient. The contribution of local institutions and non-governmental elements in provincial centers or in various settlements was important and possibly decisive. Even if most of the innovations were local, it is hard to conceive that the economic and social development of Palestine would have been able to overcome the impediment of the lack of a proper infrastructure without external assistance. As noted in the opening part of this chapter, certain scholars believe that external involvement was of secondary importance. Even if this were true, such influences were more visible during the period when the process of development was most intense, that is, toward the end of Ottoman rule in Palestine.

The question that underlies this discussion is: How did the factors listed in this chapter affect the processes of demographic transition in Palestine? Even if for some of the subjects (like medical services) the connection is obvious, there are many items for which it would be hard to prove a demographic connection. But worldwide experience has shown that demographic changes have been closely related to economic and social factors. There are, however, major problems in attempting to document or quantify the relationships between the various components. This is even more so for the nineteenth century Ottoman system. Birth, death, and growth rates are just approximations, and when actual data can be found, one must carefully check their validity and accuracy. The next chapter deals with the causes and implications of non-Jewish migrations to Palestine. The data pertaining to the size of the rural Arab population, its spatial distribution and growth rates will be presented in chapters 3 and 4.

Notes

1. Palestine Royal Commission (Peel Commission) Report, pp. 233-334.
2. See Clay for a detailed account of the process that led to the crisis.
3. See Gross, *Economic Transitions*, pp. 111, 115; see also Gross, *Not by Spirit Alone*. For a contrary view see Muslih, pp. 37-39, and Schölch, *Transformation*, pp. 110-117.
4. Schölch, *Transformation*; see also Gilbar, "Trends."

5. See the British Consul Finn's *Stirring Times*, especially chapter 9, where records of the local struggles that he reported to his superiors, were re-written.
6. Doumani, *Merchants and Peasants*, pp. 50-54. The demographic aspects of this subject are discussed in chapter 3.
7. See e.g., Oliphant, pp. 73-77.
8. See Issawi, p. 4.
9. Graham-Brown showed that Nablus soap bars were shipped by sea. By 1908 the total shipment amounted to 4,000,000 oka (oka = a Turkish weight of c. 2.75 pounds).
10. See e.g., BD/7, Acting-Consul T.D. Jago to Consul-General Eldridge, Report, Enclosure in Doc. 2714/6/1878, pp. 356-357.
11. According to Avitzur, the price of transporting wheat by camels over a distance of fifty km was equal to the price the *fallah* received for growing it. See Avitzur, *Changes*, p. 244.
12. Clay, p. 130.
13. Clay, pp. 129-130.
14. Okyar , pp. 24-25.
15. BD/7, Jago to Eldridge, pp. 356-359 (see note 10).
16. Schölch, "European Penetration," p. 37.
17. See Oliphant, pp. 79-83, for a contemporary account on the construction; Agmon, p. 127. The labor was supervised by Meizner, a German engineer, but the endeavor was viewed as an Ottoman feat, and was considered as one of the most successful projects carried out by the government.
18. CR, 1878, p. 891, September 15, 1877, Report by Hardeg, the U.S. vice-consul in Jaffa.
19. De Haas, p. 428; Gross, *Economic Transitions*, p. 120.
20. Haifa was not the first Templer settlement. It was preceded in 1866 by Samunia, in the northern Jezre'el Plain. Unfortunately, all twelve original settlers died, and the site was deserted.
21. BD/7, Jago to Eldridge, pp. 356-358 (see note 10).
22. Further information is provided, among many others, by Gross, *Not by Spirit Alone*; Schölch, *Transformation*; Agmon.
23. CR, 1889, Consul Henry Gillman, Report, 13/12/1888, pp. 168-369; see also BD/7, Jago to Eldridge (see note 10).
24. See Firro, Silk.
25. Aktan, pp. 110-111. According to the author's calculation, the urban sector, comprising only 15 percent of the population, received 54 percent of the benefits.
26. Davison, *Reform*, p. 44; Baer, *Agrarian Relations*, p. 39; Maoz.
27. During the Egyptian rule Ibrahim Pasha also imposed a head tax (*ferde*) that was strongly protested, and, along with the military draft, served as the trigger to the 1834 uprising.
28. Farm laborer's daily income in Jaffa around 1850 was between 2 and 5 *grush*. Issawi, pp. 89-90. In the late nineteenth century the *grush* was worth about a 0.01 of British pound.
29. Gerber, "Sanjak of Jerusalem."
30. Even though the new head tax (*ferde*) was bitterly opposed, the main grievance was aroused because of his draft policy. The bitter opposition to it spread all over the country, and in 1834 a rebellion broke out. Repressive measures were not a rare occurrence, but this event had unusually extreme consequences (see chapter 2).
31. Granovsky, *Tax System*, 173-90; see also Aktan.
32. Rafeq.

33. BD/7, Harrison Report, Document 21, pp. 140-171. The tax was paid in kind at least until 1927. C.O. 733/207/87275, a telegram from the High Commissioner to the Minister of the Colonial Office, 26.5.1931.
34. BD/7, Jago to Eldridge (see note 10).
35. Karpat, *Demographic and Social*, p. 241.
36. Schölch, "Demographic Development," p. 503.
37. Karpat, *Ottoman Population*, p. 11.
38. The Abu Ghosh family, whose center was in Qaryat Al-Enab, about fifteen kilometers from the city, provides a classic case of this condition. They exploited their location on the Jaffa-Jerusalem road to collect tolls from pilgrims and tourists. See also Hoexter, Doumani, "Nablus," pp. 10-13; Doumani, *Merchants and Peasants*, pp. 50-54; Latron, pp. 230-240; Firestone, "Mushā'," pp. 114-119; see also Inalcik, "Military and Fiscal"; Baer, *Fallah and Townsman*.
39. Pamuk, pp. 88-90.
40. See Clark.
41. Braslavi, Vol. 2, p. 143, where a Bedouin agreed to sell his 22.5 hectares for two goats and an *abaya* (a long robe).
42. Among the numerous references to the *musha'* system and its legal implication are Bergheim; Post; Klein; Baldensperger in PEF article; Abramson; Poliak; Ben-Shemesh; Baer, *Agrarian Relations*; Firestone,; Grossman, "Communal Holding"; Grossman, "Implications"; Weullersse; Latron; Klat; Atran; Kark, "Land-God-Man."
43. Graham-Brown, p. 126. For a strong anti-*musha'* opinion, see, among others, Patai, "Musha'," and Patai, *Arab Mind*.
44. Nadan, "Misunderstanding," p. 320; see also Nadan, *Palestinian Peasant*, pp. 261-298.
45. See Nadan, "Misunderstanding"; Kark and Grossman, "Communal Village"; Grossman and Kark, "Common Pool."
46. See e.g., Hütteroth and Abdulfattah, list on pp. 112-220 and pocket maps.
47. Volney, II, p. 338.
48. For a discussion of cotton cultivation in the eighteenth century see Cohen, *Eighteenth Century*; see also Avitzur, *Changes*, pp. 8-22. The textile industry suffered a severe blow after the Industrial Revolution (see below).
49. I am grateful to Prof. Nahum Gross for this information.
50. Tabak. See Avitzur, "Watermelons," for a discussion of the late nineteenth-century and early twentieth-century watermelon trade.
51. A decrease of from 400-500 liter of seed per hectare to only 200-300, but with marked regional differences. It would seem that in Palestine the rate was lower than for Hauran, usually not exceeding 10:1. In the 1880s Palestinian farmers averaged only a scale of 6 (6 kg wheat per kilograms of seed), although in a good year it could even reach 12:1 (ratio of yield to seed).
52. Tabak, pp. 142-146. Additional information on the rate of input to yield for farmers can be obtained from several publications. Among them, see Avitzur, *Changes*, pp. 35-52; Johnson and Crosbie, Report, Colonial Office, C.O. 733/185/77072. (The report was also published by the Mandate government and distributed in a booklet in the three official languages. Chapter 6 provides additional details on the report; see also Elazari-Volcani, *Fallah's Farm*; Abramowitz and Gelfat.)
53. Oliphant, p. 74.
54. Oliphant, p. 75. In the early 1880s the Sursouk estates of the Jezre'el Plain shipped quantities of wheat whose value was estimated at $50,000, a huge sum in contemporary prices. Another indication the economic transition was that the price

of real estate around Haifa "has risen three folds in value during five years, while export and import have increased with a remarkable rapidity, and the population has doubled within ten years." Oliphant also stated that Sursouk paid $18,000 for the 21,000 hectares, but only £6,000 of the total sum were actually recorded. To facilitate the transportation of their crops, the Sursouk family was instrumental in the laying of the rail line linking Haifa and Damascus, that was completed in 1905; see Oliphant, pp. 78-83; Inalcik and Quataert, p. 853.

55. Inalcik and Quataert., pp. 858-859.
56. Schölch, *Transformation*, pp. 88-89, 400, 428; Rosenan, pp.150-51. Fortunately, the winter staple crops suffered only light damage.
57. CR. Consul J.G. Willson, Report, 5/10/1878, p. 1134. Rosenan; BD/7, Jago to Eldridge and Enclosure 24, 26/8/1878, p. 235. For information on Willson and other consuls see Kark, *American Consuls*.
58. Rosenan; CR 1878, Consul J.G. Willson Report, 5/10/1878, p. 1134.
59. Kark and Oren-Nordheim, p. 253.
60. CR, 1889, Gillman, Report on Jerusalem, 13/8/1888, pp. 168-173.
61. Ben-Zvi, pp. 316, 396-397.
62. Sabri, p. 354.
63. CR, 1884, Part 2, pp. 553-554. Merrill also reported on a serious outbreak of influenza that did a great deal of damage to the commerce in Jerusalem in 1889/90 (RG 59, T-471, 9/12/1890, Document 202), and of smallpox that afflicted mainly Jews and Muslims in Jerusalem in 1901 (CR, 1902, Report of Consul Merrill, November, 1901, p. 1066).
64. RG 59, T-471, 24/9/1903, Document 73; 18/10/1902, Document 60; see also 12/5/1902, Document 55. An additional epidemic of cholera that also originated in Jedda, spread to Turkey and Russia in 1910, but there is no evidence of it having affected Palestine. See BD/20, 1908-1914, Document 59, pp. 364-403.
65. Panzak, *La peste*, pp. 34-35, 343-353, 623-624; see also Yapp, p. 13. According to Ben-Zvi's list, pp. 446-452, there was only one outbreak of bubonic plague in Palestine between 1800 and 1900. It centered in the Upper Galilee, and occurred from 1811 to 1813. It was described in his list as being one of the most serious incidents. It is probable that Ben-Zvi listed only the most devastating outbreaks. These events caused a decline in the population growth rates, and there is, it seems, truth to the premise that the general demographic growth rate for the first half of the nineteenth century was rather low.
66. Panzak, *La peste*, p. 481.
67. Panzak, *La peste*, for additional details, pp. 479-492, 507.
68. In order to clarify the significance of the process of eradicating the bubonic plague, one must emphasize the fact that in spite of the general success, there remained in the Ottoman Empire points of contagion even after 1844. These occurred in specific geographic locations, all of which were on the periphery of the Empire: Iraq (especially Baghdad), and other Middle Eastern areas. Panzak attempted to explain this distribution as opposed to places which had a non-permanent rodent population that could be controlled by sanitary means and quarantines. The reason for this, he explained, was the special environmental conditions in these areas, but might even have been associated with certain lifestyle modes. Panzak, *La peste*, pp. 508-510.
69. Such are the statistical data from Istanbul from 19/12/13; see McCarthy, *The Arab World*, p. 109; in 1895 (H 1330) the Empire had only one hospital bed for every 7,000-8,000 people. In the District of Jerusalem there was only one government hospital having 38 beds, one doctor and a total staff of forty-three workers; see McCarthy, *The Arab World* pp. 107-108.

70. McCarthy, *Palestine*, p. 17. McCarthy, "Fertile Crescent."
71. McCarthy, *Palestine*, p. 17; see Schölch, *Transformation*, pp. 121-122, on the events leading to the termination of the inter-tribal conflicts in 1859.
72. Doumani, "Nablus," pp. 10-15; Issawi, pp. 51-54.
73. Philipp.
74. See Schatkowski-Schilcher; see also Ben-Zvi, p. 446.
75. Volney, I, pp. 192-194.
76. Duran, p. 169; Inalcik and Quataert, p. 872; Okyar.
77. Kushnir, "The Last Generation"; Longrigg, p. 19.
78. Brawer, "Food Supply."
79. See Braudel, III, pp. 21-45, for a discussion of the concept "periphery" and the position of the Ottoman Empire as part of the world periphery.
80. The demand for bread made from wheat was mainly from urban areas; see Gross, "Economic Transitions," pp. 122-123.

2

Migrations and Settlement of Various Ethnic Groups in the Nineteenth Century

Introduction

The purpose of this chapter is to examine the migrations of various ethnic groups that settled in Palestine (Jewish migrations are discussed for comparative purposes only) during the nineteenth century, their size, the causes, geographical distribution, and their socio-economic status. The main question posed here is, what was the impact of these migratory streams on the reserves of Palestine's arable land?

Statistical data on the various components of migrations are not always available because of the absence of official registration of the mobility from one part of the Ottoman Empire to another. Overland migrations were not treated as international crossings since they took place within the borders of the Empire. However, for one category, at least, that of Muslim refugees and displaced persons, the authorities conducted surveys in order to estimate their numbers and provide resources for their resettlement. Special commissions were appointed for this purpose and, therefore, some quantitative data can be obtained on their welfare, their size and the sites chosen for their re-settlement.

The number of refugees that streamed into the Ottoman Empire during the last four decades of the nineteenth century has been estimated to be between two and three million.[1] Most of them were absorbed outside of Palestine, but the dynamic nature of this large-scale demographic phenomenon had important ramifications for Palestine.

The rural population of Palestine also absorbed many migrants who were not defined as refugees even though many of them were forced to find new means of living or refuge because of local rivalries and even official oppressors in their original territories. Many of these migrations were just local movements, but several came from distant places including Europe and other overseas countries. The dominant local wave (i.e., within Palestine) was from Hebron to northern Samaria and its adjacent areas. This movement consisted mostly of people whose lifestyle was semi-nomadic, because the climate of their home region, which was surrounded by dry-lands, was notoriously unstable. It was subject to long periods of drought, and, occasionally, even to catastrophic events that forced its inhabitants to seek new permanent homes.

Other causes for the local moves included the search for refuges from blood revenge; inter- and intra- *hamula* (extended family) strife; regional faction wars (known as *Qais-Yaman*); escape from Bedouin raids or various other communal or individual causes; and, not the least, insufficient means of subsistence. There were also many short-distance and seasonal moves for cultivation of relatively remote or inaccessible plots. But, as noted above, the most conspicuous, mostly long distance moves, were those generated by repeated droughts or other forms of food insecurity in their original homes. This type of push-generated mobility was characteristic of the *fallaheen* (peasants) who wandered to northern Samaria and to its adjacent areas from the periphery of the Hebron Sub-District.

Migrations from areas that are now termed "foreign countries" often had similar causes. Some of them had, in fact, family- or clan-based ties and retained close links with each other. This was especially the case with the east-west move across the Jordan River. In fact, both banks of the Jordan belonged, for much of the nineteenth century, to Balqaa District. Some of the mobility was the result of purely economic reasons. There were also migrants who originated in more remote areas.

The most outstanding cases were from farther areas. They came from Circassia and Chechnya, and were refugees from territories annexed by Russia in 1864, and the Bosnian Muslims, whose province was lost to Serbia in 1878. Belonging to this category were the Algerians (*Mughrabis*), who arrived in Syria and Palestine in several waves after 1850 in the wake of France's conquest of their country and the waves of Egyptian migration to Palestine and Syria during the rule of Muhammad Ali and his son, Ibrahim Pasha. The causes of each of these migrations were unique, but they had in common a strong push factor associated with inter-ethnic or international conflicts. The following section discusses the Egyptian migration and its demographic impacts. The other migratory groups and their impacts are treated later in this chapter.

The Egyptian Migration: Background and Significance

Unlike various groups of Muslim refugees that arrived in Palestine from territories lost by the Ottomans in the Balkans or in the Caucasus Regions, the Egyptian settlers did not receive any direct government aid. However, the authorities refrained from demanding any payment for the land that the migrants managed to occupy.[2] From a demographic point of view, the Egyptian "migrants" (most of them not strictly migrants, as will be shown below) were much more numerous than any of the others that preceded the Jewish migratory waves (that are called *aliyot*; pl. of *aliyah* = ascent).

The Egyptians left their impression on the map of population distribution unevenly. Because of their extreme poverty, the relative ease with which they were absorbed into the local population and the fact that the government provided no territory for their settlement, they did not leave their mark on any specific geographical zone. Their distribution reveals, nevertheless, a clear spatial pattern whose general shape closely resembles that of the later (post-1882) Jewish one. Like the Jewish migrants, the Egyptians came in a series of waves, but unlike them, they often settled in already established villages, though in some cases, as around Jaffa, they built new ones.

The Egyptians were not newcomers to Palestine. There is evidence of their arrival at the end of the late eighteenth century as a result of a severe famine in Egypt, but several waves came even earlier. The migration was bi-directional, since many Palestinians moved to Egypt for a variety of reasons, but the following discussion focuses solely on the more dominant, one-way stream, from Egypt to Palestine.[3] The push factors were numerous: natural disasters such as droughts and plagues, oppression by government officials, tax policies and the military draft. Much has already been written about these subjects, and I have delved into these questions in prior research works, but some of these migrations have never been documented at all or only partially so.[4] I believe, therefore, that the Egyptian contribution to the demography of Palestine deserves to be thoroughly studied.

The major series of Egyptian migration waves are associated with the time of Muhammad Ali's Syrian campaign. The original wave took place in 1829, about two years before the invasions, and ended in early 1841, with the forced retreat of the Egyptian army.[5] The historical circumstances that brought about the Egyptian migrations are presented briefly below. The migrations had profound demographic and socio-economic impacts. They contributed to a population increase that more than counterbalanced the loss of life caused by the harsh rule of the Egyptians.

The Egyptian invasion was caused, at least partly, when the ruler of Syria and Palestine refused to obey Muhammad Ali's demand to repatriate the Egyptians who had escaped from the forced labor projects in the Nile Delta. But, ironically, the regime's later Syrian-Palestinian development projects were accompanied by the import of Egyptian forced labor into the conquered land. The termination of Muhammad Ali's Syrian administration resulted in another wave of Egyptian migrants. The demographic impacts of Egyptian rule in Palestine occurred thus during the period that preceded it (1829), during the period of its administrative control (1832-1839), and during its termination phase (1840-41).

The motivation for these migration waves was, thus, complex. There was a strong push factor, such as escaping from forced labor, or deserting the military forces, and on the other hand—a somewhat weaker pull factor, such as personal desires for improving economic prospects. It is possible that the military desertions that accompanied the forced retreat of the army in 1840-41 were partly motivated by the desire to take advantage of the greater productive potential of Palestine, where the pressure on the land was lower. At any rate, the Egyptian population that remained in Palestine after the retreat of the army made up the largest migration that the country had known during the nineteenth century. One of the contributions of this wave was the emergence of Jaffa and its rural hinterland, although the new neighborhoods that they established were mostly slums, built of adobe bricks and other unsorted, locally available materials.[6]

But the real demographic influence of the Egyptian settlers was in less visible areas, that is, in the rural periphery. These places included the areas from which the Bedouins had been removed as a result of Ibrahim Pasha's harsh policy against the nomads in the aftermath of the 1834 uprising (see below), but the repopulation was also felt in many existing settlements. When the first wave of Jewish migrants arrived at the end of the nineteenth century, they found a land more populated than it had been during the first half of the century. What they noticed, however, was that the population of their neighboring Arab villages was increasing. This was, in fact, partly the result of a renewed migration wave from Egypt, which was generated by the increasing employment opportunities in the new Jewish colonies.[7]

As hinted above, it is ironic that Muhammad Ali's desire to stem Egyptian migration into Palestine in 1829, which some scholars believe was one of the causes for his invasion of Syria and Palestine in 1831, was, in the end, a major generator of an even larger migration wave from Egypt. The Egyptian military campaign started with Muhammad Ali's demand from Abdallah Pasha, the ruler of Palestine and Syria, to repatriate all the *fallaheen*, who had sought refuge from the burden of forced labor in his Nile Delta development project. Most of the scholars who have researched this period believe that this demand was just an excuse, but there is no agreement as to the real cause of the invasion. A possible explanation is that the incident served as a pretext to press the Sultan to fulfill the promise to add Syria to the territories under his administration. This promise was made, according to Muhammad Ali, when he was asked to participate in the 1827 Navarino maritime battle against the British navy, which ended with the Ottoman-Egyptian defeat.[8]

The uncontested fact is that when Abdallah Pasha refused to return the refugees, Muhammad Ali's troops, led by his son Ibrahim, invaded Palestine. By the end of October 1831, he had succeeded in conquering Acre and gaining control of all Palestine and Syria. Ibrahim was then appointed governor of the captured territories. In spite of the successful operation, the refugees, whose number amounted to some six thousand, and possibly even more, were not returned to Egypt.[9]

Political and Socio-Economic Conditions during Egyptian Rule

Muhammad Ali's rule in Syria and Palestine was initially welcomed. Ibrahim Pasha established security and contributed to economic development. But the high-handedness and the harshness of the Pasha's rule had some negative impacts that led to resentment and eventually culminated in fierce and bloody revolts in 1834. The uprising, known as the Fallaheen Revolt, broke out because of the resistance to the ruler's demand to draft young men into his army (Figure 2.1) and to impose a new head-tax, even though he had promised to reduce taxation when he took over as governor. The rebellion spread quickly and soon encompassed the *fallaheen* and Bedouin population. The suppression of the uprising was cruel, but the Bedouin took the worst punishment.[10] One of the tribes of the northern Negev suffered the most. Many of its members were killed, and the survivors fled to other locations including to the southern Sharon.[11]

Ibrahim Pasha exploited the situation to increase his authority over the Bedouin, to break their power, to prevent their traditional raids against their neighbors and to improve the security of life and property throughout the country. In the Hebron zone, one of the uprising's main centers, he ruled with a brutal hand, and many of the Muslims fled to peripheral areas. The Jews and the Christians were spared because they

Fig. 2.1
Ibrahim Pasha's military camp near Jaffa, 1836

Source: W.H., Bartlett, *Jerusalem Revisited,* 1855. Reprinted in R. Kark, *Jaffa, A City in Evolution, 1799-1917,* Jerusalem: Ariel Publishig House, 2003,1976 p. 16 (Hebrew). By courtesy of Professor Ruth Kark and Mr. Ely Schiller, the publication rights holders.

were not subject to the draft and, therefore, had not joined the rebels. On the other hand, he singled out the Druze, who had joined the revolt and exploited the disorders to pillage Safad (Tzefat) and its Jewish population. Fearing his eventual revenge, many of them escaped to the Hauran Mountain (which is still called Jabal Druze) and several of their villages in Palestine were partly, or even completely, deserted.[12] These harsh steps caused a demographic decline, but it was more than offset by the net Egyptian migration into the country.

Politically, the stabilization that followed the revolt had positive results. The defeat of the Bedouin allowed the government to extend its rule to frontier areas, to allocate the vacated territories to potential settlers and to enhance other development plans. Among the latter were the northern Negev, certain parts of the poorly drained areas in the Ramla zone and the Syrian Desert. In the Ramla area, a group of Jews from Jerusalem tried to buy land (see below), but the initiative failed. At any rate, despite the harsh "ethnic cleansing" of the Bedouin, the net demographic impact of Egyptian rule is generally considered, on balance, as positive. In his own time, however, there was no universal agreement that Ibrahim Pasha's rule was benevolent. In a survey conducted among the British consuls in 1836, the answers to a question on this subject varied widely.[13] Even so, there is no doubt that the harsh punishments meted out by Ibrahim reduced Bedouin raids, suppressed the traditional of blood vengeance custom and prevented inter-tribal wars. But these advantages were only temporary. The violence was only postponed until after the retreat of Muhammad Ali's troops, and was renewed even more forcefully during the 1840s and 1850s, probably Palestine's most violent and unruly decade.

The Egyptian Military Retreat: Its Demographic Impact

The favorable impacts described in the last few paragraphs did not alter the policies of the British and their allies, who supported the Ottoman Sultan's desire to force Muhammad Ali to retreat from Syria, but they hesitated to actively engage in another naval operation against Muhammad Ali. Ibrahim's invasion of Anatolia and his advance toward Istanbul brought a definite change of policy. The British agreed to the Sultan's request to act against the threat, and Britain and Austria managed to force Ibrahim's army to retreat to Lebanon. His failure to defend the Lebanon coast against the British invaders and their bombing of Acre ended in his complete defeat and his hasty retreat to Egypt that lasted from December 1840 to January 1841.

The disorderly retreat had strong demographic significance. It magnified the number of the Egyptian "refugees" in Palestine. The many deserters, particularly from auxiliary units, also included civilians who accompanied the army. The deserters' total number probably exceeded that of the "refugees" whom Muhammad Ali had originally demanded be repatriated in 1831.

The remainder of Ibrahim's forces left Damascus in three columns and tried to avoid the populated centers as much as possible. Ibrahim's own forces traveled by the Trans-Jordanian desert route, but in spite of their precautions, he and his officers could not evade confrontations with hostile local inhabitants and many Bedouin tribesmen who kept attacking his depleted and suffering troops.[14]

Many of the returnees who managed to reach Egypt were wounded or sick with dysentery, typhus and malaria. When they entered Egypt, many were sent to hospitals where, according to eye-witnesses, conditions were very poor. Muhammad Ali had foreseen the dangers to his son's troops, but his appeal to postpone the withdrawal until the spring was rejected by Commodore Charles Napier.[15] An intelligence report of that time compared the retreat of the Egyptian forces to that of Napoleon's retreat from Moscow. This comparison may be exaggerated, but it effectively represents the pitiful impression that the defeated Egyptian army made on its observers.[16]

This impression has some bearing on one of the questions that concerns us: What was the number of the Egyptians who stayed in Palestine after Muhammad Ali's retreat? There are no documents that allow us to precisely determine the number of soldiers who returned from Syria and Palestine to Egypt, and how many deserted the ranks during the retreat. The exact answer to this question may never be known, but we may arrive at a reasonable estimate by consulting the archival records and the scientific literature that is available on this historic event. British and other European intelligence reports provide some information on this issue.[17] Using the largest estimate, we can infer that the number of army dropouts, deserters and absentees amounted to some 94,000, but there were also a number of documents that quote lower estimates.

Qualified researchers who quote the Egyptian archives supply information that seems to be fairly close to reality.[18] Despite the diverging numbers, it is fair to conclude that those who defected or were left behind by the retreating army amounted to more than ten thousand. Many of those who failed to return either perished in battles or were stricken by various diseases and by the angry *fallaheen* and Bedouin who trailed them on the arduous way back. However, many others must have stayed in Syria and Palestine.

Clearly, the Egyptian army was not exclusively Egyptian. Many of the soldiers were forcibly recruited from many locations outside of Egypt, mostly in Palestine and Syria. The 1834 revolt included many persons who must have been happy to take the opportunity of the chaotic conditions to return home. None of these "foreign" troops had any reason to "return" to Egypt.

The number Palestinian and Syrian draftees in 1835-36 was estimated by one source to be 36,100 men. Of this number, the Palestinians, excluding the Bedouin and other draftees, were about 10,000.[19] These non-Egyptian soldiers most probably returned to their original homes, and should not be counted among the other deserters. They, though not all the 36,000, must be subtracted from the number of soldiers who did not make it back to Egypt in 1841. If we accept the estimate of the surviving high estimate of 94,000 dropouts (see the intelligence reports quoted above), and subtract the 36,000, the remaining Egyptian dropouts must have been about 58,000. It is almost certain, however, that the Palestinian share was at least 20,000.

This statistical assessment does not include the many Egyptians who had managed to settle in Palestine after 1829 and during the decade of the 1830s.[20] It also does not include those civilians who arrived during the decade 1830-1840, when many Egyptians were employed by the authority's development projects and other public works. Nor does it consider the various migration waves that took place either before 1830 or after 1840. In fact, the Egyptian migration accelerated during the late nineteenth century and particularly during the British administration (1917-1948) period. Certain articles found in Jaffa (figure 2.2) left physical evidence of their former homeland.

The Distribution of Egyptian Settlers in Palestine

One way of bypassing the difficulties that are inherent in the poor migration statistics is to look at the destinations rather than the sources. Instead of counting the number of returnees to Egypt, I will now try to study the distribution of Egyptians in Palestinian destinations. This method is, admittedly, more difficult than any statistical data that are based on administrative counts. The mostly illiterate Egyptian settlers did not leave any documentation, and it is impossible to discover from

Fig. 2.2
Egyptian cameo found in Jaffa

Source: Found in Jaffa. Courtesy of Professor Ruth Kark who holds the copyrights of its publication.

the scant literature that refers to them where they settled. However, in spite of these limitations, the spatial distribution of the Egyptian settlers is fairly well known. The next discussion deals only with their destinations west of the Jordan River. The main spatial factors that account for their rural diaspora are:

a. proximity or accessibility to Egypt;
b. similarity to the Egyptian landscape;
c. the possibility of employing irrigation methods known from the Nile Valley;
d. the availability of land reserves that could be used for agriculture and grazing.

In most cases the Egyptian army dropouts and the other Egyptian settlers preferred to settle in existing localities, rather than to establish new villages. In the southern coastal plain and Ramla zones there were at least nineteen villages which had families of Egyptian origin,[21] and in the northern part of Samaria, including the 'Ara Valley, there are a number of villages with substantial population of Egyptian stock.[22]

The Coastal Plain Settlement Zones

The southern coastal plain (Philistia) met at least two of these spatial conditions. It is accessible and has underground water that lies reasonably close to the surface that can be reached by means that were well known in Egypt. However, it was densely settled and, therefore, its land reserves were low (map 2.1).[23]

In Jaffa, according to one source, there were some five hundred or more Egyptian families, that is, a population of over two thousand people.[24] On the town's periphery there was a ring of new *saknat* (neighborhoods; pl. of *sakna*) which grew up as a result of the Egyptian settlement (map 2.2). The largest was *Sakna(t) al-Misriya* (i.e., the Egyptian Neighborhood, its location along the Mediterranean coast). It spread out along the seashore cliffs north of Jaffa, parallel to the future new town of Tel Aviv (founded in 1909). Other *saknat* (map 2.3) developed along roads and within the citrus fruit belt, where seasonal employment was available. The *saknat* consisted of poorly built huts of assorted materials, with no planning or public control.[25] These "squatter" communities contributed to the demographic growth of the town and are at least partly responsible for making Jaffa the leading commercial center of Palestine.

Some ancient ruins were also resettled by the Egyptians, but most of their migrants found their way into the existing peri-urban ring. A major settlement center was in the low hills of the Ramla zone. Some indication of its role as an Egyptian destination is available from an agrarian

Map 2.1
Egyptians in the coastal plain

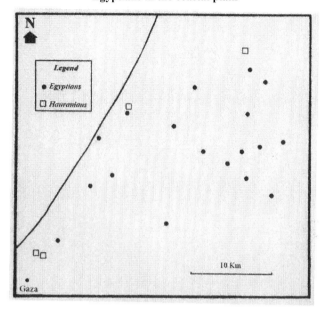

Source: Drawn by David Grossman.

survey conducted in five villages of this Sub-District in 1944, where the inhabitants of one of them were migrants.[26] At least three other Ramla villages are known to have been settled by Egyptians migrant in the same zone. Many of these settlements were recorded in contemporary publications of Jewish writers or settlers who employed the Egyptians as day laborers in their vineyards and citrus groves.[27]

At a location east of the main Jewish settlements, a group of Jerusalem Jews tried to acquire part of this land. They wrote a detailed letter to the London-based philanthropist, Sir Moses Montefiore. They requested him to help them purchase land from which the Bedouin had been expelled several years earlier,[28] but landless Egyptians migrants took over this territory. Just before the World War I started, however, part of it was acquired for Jewish settlement.[29]

The largest of the Egyptian rural concentrations were in the Sharon and the adjacent areas to the north of it along the piedmont zone (i.e., the hilly areas between the central mountains and the coastal plain.). The malaria-infested swamps northeast of Jaffa, where the Jewish rural settlement was established in 1878, and similar rural areas south of Jaffa, were also settled by dropouts of the Egyptian army.[30]

Map 2.2
Jaffa's *saknat* (detached neighborhoods)

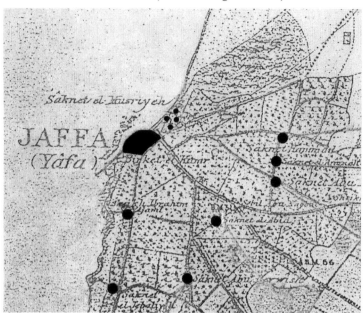

Source: Palestine Exploration Fund, Sheet 13 of 26 sheets, 1878, modified by David Grossman

The number of Egyptian families who moved to the adjacent Sharon was most probably even higher than that of the adjacent Samaria zone. Many of the families were absorbed in the Sharon's existing villages or on the eastern periphery foothills of Samaria where the soils are of higher quality and the villages are larger and more stable. In the Sharon proper settlement stability was lower. There were frequent fluctuations of population, and the Egyptian migrants had to adapt to the low soil quality of the area. At least three semi-nomadic Egyptian clans, that led a lifestyle resembling that of the Bedouin, grazed their flocks and cattle in the southern part of the Sharon and several others have lived in other parts of the region.[31]

Bedouized Egyptians were also widespread in the northern Negev region, where they became sharecroppers of the Bedouins. Most of them, however, as also those of the Sharon, eventually settled down in permanent places located in the foothills. In the Negev they were instrumental in introducing methods of dry farming and some irrigation techniques that they adapted to local conditions (see the next section).[32]

Map 2.3
Saknat Abu Kabir and the surrounding citrus groves

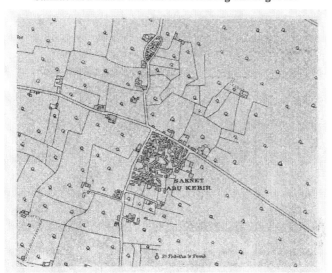

Source: Professor Ruth Kark, "Jaffa, from village to town, changes in urban structure,"
David. Grossman (ed.), *Between Yarkon and Ayalon, Studies on the Dan zone and the
Lod Valley*, Ramat-Gan: Bar-Ilan University Press, 1983 (Hebrew), p 114. Courtesy of
Professor Ruth Kark who holds the copyrights of its publication.

The Internal Valleys, Samaria and the North

The 'Ara Valley connects the Sharon with the Jezre'el plains. Geographically, it is the physical boundary between northern Samaria and
the Carmel's foothills (the Ruha Heights), where additional Egyptian
families settled (map 2.4). A descendent of an Egyptian migrant whom
I interviewed in a large village (now a town) in this valley told me how
his family had migrated from its Hijaz origin through Egypt, then to
the southern coastal plain. From there one of his ancestors' branches
wandered to the 'Ara Valley. He pointed to an olive tree that, according
to the family tradition, was planted by the first settler and was about
150 years old (that is, probably about the time of the Egyptian retreat).[33]
Stories of similar "leap frog" migrations, though not as detailed, were
obtained in other places as well.

North of the 'Ara Valley, in the Ruha Heights (in Hebrew: Ramat Menashe) there were also many Egyptian settlers. In two of its settlements,
the Egyptian presence was significant. It is likely that a large segment
of the scattered population of the area's small hamlets included other

Egyptian migrants. The soils are shallow and poor, and most of it was unsettled before the mid-nineteenth century (see chapter 5).[34] Much of the land was subsequently sold out to absentee owners (*effendis*) who settled their sharecroppers in new hamlets. After 1937 these owners sold much of their properties to Jewish settlement organizations. The rest were seasonally inhabited by semi-nomadic clans of Turkmen origin.

'Ara Valley and its vicinity also acted as interim stops for migrants moving to inland locations. An example is an extended family of a large village in the Lower Galilee called 'Araba. Like the 'Ara Valley, the person who originally "leap frogged" into 'Araba settled by taking advantage of the Land Registration Code in 1864, and officially privatized his communal holdings. His *hamula* is now the owner of as much as one third of the land of the Natuf (Hebrew: Beit Netofa basin; see chapter 5).[35] It is likely that the reason for his successful claim was that much of the basin is poorly drained and is almost totally flooded in wet winters. It is mostly unfit, therefore, for raising winter grain crops. Now, because of the possibility of marketing summer crops in the Israeli market, it

Map 2.4
Egyptian families in Samaria

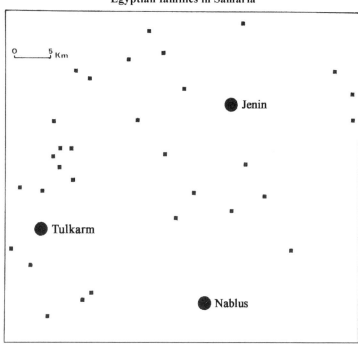

Source: Drawn by David Grossman.

fetches a substantial income from growing high quality watermelons without artificial irrigation.

Poorly drained swampy lands located in a plain northeast of modern Haifa also attracted the displaced Egyptians. Some of the occupants of these swampy areas were descendents of tribes or fractions of tribes of Sudanese origin that had occupied these areas, as they also did in the Sharon, long before the nineteenth century. Even more extensive swamps were in the Hula Basin of the northern Jordan Basin. The dwellers of these unhealthful lands resided in huts constructed from reeds, and subsisted mainly on the products of their water buffaloes. They were afflicted with malaria and other diseases and were regarded by their neighbors as the lowest stratum of the rural population. They were indeed the poorest population of Palestine. Because many of them had dark skin they were considered to be of Sudanese origin, but in fact they are of heterogeneous sources that had arrived in the marshlands at various times. Many of them probably preceded even the arrival of the Ottoman administration.[36]

The approximate Egyptian dispersal pattern is depicted in map 2.5, but persons of Egyptian origin were scattered, in fact, throughout Palestine. They were also found in villages of the Beisan (Beit She'an) Valley, in Hebron and in the Jerusalem Mountains. The major zones of Egyptian settlement had deficient resource bases: rocky fields (northern Samaria), poor red sandy soils (Sharon), thin soils in the Ruha Heights, and swamps (Hula Basin, the northern Sharon and other plains).

These destinations were, in short, mostly "leftovers" with low density. This generalization also applies to many of the Jewish settlement zones, which in many cases followed on the heels of the Egyptians (map 2.6; compare with map 2.5). The correlation between population density and resources will be covered in greater detail in the coming chapters.

Estimating the Number of Egyptian Settlers in Palestine

In an attempt to estimate the number of these migrants, I consulted the Israeli official population registration. According to this register there were 20,185 persons whose family name contained the words *Masri* and *Massarwa* (i.e., *Egyptian*) or some variations of these names.[37] I also counted the people listed in the Israeli 2007-8 telephone books that have such names. The total tally of the latter was only about 2,000, but 63.6 percent (i.e., 1,271) of the total was accounted for by three settlements of the Sharon and the 'Ara Valley.[38] This is certainly not a representative sample. The West Bank and Gaza Strip were not counted, and it is evident that most Egyptian families have no identifiable names. Combining the findings of a number of sources, which unfortunately do not provide population data, it can be concluded that of the total number of "fixed" settlements (excluding Bedouin) within the area of present-day Israel was at least 64. The *Masri-Massarwa* list accounts for about 2 percent of the 2006 Arab population of Israel.[39]

Map 2.5
Egyptian dispersal and settlement process in Palestine

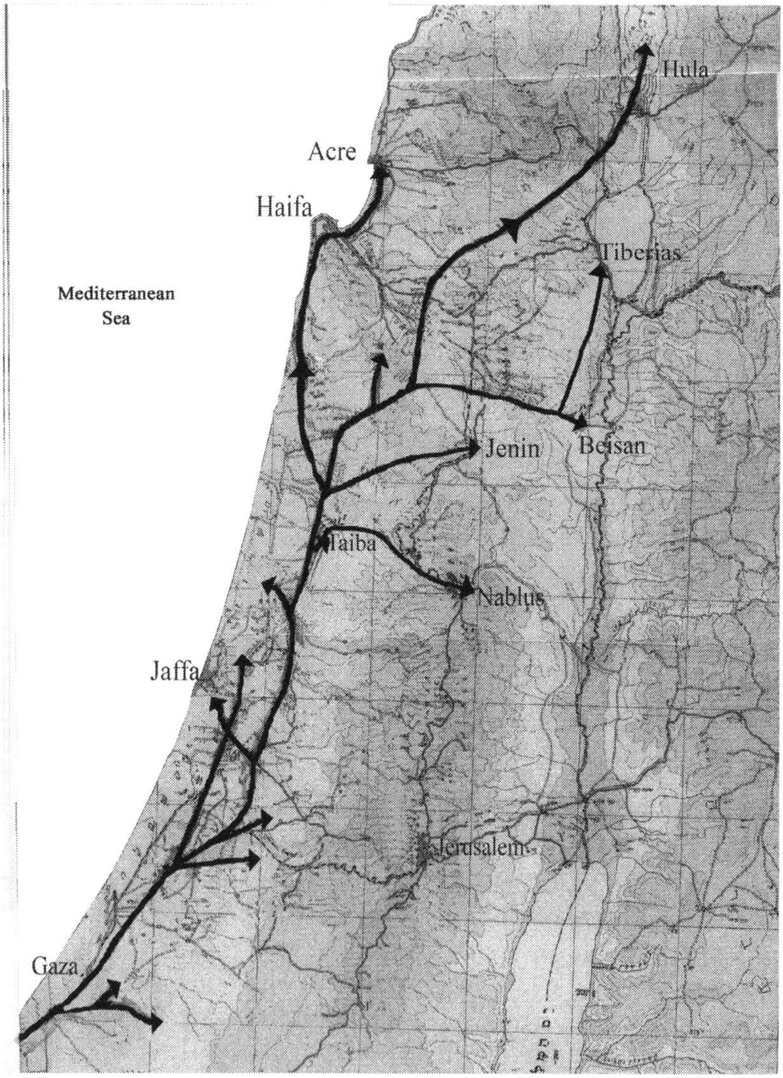

Source: Drawn by David Grossman

Map 2.6
Jewish settlement distribution in the period 1918-1948

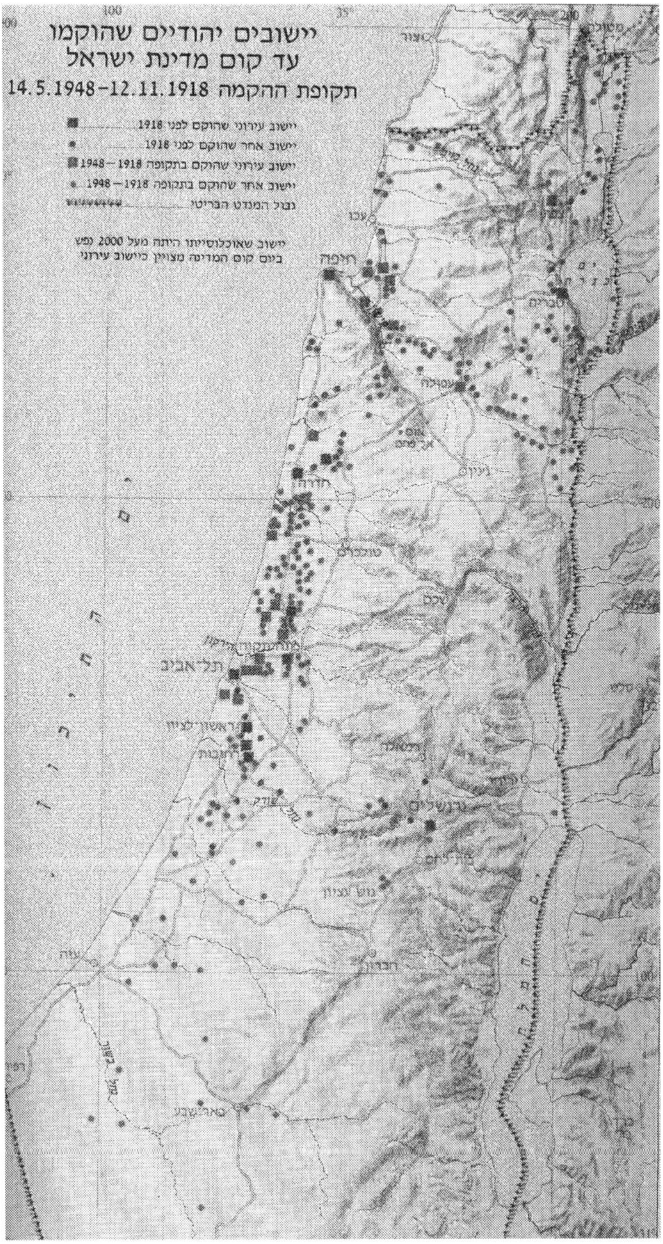

Source: *New Israel Atlas*, Tel Aviv: Survey of Israel, 1995 (Hebrew), p. 46. Courtesy of Survey of Israel. All rights reserved by the Survey of Israel © 2010.

I was also able to obtain fairly reliable information on the semi-nomadic Bedouin tribes who claim to have Egyptian ancestry. In the Negev their total number in the official voter registration records of all the Negev tribes was, in 2006, about 44,030 (approximately one third of the entire Bedouin population of the Negev).[40] The Bedouin diaspora in other parts of Israel is concentrated in urban areas. Its "Egyptian" share is not known to me. The Galilee has many Bedouin, but it is not likely that it included descendants of "Egyptians."

Another approach is to consult historical records on the Bedouin demographic data. According to the Israeli census of 1961 the number of the Negev Bedouin was about 17,000. This estimate includes tribes which moved out of their territory (*direh*) either because of severe droughts and other natural calamities, or because of blood revenge and inter-tribal warfare. The latter events resulted in "chain reaction" mobility: a defeated tribe pushing neighboring tribes out of their territories in an effort to compensate for its own losses.[41]

Not all the Negev Bedouin who originated in Sinai were descendents of "genuine" migrants, or of permanent movers who were pushed out of their home territory. Many of them arrived in Palestine as a result of regular seasonal mobility. These Bedouin were omitted from the above counts, but while the arrival date of most tribes is uncertain, the tradition of at least one tribe (about 10,000 people in 2006) holds that its ancestors were descendents of laborers employed by Ibrahim Pasha. On the basis of the scant data I assume that a century earlier the Egyptians stock numbered only about 6,000 souls.[42]

We have to add to this figure the non-Bedouin rural and urban "Egyptians." In Jaffa, the number of the Egyptian 1830s settlers was about 5,000. There were also many others who settled in other towns and villages. It is difficult to estimate their exact number, but on the basis of the crude statistics of 1829 to1841, they must have exceeded 15,000. My best guess is that the entire number of the Egyptian stock was at least 23,000 and possibly even 30,000, but, in the absence of documentation, the number remains undecided (see this and previous notes).[43]

This estimate excludes the even larger number of the Egyptians who migrated to Palestine between the late nineteenth century and 1948. The number of the Egyptians in Palestine substantially increased after 1882 (the Jewish First *Aliyah*) and again during British Mandate. During World War II there was a large wave of migrants, as a result of the increased demand for labor for building camps and other military facilities in the Palestinian coastal plains.[44]

Most of the Egyptians who arrived during the 1830s provided a reservoir of sharecroppers employed on absentee landowners' estates and on Bedouin land. As noted above, they were also employed as laborers at the Yarkon water mills (figure 2.3). Some of them, mostly from Sudan, raised water buffaloes along this river and several other streams and swamps.[45] They eked out a living by whatever means they managed to find, and belonged to the lowest class of the rural dwellers, but there were also some notable exceptions.

One of the migrants became a rich landowner by "agreeing" to register large tracts of land in his name when the 1858 law was implemented (see chapter 1). He even possessed a large property near Jaffa, where he owned an impressive *buyara* (literally a well house) where his permanent staff was housed. Near it was a water mill (*saqya*; *antiliya*) that pumped the water from an underground well (figure 2.4).

His descendents eventually made a large fortune by selling land to the Jewish National Fund. This was not the only family of Egyptians who were able to acquire wealth. There were similar cases in the Sharon and, as already noted, in the Galilee. These were, however, a minority of the otherwise impoverished Egyptian migrants.[46]

The present discussion has concentrated on Egyptian migrants, and focused mainly on the drop outs and deserters of Muhammad Ali's army. But, as was pointed out, this was not the only wave of Egyptian migrants. Others pre-dated Muhammad Ali and some arrived as late as the Mandate era, all

Fig. 2.3
Ruins of a watermill in Mir

Source: Professsor Shmuel Avitzur, *On the Banks of the Yarkon River, 1947*, Tel Aviv: Dvir, 1980 (Hebrew), p. 91. Courtesy of Ms Nili Keinan, heir of the late Professor Shmuel Avitzur, who holds the publication rights of this book.

of whom substantially increased the overall number of the population of Egyptians and their descendants. There is no reason to believe that Everett Lee's principle, that every migration has a counter stream, does not apply to Palestine, but the likelihood of a large return migration is doubtful.[47]

The rural Egyptian settlers were the most important non-Jewish settlers. They resembled the Jewish migrants in their settlement pattern. It can be represented by a simple model consisting of irregular articles or other rough particles that are thrown into a vessel that already contains many similar articles. The new pieces fill in the residual empty, or partly occupied, spaces that are mostly the less attractive ones.

This model is particularly suitable for describing the non-regulated Egyptian settlement pattern. It cannot be applied to other migratory waves which are discussed below, whose settlements were mostly predetermined by the Ottoman administration or by kinship and business considerations. However, unlike the latter that are mostly well recorded, the Egyptian process and pattern is poorly documented. It clearly deserves additional studies to overcome this lacuna.

Migrations from Other Locations: A Review

Throughout the entire Ottoman period, there had been many migratory streams. In almost every village it is possible to find families that were from various external locations. The places of origin varied. Aside from Egypt, the largest external groups came from eastern Trans-Jordan and the Arabian Peninsula. There were also families from Libya, Algeria, Sudan, Iraq, Syria, Lebanon, Turkey, and Iran. Among the nomads there

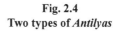

Fig. 2.4
Two types of *Antilyas*

Source: Professsor Shmuel Avitzur, *Man and His Labor, Atlas of the History of Work Tools and Production Equipments in Eretz Israel*, Jerusalem Carta, 1976 (Hebrew), p. 63. Courtesy of Ms Nili Keinan, heir of the late Professor Shmuel Avitzur, who holds publication rights of this book.

were mainly Turkmen and Kurds. The Galilee contained many scattered tribes or parts of tribes, who lived in tents. Their vast majority moved to permanent houses built in their own villages, but most of the migrants were originally *fallaheen* who were absorbed among their host villages and, therefore, it is difficult to map their distribution.

The Turkmen nomads subsisted mainly on flock herding in the northern Sharon and on the fringe of the Jezre'el Plain, using Ruha (a-Ruha) as a land bridge between the two locations. The poor, short grass of the Ruha Heights is probably derived from the Arabic root *RUH* = go (or walk), and was probably given to it because it was primarily used as a walking zone between two terminal places rather than as a location which had its own significance. During the late nineteenth century, the Turkmen started to fix a couple of camp sites. They also had a number of villages in Samaria.[48]

The most significant bi-directional migrations took place across the Jordan. This suggests there existed strong historical ties between the western (Nablus) and eastern (Balqaa) zones. The social and economic ties between the eastern and western banks were also linked until 1887 by a common administration. Nablus and Balqaa were joined in a single district during much of the nineteenth century (until 1887). During the late nineteenth century the movement from Nablus surpassed that from the opposite direction.[49] As will be shown below, the Nablus-to-Balqaa or to Zarqa movement generated a sustained development process in the sparsely settled eastern bank of the Jordan River. The change was the result of better security that was generated, in part, by the policing activities of relatively new groups of migrants, the Circassians and the Chechens. The impact of this migration will be discussed in some detail.

These migrations were not limited to Palestine alone and in most cases their demographic influence on other parts of the Empire was stronger than that in Palestine. The official aid was mostly granted for the rehabilitation of the Muslim refugees who had been uprooted from their homes during the Balkan and the north Caucasian wars.

The assistance policy that operated during the *tanzimat* (the 1839 and 1871 reforms) had additional purposes. It also encouraged the migration of non-refugee European and American migrants who were familiar with modern agricultural methods. They were directed to the Empire's sparsely settled and peripheral land and were expected to promote their development by settling them and increasing the population. The government believed that the economic backwardness of these territories was due to under-population, and that the European settlers would be able to help in the development of these peripheries. A special law enacted in March 1857 encouraged Europeans to settle in the empire. The permission was conditioned on the submission of proof that the potential migrant had substantial financial resources and would be faithful to the laws of the Empire. The government promised to grant the migrants the best land available, and even to pay for the building of churches or other prayer houses. This offer raised wide interest throughout the Christian world.

The Templer movement was one of the first to take up the proposal. The Templer members established their first (though unsuccessful) colony on the northern fringe of the Jezre'el Plain in 1866, and two years later they settled in Haifa, which became the main springboard for their later expansion. Their plan was mainly religiously motivated, but later became infused by strong social-nationalistic ideology. Its stated goal was to bring to Palestine a large number of Germans.[50]

The Jews, on the other hand, did not rush to accept the challenge. The Jewish migrants, the *olim* of the Hovevei Zion (i.e., Lovers of Zion, the movement favoring the migration to Palestine, active long before 1897, the year of the first Zionist Congress), discovered the law's potential only several decades later. The first Jewish rural migration began only in the 1880s. But when the government found out that the fast-growing Jewish migration was motivated by nationalist aspirations, the policy was changed, and in 1906 the Jewish *Aliyah* was prohibited. The initial restrictions on migration began even earlier. In 1886 the Jerusalem District governor opposed the granting of migration permits to a group of forty American families, but officially, the rules were not specifically aimed against Jews.[51]

The emerging European nationalistic movements and the vehement anti-Semitism that accompanied them had strongly affected Jewish aspirations. The unification of Italy and Germany and the growing number of Balkan states, which succeeded in reaching their aspirations for independence in the last quarter of the nineteenth century, strengthened the emerging Jewish nationalist ideology. Both push and pull factors were responsible for the growing Jewish migration waves that started in 1882.

The Jewish migrants, like the others, took advantage of the existence of relatively large tracts of sparsely populated territories. Like the Egyptian migrants, they helped to alter the settlement distribution and expanded the settlement frontier of Palestine. The following discussion focuses on non-Egyptian Muslim migrants, whose demographic impact was somewhat different.

The Algerian Migrants: Size and Distribution

Despite the relative heterogeneity, the majority of the nineteenth century migrants were Muslims. The Ottoman Empire had to cater to refugees from Algeria (*Mughrabis*) and later, after 1850, it was faced with numerous refugees from the Caucasus and the Balkans. The receiving areas where they were settled in Palestine were thinly populated. The reason for the availability of the land was, in many cases, that it was characterized by some form of ecological deficiency. Internal violence might also have been a factor.

As noted above, the Ottoman government absorbed many Muslim refugees during the second half of the nineteenth century. Among them were those who had joined 'Abd al-Qadr al-Jazairi, the head of the failed revolt against the French 1830 conquest of Algeria. After his defeat 'Abd al-Qadr was expelled to Paris and was later allowed to migrate to the Ottoman Empire. In 1855 he reached Damascus, and from there he and his followers moved to Palestine. The number of Algerian migrants later increased for various reasons. One of them was the compulsory military service that the French colonial regime imposed in 1883 on the Algerian population. This gave rise to one of additional four migration waves that occurred after 1855. The last wave started in 1900 and lasted to 1920.

The Ottoman authorities granted the migrants ten villages and two additional hamlets near Haifa, and also settled them in additional locations within Palestine. Husha', one of the two hamlets near Haifa, proved to be problematic. It was located on mostly rocky land, and the Algerians' relationship with their neighbors was not amicable. They had long disputes with the local Arabs over the extent of their territory and on the possession of some of the olive groves of the area. The relatively close proximity of the developing Haifa town was, however, an advantage. Some of them found employment there.[52]

The villages granted to the Algerians were at that time either totally vacant or under-populated. The devastating earthquake of January 1, 1837 may have been the cause of the low population of the Safad area. The Tiberian villages were also hit by the quake, but they were probably also the victims of Bedouin raids and tribal warfare,[53] or of severe climatic conditions. The Safad villages included two localities which were in the malaria-infested Hula Basin. The rest were in the relatively flat area north of Safad or on the eastern slope facing the Rift Valley, where the terrain was rugged and rocky (map 2.7). The census records of the Mandate period revealed that the population of several of these villages was mixed, and their inhabitants contained, besides the Algerians, Kurds, and local Arabs.

The Tiberian villages were mostly in better locations. All four of them were in a single, well defined area of the eastern Lower Galilee, which was relatively flat and had tillable soils. But the agricultural resources were somewhat problematic, because the precipitation was relatively low and the soils tended to crack and lose their moisture after short dry spells. The property of the Emir 'Abd al-Qadir and his descendents was located in an area of ruined villages and powerful Bedouin tribes. This suggested that there was some inherent instability in the region.

Most of the original Algerian settlers eventually left the area after the son of 'Abd al-Qadir (the Emir) sold his properties to the Jewish Colonization Association (ICA) and, later, to the Jewish National Fund (JNF) and other Jewish companies, in a series of transactions conducted during the early part of the twentieth century. The Emir promised to transfer the Algerians to Syria where he owned other large land properties, and many left with him. These deals led to an eventual transformation of most of the eastern Lower Galilee into a contiguous Jewish territory that included a number of Jewish settlements. Statistical records reveal, however, that as late as 1945, most of the ten villages that were originally granted to the Algerians were still inhabited. It is not known, however, how many of the people residing there were of Algerian extraction.[54]

Map 2.7
Algerian settlements: Distribution pattern

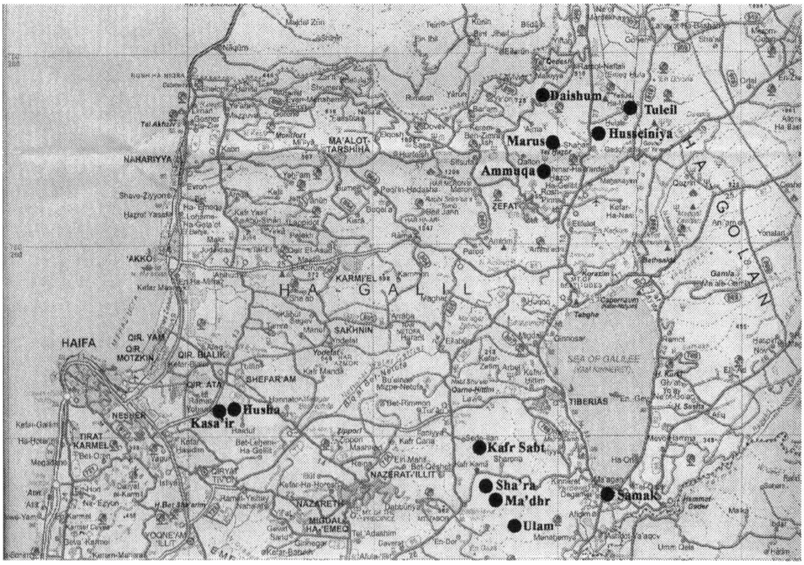

Source: Drawn with major alterations by David Grossman.

Circassian Distribution: Location and Settlements

The Circassian refugees were also granted agricultural land in the Galilee. The grantees consisted also of a few Chechens who migrated into the Empire mainly after the Russians conquered their last northern Caucasian stronghold in 1864. But the larger waves of these migrants were settled mostly outside of Palestine, including a substantial number in territories surrounding Palestine. Their total number in the Ottoman Empire was about one million.[55]

The Circassian diaspora included the Danube area and other locations, where Circassians acquired a reputation for their military expertise. They proved to be loyal to the Ottomans and were employed as guards and policemen. But their violent nature was resented by most of the often brutally treated population. They refrained from forming close relationships with the local inhabitants even though they were Muslims, maintained their former culture and refrained from marrying local inhabitants.[56]

To counter these, the Circassians proved to be good farmers and efficient settlers. The few villages that they were given in Palestine have been more successful than those of the other migrant groups but, as will be shown below, they deserted the three settlements which were originally granted to them in the northern Sharon. Unlike many of the Algerians, they held on to their farms and have managed to stay there to the present day. They reside now in two villages, one north of Safad and the other in the Lower Galilee, not far from the villages of the Algerians.

In Palestine, as in the Danube zone, the Circassians were not liked by their host populations. They had a reputation for violence and lawlessness. A few settlers of a southern coastal plain village, some "eight hours" by horse from northern Sharon, complained about the Circassian habit of extorting them by repeatedly demanding food and money, and by threatening them with violence if they refused to comply.[57] An even more extreme complaint about the Circassian violence was expressed by the journalist and writer Laurence Oliphant. He described them as highwaymen and horse thieves and complained especially against their violent activities against the Templer settlers of Haifa.[58] Ironically, he noted that "the people who committed the Bulgarian atrocities [were settled] within three or four miles from the colonists belonging to the same race they massacred."[59] He was not aware, however, that both Bosnian and Circassians were Muslims, while the "atrocities" were committed against Christians who were not loyal to the Ottoman rulers. In fact, several Bosnian families settled in the Circassian Galilee villages.

The geographical proximity that Oliphant was alluding to was the zone of the northern Sharon, where the newly arrived Bosnians had been settled in a new planned village within the ruins of ancient Caesarea (map 2.8), not far from the Circassian colonies. To the west of it there were two estates, one Bosnian and the other Circassian. The distance between them was about one mile.

Grants of land to the refugees were not an innovation. The government used its legal means to favor the refugees by reserving the vacant or neglected lands for their rehabilitation, and by not granting them to any other potential settler. As noted above, this policy was applied also in the case of the Algerians, and was provided by the authorities in areas of relatively low population in the Balkans, in Trans-Jordan and in Syria, along with financial assistance. The settlers were freed from taxes for eight years and also from obligatory military service. The lands they received were state property (*miri*), but no claimant could obtain permission for their use until the refugees could be properly settled.[60]

The Circassian hamlets of the northern Sharon did not survive very long.

The cause was, probably, endemic malaria infestation. They moved out and were re-settled instead in two Galilee villages. The first was settled in 1873, before the war of 1878, while the other was founded only in 1880.

In the neighboring Muslim countries, the Circassians and Chechens were more effectively absorbed. In the quarters of Beirut and Damascus there were more than 55,000 Circassian families. After 1873 most of them were united in Damascus, but quite a few were settled in arid, sparsely populated rural areas of the Euphrates Valley and in the Golan Heights. In Trans-Jordan they settled in several places. They were, in fact, those who converted Amman, a former *khirba* (ruin) that functioned mainly as a watering point for Bedouin flocks, into a permanent town that later became the capital of modern Jordan.

In Palestine, their previous Sharon lands were eventually acquired by Jewish companies. The Jewish settlers arrived in 1900, but were soon hit by the endemic malaria. About half of the population perished from the disease. But despite repeated calls by the Jerusalem Jewish community to leave the "cursed place," they insisted on remaining. The place they founded was a large swamp named Hadera (green in Arabic). This name was retained, and it is now a central transportation hub of the Sharon plain.[61]

Map 2.8
Distributions of Circassians and Bosnians in Palestine

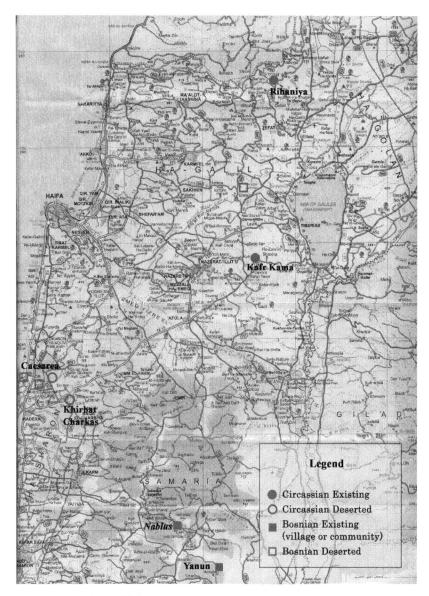

Source: Drawn by David Grossman.

The Bosnian Distribution: Locations and Settlements

The other ethnic group that found refuge in Palestine was the Bosnians (locally known as *Bushnak*). Their arrival was the result of the detachment of Bosnia from the Ottoman Empire in 1878, but their first appearance in Palestine was apparently after their failed uprising in 1864.[62] Many Muslim Bosnians, who preferred to be under Islamic rule, were also given large landed estates. Their central settlement was in ancient Caesarea, where they built a newly planned village inside the ruins. The village had, in 1887, "22 well built houses with tiled roofs" (figure 2.5).[63] It became, in fact, the first permanent habitation of Caesarea since its destruction in the thirteenth century, and was declared the center of the newly formed *nahiya* (the smallest administrative unit, see chapter 4), headed by a Bosnian settler (map 2.9).

The Bosnians were also granted several other estates in the new *nahiya* and a few of them resided in other parts of the country. The residence of the former *nahiya* head (*mudir*) is shown below (figure 2.6). Unfortunately, it was totally demolished in the late 1980s. Eventually these properties were also acquired by Jewish companies, and several new Jewish settlements emerged on them.[64] There are still a few isolated *Bushnak* families in the Nablus District, where they had an estate and a small village on the outskirts of the town, but most of them dwell in the town. A few families have also migrated to the Galilee, where they resided in the two Circassian villages, but the village they established there did not survive for long (map 2.8 above). It is now inhabited by Bedouins.

The Bosnian and the Circassian migrants left a lasting mark on the country. The Bosnians pioneered in reviving ruins. They also constructed large farm buildings, one of which includes a big yard, surrounded by several rooms for permanent workers, storage and animal watering places. The structure was surrounded by twenty huts and there were sixty additional huts in three other new settlements in the vicinity.[65]

The settlements of the Circassians successfully accomplished the task that they were expected to fulfill: to subdue the Bedouins. Most previous migration movements between Nablus and Balqaa were one way streams (i.e., from Balqaa to Nablus). The opposite stream (from Nablus to Balqaa) was an innovation that was due to the Circassians. The pacification accomplishment contributed thus to the success of an additional migratory wave that soon grew and included enterprising businessmen who invested mainly in the region's agriculture. Wealthy migrants and notables from this city helped to develop and enlarge the East Bank city of Salt that grew up to become an important economic and political center.[66]

Map 2.9
Plan of Bosnian village in Caesarea, drawn by G. Schumacher

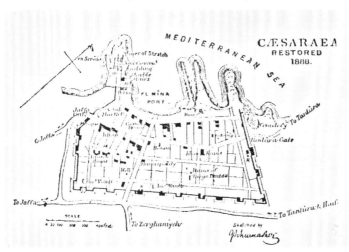

Source: Zvi Ilan, Turkmen, "Circassians and Bosnians in the northern Sharon," David Grossman, Avi. Degani and Avshalom Shmueli (eds.), Hasharon Between Yarkon and Carmel, Tel Aviv: Eretz and Ministry of Defense, 1990 (Hebrew), p. 282. Courtesy of Professor Avi Degani, Editor of Eretz Series, who holds the rights of publication of this book.

Fig. 2.5
The Bosnian village inside ruins of Caesarea

Source: Zvi Ilan, "Turkmen, Circassians and Bosnians in the northern Sharon," David Grossman, Avi. Degani and Avshalom Shmueli (eds.), Hasharon Between Yarkon and Carmel, Tel Aviv: Eretz and Ministry of Defense, 1990 (Hebrew), p. 285. Courtesy of Professor Avi Degani, Editor of Eretz Series, who holds the rights of publication of this book.

Fig. 2.6
The house of the former Bosnian *Bek* of the *nahiya* of Caesarea

Source: Zvi Ilan, "Turkmen, Circassians and Bosnians in the northern Sharon," David Grossman, Avi. Degani and Avshalom Shmueli (eds.), *Hasharon Between Yarkon and Carmel*, Tel Aviv: Eretz and Ministry of Defense 1990 (Hebrew), p. 281. Courtesy of Avi Degani, Editor of Eretz Series, who holds the rights of publication of this book.

The impact of this migration was felt mostly in the few existing towns of the East Bank which were close or easily accessible from Nablus.[67] Even though the official record of the Circassians' number in the West Bank (Palestine proper) amounted to only 1,333 persons (450 households),[68] their overall impact on the country's security clearly exceeded their demographic strength.

Summary and Conclusions

Of all the refugees and migrants that have been discussed above, only those from Egypt substantially affected the settlement distribution map of Palestine. The influence of the deserters from the army of Ibrahim Pasha can be encountered even today in most parts of the country. They had reached these destinations before the arrival of the Jewish rural settlers. Many of the settlement zones were marginal. The correlation with the Jewish settled areas is conspicuous. Like the latter, the Egyptian migrant tended to follow a pattern that approximates an **N**-shaped belt that stretched from the Upper Galilee Prong southward through the Jordan Valley to the Beisan Basin, from there in a diagonal line through the Jezre'el Plain to Haifa Bay and then southward again through the Sharon plain and to the southern Ramla area (map 2.6).[69] The main differences between the two are, however, that the Egyptian migratory zone extended deeply into northern Samaria and that the western "leg" of the N was thicker. It stretched into the southern coastal plain, where few Jews were able to acquire land, and much deeper into the Negev.

The socio-economic differences are clearly more essential than the broad spatial ones. The Egyptian migrants tended to mingle with the local inhabitants in existing villages. The Jews, on the other hand, resided in separate villages and usually also in more definite concentrations that grew around a pole in a form of a spreading ink blot.[70] The Jewish spatial pattern was the fruit of a long process, even though its form was already taking shape by the early twentieth century.

Similarities of the settlement distribution between the other migrant groups (Bosnians, Circassians, and Algerians) were not so striking, mainly because the number of their villages was small. Even so, their distribution was also based on "leftovers" and, consequently, on a relatively low resource base. This is fairly evident in the eastern Lower Galilee and the northern Sharon which functioned as parts of the cradle of Jewish rural settlement.

The "leftover pattern" was the outcome of varying processes. The Ottoman government granted some of the migrants empty lands in areas of sparse population, while others, like the Egyptians, moved into such lands on their own by squatting on vacant plots. They did not legally buy the properties from local inhabitants. But parts of the land granted to them were eventually sold to the Jews.

We do not have sufficient data on the processes of settlement of the Egyptians, but since they had little or no land resources many of them became semi-nomads while others lived in existing villages with no land rights. They suffered from an inferior socio-economic status, and had to survive as sharecroppers or day laborers.

The Jewish experience was very different. The settlers insisted on the legal purchase of land and usually did so by grouping together or by acquiring land by specialized private or public companies, settling organizations and philanthropists. But they too could not be very choosy. Supply was limited to unoccupied land, and availability rather than quality was often the deciding factor. There is already a large volume of literature that details these acquisitions and it is not necessary to deal with them here. The conclusion presented in this section is a generalization. It is not meant to apply to any specific case.

In the next chapter I will focus on some of the main characteristics of Palestine's population geography. More specifically, I will attempt to arrive at a close estimate of the population size by a critical analysis of the available sources and research findings.

Notes

1. Karpat ("Ottoman Population", p. 246) estimated the number of the Caucasus refugees at about two million. Lewis, Nomads, quoted a figure of three million for the total migration, including that from the Balkans.
2. Kressel and Aharoni, p. 229.
3. Volney, I, pp. 193-194.
4. Among the sources are Volney; Baldensperger, in book. Some of the later studies on the Egyptian migrations are: Marks; Bailey; Avneri; Mendelsohn Rood; Kressel and Aharoni.
5. The term Egyptians commonly used for denoting Muhammad Ali's rule. I will also use this term in the following discussion. Strictly speaking, however, Muhammad Ali was Albanian, not Egyptian.
6. Kark, *Jaffa*, pp. 114-115.
7. References to this population growth can be found, e.g., in Ya'ari, *Memories*, pp. 25-26; Ya'ari and Harizman, *Petah Tiqva*, pp.13-14; see also Grossman, *Expansion and Desertion*, p. 155, notes 50 and 51.
8. Marsot, *Egypt*, p. 222; Marsot, "Muhammad Ali," p. 66.
9. The number according to Sabri, *Empire*, p. 191, was 6,000; see also Marsot, *Egypt*, p. 222 and De Haas, p. 395. However, Gideon Kressel, "Bedouin Population," stated that the number of refugees was about 18,000. This outcome is based on a table listing the major events of Palestine during the Ottoman period. Ben-Zvi (p. 448) stated that the Egyptian migrants numbered 12,000. Ben-Zvi based this figure on Sabri, whose discussion of the causes of the 1829 events mentioned the event twice. This is apparently why Ben-Zvi arrived at 12,000. But Kressel also cited Rustum, who said that in 1831 there was another migration wave from Egypt (Rustum, pp. 25-26). It seems that by doubling Sabri's data and adding the 1831 wave, he arrived at the total of 18,000. See Kressel, "Beduoin Population." I found no reference to this number in the publication of other researches which preceded Kressel (Zvi Hershlag, p. 92; Aaron Cohen, p. 324; Arnon Soffer).
10. Manna'. The reforms instituted by Ibrahim Pasha are detailed in Yazbak, pp. 29-43, who described the administration of Haifa during the decade of "Egyptian" rule. Yazbak noted that Ibrahim Pasha's rule improved Haifa's status. This could be seen in the appearance of consular representatives in the city, and the transfer of many businesses from Acre to Haifa.
11. Al-Araf, pp. 122-124; Bailey, pp. 51-69.
12. Yisrael Beck received the village of Jermak from the governor when its Druze inhabitants abandoned it. See Ya'ari, *Memories*, pp. 144-145; Guérin, Vol. VII, pp. 82-84; Firro, *Druzes*, pp. 166-167.
13. Bowring, p. 43.
14. FO 406/6, Ponsonby to Palmerston, 8.6.1840, Doc. Paper 66, pp. 64-65.
15. FO 406/5, Napier to Stanford, 11.1.1841, Doc. Paper 146, and Doc. Paper 65. In June, 1841, the Sultan published an Imperial decree limiting Muhammad Ali's

army to 18,000 men. See Clark, p. 72; see also FR, 1.12.1879, Comanos to Evarts, Doc. 485, p. 1032.

16. FO 406/6, Doc. Paper 2, Part 4, dated 26.3.1841, pp. 2-3. To the problems of the Egyptian army there was an added one that was caused by Muhammad Ali himself: He deducted a full year's salary from the soldiers in order to finance the purchase of lost equipment and to pay the officers and the European advisors.

17. According to one intelligence evaluation, marked by the agent as "hypothetical," in February 1840, the army, before the commencement of the retreat, numbered 221,460 troops. Of these, 125,000 were stationed in Syria. In 1841, after the retreat, the army numbered only 87,500 men, but of the units that had been stationed in Syria, only 33,352 remained. See Ponsonby to Palmerston, above. The number of soldiers that returned from Syria had diminished by 94,000. This estimation is not much different from the intelligence document included in Document 2, cited above, that estimated the sum total of Egyptian forces at some 100,000 soldiers. According to one of the intelligence assessments, after the reorganization of the Egyptian Army in March 1841, there remained no more than 50,000 regular troops in the entire force, aside from 5,000 naval men. Another estimate, whose source was in the U.S. Consulate in Cairo, claimed that in 1839 there had been only 140,000 men in Ali's army, and not 220,000; see Comanos to Evarts above, various documents in pp. 1018-1091.

18. De Haas, relying on Commodore Napier, wrote that at the onset of the retreat, Ibrahim Pasha's army had 85,000 men; see De Haas, p. 398. This number seems to reflect the defections that had begun even before Ibrahim Pasha's defeat in Acre (see below). Kamal Suleiman Salibi gave an even lower number: 30,000 before the battles and 10,000 afterwards, but he did not cite any source for these figures. See Salibi, p. 34. The most acceptable estimate is found in Sabri. He maintained that the forces in Damascus before the long journey to Egypt began amounted to some 50,000 men. He also did not cite any source.

19. Bowring, p. 130. Of the ten thousand, nine thousand were from Jerusalem, Jaffa, Jericho and Nablus. The rest came from other localities in Sidon, Beirut; or Syria.

20. Soffer estimated the total number at 25,000.

21. Grossman, Historical Migration in Samaria, pp. 402-403; Grossman, *Process-Pattern*, p. 108.

22. See Golani; see also Gorkin, pp. 17-18.

23. Grossman, "Southern Coastal Plain"; Grossman, *Process-Pattern*, p. 108.

24. De Haas, p. 419.

25. See Kark, Jaffa, for a comprehensive treatment of this subject.

26. *Survey of Social and Economic Conditions*; see also Kark and Shiloni.

27. See Ya'ari and Harizman, *Petah-Tiqva*, pp. 13-14; see also Brawer, "Migration."

28. The area was located south of Ramla. Despite the failure, several Jerusalem Jews established a partnership with Arabs who lived in the proposed area; see Bartal, "Old Community," pp. 203-204; see also Bartal, *Travel Diary*, pp. 150-151; Ya'ari, *Letters*, pp. 409-422; Kark, "Agricultural Land"; Kark and Oren-Nordheim, pp. 315-316.

29. Kark and Shiloni.

30. Grossman, "Arab Settlement Process in Ottoman Times"; Ya'ari, *Memories*, pp. 243-245; Ya'ari and Harizman, *Petah Tiqva*, pp. 13-14.

31. Grossman, "Yarkon-Ayalon," pp. 88-93, Grossman, *Expansion and Desertion*, pp. 213-241. Grossman, "Arab Settlement Process in Ottoman Times"; see also Ashkenazi.

32. Marx, pp. 70-71. On Bedouin agriculture see Kressel and Ben-David; Ben-David.

33. Interview with *Sbih*, *Abd al-Wahab*.

34. See Shechter, pp. 152-154; Ilan, Turkmen. Grossman, Goldshlager and Bar-Cohen., pp. 42-44.

35. Interview with Hussein Yassin, Khirbat Maslahit. See Grossman, *Expansion and Desertion*, p. 97.
36. Some scholars believed that the Hula swamp dwellers (called *Ghawarna*, as the other swamp inhabitants) reached Palestine during Muhammad Ali's occupation. Karmon, Hula, based this hypothesis on the fact that Robinson and Smith (Biblical Researches) who visited the place in 1838 did not mention the *Ghawarna*'s existence, but this is clearly not solid proof that they were completely absent. The dark-skinned people of the Sharon who, like the Hula dwellers, subsisted on water buffalo, and were also considered to have originated in the Sudan, had been occupying the swamps for several centuries. See 1596/7 tax lists in Hütteroth and Abdulfattah, p. 158.
37. I am indebted to Ms. Liora Binyamin of the Israel Ministry of the Interior for providing this data.
38. The number in the three villages was: a 781; b 97; c 393. During the count of people listed in the 2007-8 telephone book of the eastern Sharon having various spelling versions of *Masri and Massarwa* (*Egyptian* in Arabic), I found that the percentage having these names in the three settlements varied from 5 to 15 percent. The largest was found in a town of about 30,000 inhabitants where the total number of *Massarwa-Masri* names was 781; see De Haas; Soffer; Kressel and Aharoni; see also Brawer, "Migration," for many additional names of extended Egyptian families which form a significant proportion of many villages. In my own telephone-based records, there was a family named Yassin which accounted for 5 percent (134 persons) of a single town. Additional Egyptian names appear in publications that do not specifically deal with this topic.
39. Maps 2.1 and 2.4, based on my field work and partly on Dabagh, contain at least 50 villages which have Egyptian population. See also Kressel and Aharoni's article for additional places. A person named Masarawa is mentioned by Nadan, *Palestinian Peasant*, pp. 116-117 and p. 209, as one of his informers. If we assume that this proportion (2 percent) also prevails in other parts of Palestinian Diaspora (i.e., a total of at least 4 million), this segment of the Egyptian stock numbers not less than 80,000. In c.1850 the same percentage represented about 7,000 people. This was, probably, only a fraction of the total Egyptian villager-settlers. The total sedentary Palestinian population was estimated at that time to be about 350,000 (see chapter 3).
40. I am grateful to Dr. David Sivan, who collected this information from Bedouin informants.
41. See Bailey.
42. See Meir, Demographic Transition. According to the 2004 Bedouin Yearbook, the Bedouin population in 2006 was 126,600. If it is multiplied every fifteen years must have reached about 136,000 by 2006 (but the doubling rate could have been even twelve years). During the 1961-2006 (i.e., forty-five years), it grew at a mean rate of 12.5 percent (from 17,800 to 136,600). If the Egyptians were one third of this figure, they counted about 45,000 persons. The demographic growth rate during the pre-1961 era (about 130 years) was certainly much lower. It is not easy to find out what the figures were, but in 1931 (the only census of Bedouin during the Mandate era), the Negev Bedouin population was 47,981. However, many of them left Israel after 1948. For c.1870, Ben-Arieh estimated them at 30,000 (see chapter 3), i.e., during 1870-1931 the Bedouin population grew at a rate of 0.78 percent. The 1840-1870 Growth Rate was most probably lower, not more than 0.5 percent. This yields an 1840 population of about 23,000. The original Egyptian settlers in the Negev should have numbered about 8,700. In fact, the number was lower. It is unlikely that it exceeded 6,000.
43. Adding all the above figures in order to reach a reasonable total population estimate seems to lead to an under-count. If the total number is arrived at by using the three geographical destinations, a. Urban (mainly Jaffa); b. Rural places; c. Bedouin:

(i.e., a. 2,000 + b. 15,000 + c. 6,000) the number of the early settlers was about 23,000.

44. E.g., Ya'ari and Harizman, *Petah Tiqva*, pp. 13-14; see also Brawer, "Migration"; Peters; Gottheil, "Arab Immigration."; Gottheil, *The Smoking Gun*, Gottheil argued that McCarthy, *Palestine*, deliberately ignored the large Arab migratory waves during the Mandate era. Gottheil contended that this gap is due to external migrations. By subtracting the average number of the presumed natural population growth for this interval from the total population growth of the inter-census period he concluded that the net number of non-Jewish external migrants into Palestine during this short period amounted to about 60,000 people. He attributed the differences between the two censuses to the economic attractiveness of the Jewish settlement zone. A study by Avraham Vilan, pp. 21-25, also based on an analysis of inter-census data supports Gottheil's arguments.

45. Avitzur, *The Banks of the Yarkon,* pp. 34, 146-149.

46. Grossman, *Expansion and Desertion*, pp. 201-203.

47. See Lee. Large emigration from Palestine was unlikely because of the existing urban opportunities. De Planhol noted that the out-migration from rural areas, which resulted in depopulation in Europe, had been avoided in the Middle East. This observation certainly applies to Palestine where the 1922-1931 growth rate was 34.4 percent, but the coastal areas grew at a faster rate than the general population. Jaffa Sub-District grew by 98 percent and Haifa Sub-District, by 80 percent. See Central Zionist Archive, A202/146א. Memorandum in response to French report, by Haim Arlozorov, p.15; see also Brawer, "Migration"; von Mülinen, v. 31, p. 195; Grossman, Goldshlager and Bar-Cohen, p. 53, where Arab employment in the Jewish rural sector of the Carmel zone is discussed.

48. Grossman, *Expansion and Desertion*, pp. 169-175.

49. Grossman, "Historical Migration in Samaria," pp. 402-104.

50. There were several other religiously motivated Christian groups, like the Millenarians, who also preached to their followers to migrate to Palestine. See Thalmann; Kedem; Gawler; Bartal, "Gawler's Plan."

51. Karpat, *Demographic and Social Characteristics*, pp. 62-64.

52. This information and most of the following accounts are based on Abbasi's comprehensive discussion of the Algerian migration to Palestine. Additional sources are Thompson, pp. 261, 267, who described the poor appearance and the pitiful condition of the arriving Algerians; see also Braslavy (Braslavsky), Vol. I, pp. 375-377; Avneri, p. 16.

53. Thomson, p. 443-444.

54. Two villages were entirely deserted after 1927, but one of them was resettled after 1931 by local Arabs. The entire 1945 population of the ten villages was 3,352. Abbasi, pp. 51-52.

55. The process of the Levant refugee settlement was, as noted above, part of a wider refugee problem. According to an 1864 estimate, the number of Circassian refugees reached 600,000, and between 1864 and 1866, another 400,000 Circassians (and Chechens) arrived in the Ottoman Empire. The government spent much energy in trying to absorb them. The Muslim refugees, who arrived after the Empire's 1878 defeat, became the adversaries of the Circassians, because the latter were employed to police the boundary in the Danube area and were blamed for committing many acts of violence. Madhat Pasha, the governor of the Danube region at the time (and later the national Prime Minister), did much to rehabilitate them. See Schilcher, "Grain Economy," pp. 178-179.

56. A detailed account of the Circassian settlement process is provided by Davison, pp. 151-152.

57. Hapoel Hatzair, pp. 11-12; Izraelite, pp. 27-28; I thank Mr. Yuval Ben-Basat who assisted in obtaining these sources. See Ilan, "Turkmen."
58. Oliphant, pp. 220-224.
59. Oliphant, p. 238.
60. Originally *amiri* (the Emir's land), that is, state land, which according to the 1858 Land Code, was subject to registration of use rights by those who could prove that the land had been used by them for at least three consecutive years. Its ultimate title was, however, held by the state. The refugees received, along with the land, houses, farm animals and basic necessities. Davison, pp. 151-152.
61. While touring in Jordan I was informed by a Circassian tourist guide that there are now (2007) approximately 150,000 Circassians and 50,000 Chechens in the Kingdom of Jordan. According to Lewis, p. 98, the number of Circassians who arrived in southern Syria by 1878 was 25,000. Additional Syrian Circassians (1,949 families) arrived in Quneitra in 1906 (Lewis, p. 101), where they were housed in the local khan and received plots ranging from seven to thirteen hectares per family. Until then the Golan had served as pasture land for the local nomadic tribes. There were harsh disputes between the Circassians and the Golan's Druze. Lewis, pp. 96-123, provides many details about the Circassians and the Chechens. His accounts suggest that most of these migrants were poor and suffered from appalling sanitary conditions. He provides specific statistical data on their high death rates and their extremely high child mortality levels. Lewis also provides, however, a picture of a Circassian village with its clearly European style layout, which very different than the Arab villages. (I am grateful to Mr. Seth Frantzman for this information.)
62. Oliphant, pp. 220-224.
63. Schumacher, "Caesaria," p. 84. According to the 1922 census there were thirty-two Maronites in Caesarea. I am grateful to Mr. Seth Frantzman who turned my attention to this information.
64. Ilan, "Turkmen," pp. 281-284; see Ben-Artzi and Biger, p. 444 and Parkes, p. 211, for minorities distribution maps.
65. Schumacher, "Caesaria," pp. 83-84. Schumacher also reported the existence of "130 houses, built in European style." This description refers to Zichron Ya'akov, then a newly founded Jewish settlement; now a Jewish town in the southern Carmel range
66. Rogan, p. 256. The traditional ties between Nablus and Jabal Balqaa are treated in detail by Nimr.
67. Al-Jaludi and Al-Bakhit, p. 48.
68. McCarthy, Palestine, p. 11. McCarthy quoted data published in 1884-85 by the Ottoman commission appointed to assist the refugees. The 1922 Census of Palestine reported that there were only 656 Circassian language speakers.
69. Ruha Height (Ramat Menasheh) was a latter addition to this pattern.
70. See Weitz; Reichman.

3

The Population of Palestine: Distribution and Density in the Nineteenth Century

Introduction

In the minds of many Europeans, especially Zionist Jews, Palestine was "empty" before the arrival of the first wave of Jewish settlers in 1881-84. "Emptiness," of course, did not denote, except for the most ignorant, the physical absence of the native population. Rather, it meant the absence of "civilized" people, in the same sense that the Americas and Africa were portrayed as virgin territories ready for waves of pioneers.[1]

This quotation, from Doumani's article, is rather unrepresentative of his sophisticated and well-documented reviews of Arab and Jewish writings on Ottoman Palestine. But here he has overly generalized and, at best, attributed to those that are not "the most ignorant" a view that is even more insulting. It implies that educated "Europeans [and] Zionist Jews" are unable to distinguish between "the physical absence of the native population" and that of "civilized people."

Doumani is right in stating that in the nineteenth century Palestine was mostly populated by ignorant people. This is a fact that can hardly be challenged. Doumani might have also been right if he had phrased his statement to say that this factual condition led to a feeling of superiority that was widely shared by most Europeans, and naturally also by European Jews. However, he confuses these perceptions with factual demographic characteristics.

The use of the term "emptiness," which was purposely chosen, is also inappropriate and misleading. The proper term should be "sparsely populated." To set the record straight, educated people had a fairly good knowledge of the country's geography, and were able to distinguish between the settled and the sparsely settled areas of the country. This important regional differentiation is a major component of this volume's purpose. Zionists (the term does not strictly apply to the Jews who settled in Palestine before 1897; see below), as also the many non-Jews who shared the idea of the Jewish right to return to Zion, were broadly familiar with Palestine's regional demographic variations, even though they naturally had no accurate knowledge of the relevant statistical data. The importance of this distinction has already been presented in chapter 2. The 1857 Ottoman official invitation to Europeans to settle in the sparsely settled parts of the Empire cannot be attributed to "ignorance." Nor can "ignorance" explain the fact that Muslim refugees were granted vacant land in Palestine.

I do not rely on the vast literature of the travelers, archeologists, missionaries, consular officials, distinguished writers and many others who visited or resided in Palestine, though I critically refer to some of them. The quality of the many documents that they left us is varied, and I have selected only those that seem to be of great value for this discussion.[2] The scholars that I trusted did not confuse "physical absence" of human beings with "uncivilized" or with any other negative social and cultural characteristics.

I focus on the demographic and geographic facts and, to avoid as much as possible a discussion of political and emotional perceptions, I intend to present a well-documented picture of the country's population distribution by carefully studying the existing official data and the various population estimates of official and unofficial sources. Much of this and the following chapters are concerned with assessing the reliability of the sources, their validity, and accuracy. On the basis of this examination I intend to map the most probable population densities in the various regions of Palestine and their regional growth rates during the last half-century of the Ottoman rule of Palestine, that is, from about 1870 until 1922, when the British Mandate administration held the first population census. The last part of the book is concerned with the thorny issue that has clouded the Arab-Jewish conflict since 1882: agricultural density and the related problem of land pressure. Throughout the book, the focus is almost exclusively on the rural sector.

Various Demographic Estimates: Methodological Problems

The growing interest in the condition of Palestine and its population among the travelers, tourists, and pilgrims is evident in the increasing number of publications (starting from c. 1870) that contained attempts to estimate the size of the country's population. These estimates include government records which were based on some official sources or, more often, on guesses which were often biased or even deliberately manipulated by the authors. Underestimates were more frequent than exaggerations, because many European visitors, diplomats, and even scholars were affected by prejudice fortified by the prevailing negative manifestation of a poverty-stricken people who asked for handouts and behaved in other unpleasant ways because of their desperate condition. Diplomats had various additional reasons for their biased approach. But these attitudes do not necessarily imply that they deliberately falsified their reports on Palestine's demography.

A related factor that affected their conception was their exposure to the biblical references to the Holy Land as "flowing with milk and honey." Many of the Westerners were profoundly affected by the Bible, and tended to compare the land they saw with Scriptures. This applied not only to religious writers who were obviously eager to prove that the harsh prophecies about the fate of the land and its people had come true. Scholars, particularly archeologists, tended to compare their findings with the ancient records, while the consular officials were inclined to "illuminate" their factual interpretation with some scholarly reference. The lay tourists were also anxious to demonstrate their knowledge and personal talent by offering intellectual assessments and interpretations and by quoting past records. Jews could have been in any of these categories, but it was only during the last quarter of the nineteenth century that the members of the Hovevey Zion movement started to develop their own nationalistic ideas about the country and its people. These ideas acquired wide popularity and a political ideology in 1897, when the First Zionist Congress was convened.

Despite the powerful impact of past experience and the tendency for prejudice, there were many demographic estimates that were reasonably free of bias. The main problem was the scant or poor quality of the available data, but it was only in the mid-twentieth century that deliberate attempts to manipulate the facts were made. The motive was the growing impact of the Jewish-Arab conflict. Demography became a strong political tool that was used by Arabs and Jews. An extreme example of a "demographic" study of this kind is that of Ernst Frankenstein, whose peculiar calculations led him to arrive at a figure of no more than 106,000 Palestinians (his term for indigenous Moslems) in 1882.[3] Among the sources upon which these statistical data are based is *Murray's Tourist Guide*, 1858 edition, and Vital Cuinet's book of 1896 that deals with Palestine's geography (then part of Beirut Province).[4] The latter book is considered by Frankenstein as a most reliable and accurate source, but, as will be shown below, its data are now considered to contain serious errors.

Another well-publicized study was written by Joan Peters. Her nineteenth-century demographic data were also based on Cuinet, but at least some of her data and her own interpretations were based on questionable facts. The result is that this subtracts from, rather than fortifies, her arguments. She also subtracted the estimated number of non-Jewish migrants, but her statistical analysis is not as extreme as that of Frankenstein. Her main conclusion is that the "Jewish settlement area," defined largely on the basis of selected Jewish-dominated sub-districts, had, in 1893, a total of 92,300 Arabs.[5]

Peters' thesis generated great interest and support not only from the general public, but also among members of the academic community. She had, however, many critics. The most outspoken was Yehoshua Porath of the Hebrew University. His criticism centered on her methods, but he was also unhappy about Peters' distortions and illogical conclusions. Porath points out for example, that Peters quoted Cuinet even where it was evident that he had deliberately falsified his data (mostly for increasing the number of the Christian population). [6] I agree with most of Porath's critical comments. My own impression was that in many places particularly in her discussion of the Arab acts of violence toward Jewish settlers, her descriptions were taken out of context. My main objection, however, was directed to her definition of the "Jewish settlement area" and her statistical method of defining its borders..Her conclusion that the total 1893 population (including non-Muslims, Bedouin, and relatively recent migrants), amounted to about 92,300 people is, in any case, too high. This is the result of the use of official territorial units for which she offered no full explanations.[7]

In chapter 4, I present my method for defining the territorial areas where it was difficult to delineate their boundaries by the use of official units. I will briefly say here that I marked the Jewish territorial boundaries, where possible, on official boundaries, but where such boundaries were not helpful, I delineated the boundaries according to land which had been purchased by Jews and was fully settled by 1948. Peters' system, on the other hand, used boundaries that coincided exclusively with official Mandate ones. Her data, based of on Cuinet, referred to 1893 rather than to the early 1870s. As already noted, I have refrained from using his data. The reasons for this are provided in some detail below.

Cuinet's Statistics and Other Western Sources

The first census taken in the Ottoman Empire dates to 1830, but it was, in fact, no more than a rough estimate. The problems that faced the authorities in taking a reliable count of the population were critically discussed and analyzed by Kemal Karpat and by several other demographers.[8] I begin by looking in some detail at Cuinet's demographic contribution.

Cuinet's findings, published in 1896, were accepted in his time as very accurate, and were thought to be an authoritative scientific contribution by many scholars of Palestine and Syria even in the 1980s, some eighty years after their publication. It is conceivable that the positive reaction that he received was based on the fact that Cuinet was one of the first Western scholars who bothered to gather statistical information about the Middle East. Indeed, aside from the demographic data that his book encompassed, it also dealt with a wide variety of subjects: administrative systems, agricultural produce, animal husbandry, etc., but the major deficiency of the book is that it does not reveal the sources of the data or the methods he employed. McCarthy states that Cuinet used a Beirut Yearbook, with data dated H 1308 (1890-91) and multiplied the registered male population data by four; that is, he doubled the number of males twice.[9] At any rate, Cuinet presented no explanation in his book for his calculation, or the reasons for amending the original data. Interestingly, however, even leading Turkish researchers had a highly positive appreciation of Cuinet's work. Kamel Karpat considered Cuinet's scientific research as completely trustworthy.[10] Yehoshua Ben-Arieh, however, strongly disagreed. He asserted that Cuinet's data did not mesh with the information we have from other sources, and should not be accepted at all as a basis for population estimates for the end of the nineteenth century.[11] This opinion was shared by other recent researchers, including Justin McCarthy.[12]

Even a superficial examination of Cuinet's data for Palestine shows them to be unsupportable. Comparing them with any other source shows clearly that his data for the Galilee (Acre District) and Nablus (which was separated from Balqaa in 1887), and more especially those for the rural areas, are under-counts, while the data for the Jerusalem District are definitely over-counts. In other regions of Palestine, the number of rural residents was larger than that of the urban dwellers, but for Acre, Cuinet presented an opposite situation, where the rural residents were fewer than the urban ones. This picture contradicts the demographic data presented practically by all the studies of the late nineteenth century.

The population estimates made by travelers and consular officials are no better than those of Cuinet. The major problem of their reports is lack of solid and reliable sources. There are, nevertheless, some diplomatic population estimates that are not based on official counts. It is doubtful, though, if they are any better.[13]

Estimates included in the traveler books are even less reliable. Fred Gottheil provides several examples: At least four of the travelers' references that he consulted wrote that the population of Palestine was between 1,180,000 and 1,200,000, whereas the official estimate for the period before 1880 was no larger than 450,000. These exaggerated reports were not attempts to present fabricated data. They reflect, rather, a lack of access to information (possibly because of insufficient knowledge of the official language), or the realization that the available information was not reliable. Gottheil did not accept these estimates. As will be shown below he based part of his estimates on the "census" that the engineer Gottlieb Schumacher took for the District of Acre government.[14]

The Population of Palestine before the 1870s

Several researchers attempted to estimate the population growth rates by using various indirect means. Haim Gerber used tax rolls of the 1830s and compared them with reports of travelers or missionaries who spent long periods of time in the Middle East. His conclusion was that before 1857, Palestine and Syria enjoyed a moderate population growth rate.[15] The dependence on unofficial sources of this kind was due to the absence of any official data on population changes or on vital statistics. Even after H 1268, when the first Syrian provincial yearbook was published, the data referred only to lists of persons or households.[16]

Another approach to the development of natural population growth of Palestine was offered by Bashara Doumani. He analyzed the methods of the censuses taken in certain limited areas (the city of Nablus and its hinterland). Like Gerber, he also concluded that during the first half of the nineteenth century the growth rate exceeded that of the rest of the century. He argued that the census taken in 1850 (or 1849) showed that the Nablus urban population was larger, by some three to four thousand people, than that estimated by either Ben-Arieh or Schölch (which will be discussed below). Data from later censuses showed that the population did not continue to grow at the same rate as it had at the beginning of the century. His explanation for this was that the decentralization of the Ottoman authority, that is, the fact that the local rulers were more effective than the central government before the era of 'Abed al-Hamid

II was a blessing. It had positive, rather than negative, economic impact that made possible the improved demographic trend.[17]

The assertion that there was low population growth after the mid-nineteenth century is accepted by some researchers, but the report of John Bowring does not support Doumani's hypothesis. In 1836 Bowring was instructed by the British government to conduct a survey of the territories that were under Ali's rule towards formulating British policy concerning Muhammad Ali's activities in Syria and Palestine. Among other informants, he consulted the British consuls on demographic issues and asked them to provide data on population size. As the rest of this chapter reveals, most of the respondents provided fairly low population records when compared with the 1870s (see table 3.1).

Bowring's report on Syria contained data, position papers, and evaluations on various political, social, and economic conditions. It also contained, naturally, some statistical data on the demographic situation. The information was obtained by contacting the British consuls posted in the area's main centers. The following Palestinian statistical data are part of the document that was transmitted by Consul Werry. The data are based on lists of taxpayers that Bowring was able to obtain from the authorities. They deal with the two southern Syrian districts: Jerusalem and Nablus (table 3.1).[18]

The statistical data dealt only with taxable persons. In order to calculate the whole population, Consul Werry used two different multipliers. For most places he used the 3.5 coefficient (multiplier). However, probably because of what he considered to be an under-count of the Nablus District population, he preferred to multiply the number of taxpayers of this district by 4. According to his calculation, the resulting total population of the two districts was 238,891.

Mordechai Abir used similar information, apparently from a like source.[19] He quoted an official British Foreign Office document for the Districts of Jerusalem and Nablus, which provided data on the number of taxpayers: males above the age of fourteen. In the two districts there were 466 villages. The author of the document believed that the number of above-fourteen-year-old males was about one third of the total population, and, therefore, preferred to multiply the total by 3. However, Abir himself thought that this multiplier was too low, and suggested using 4 as a more reasonable multiplier. He concluded, therefore, that the total population of the two districts was 145,600.

These estimates can be compared to additional statistical data that deal with the situation that prevailed about ten to fifteen years later. One of them was supplied by the French consul and the other by the Prussian consul. Both were probably obtained from the local authorities. Despite his use of this relatively high multiplier, the total figure for the 1830s was much lower than the official 1849 records for the two districts.[20] It is clearly not reasonable to suggest that the population growth rate was as high as this 1836-1849 difference suggests. The French records were the only ones that provided statistical data on the total population (see table 3.1).[21]

This report tends to support Doumani's claim that during the first half of the nineteenth century Nablus had more people than later. But Werry's estimate, which was based on the taxation lists, does not seem to confirm this contention. However, both estimates suggest that the total population of the two districts experienced little change from 1830 to 1870 (see more on this subject below). Unlike the French data, which referred to the total population, the Prussian data had to be doubled since the original figures (146,542) referred to males of all ages, including children.[22]

Since Acre was part of the Saida (Sidon) Province,[23] its demographic data were not included in the above statistical records (map 3.1). Edward Robinson and Eli Smith's book, that summarizes their findings of their second visit to Palestine in 1852, enables us to fill this lacuna,[24] though the figures they quote seem to be an overestimate.

Table 3.1
The population of Palestine from the late 1830s to the early 1850s

District or Sub-District	Abir 1836	Werry 1836	F French 1847	Prussian 1849
Nablus & Jenin S.D.	15,800	18,218	101,600	57,122
Jerusalem District	20,600	47,434	149,000	89,420
Total recorded	36,400	65,652		146,542
Total estimated				
Population	145,600	238,891	250,600	293,084
Multiplier				
Nablus S.D.	4	4	1	2
Jerusalem District	4	3.5	1	2
Robinson Galilee Data	**Multiplier**			
Acre District		36,400		
Total estimate population	2	72,140		

Source: According to five sources (see text).

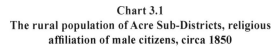

Chart 3.1
The rural population of Acre Sub-Districts, religious
affiliation of male citizens, circa 1850

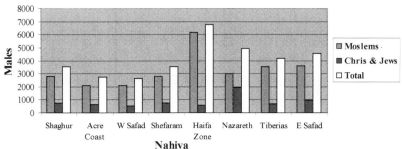

Chart 3.2
The rural population of Jerusalem District and Nablus-Jenin zones, religious
affiliation of male citizens, circa 1850

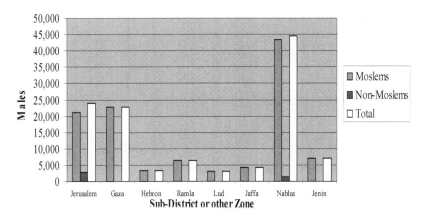

These, like the Prussian's document on Jerusalem and Nablus (cum Jenin; table 3.1), had to be doubled in order to estimate the total data.[25] The following chart presents the data for southern Palestine, according to the Prussian source and for northern Palestine (Acre District), according to Robinson and Smith (chart 3.2). Both sources provide breakdowns by sub-districts and by religious affiliation.

Table 3.1 presents the data for the rural and urban areas, but the urban population in this table is for central cities only. Therefore, it over-states the rural population. Nevertheless, these statistics suggest that the population of all the Palestinian districts at the middle of the nineteenth century amounted to some 365,000 people.[26] The conclusion

Map 3.1
Map of districts and sub-districts: Palestine and Trans-Jordan

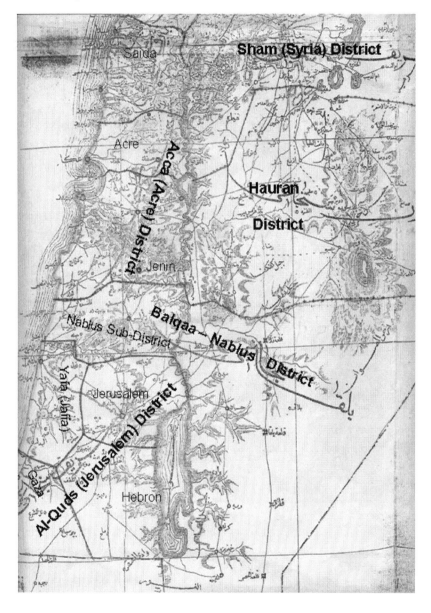

that the population of Palestine, excluding the Bedouin and non-Ottoman citizens, was between 340,000 and 370,000 people will not be far from reality. This figure does not include most of the Bedouin. With them, the total population was probably about 400,000.[27]

A group of people that was not included in the official lists was the non-citizens. Included in this category were many Jews of European extraction who preferred to remain citizens of one of the Western countries. The main question concerned, however, the accuracy and the reliability of the data.

As we noted above, it seems that Robinson and Smith's source is an overestimation. It is probable that the other estimates are also not free of errors. Even so, I feel that it is better to have some statistical approximation than nothing at all. A related problem is the very definition of Palestine and its internal administrative units. There were frequent changes in the boundaries, and there is no easy way to overcome the difficulties that these alterations entail. This problem, too, will accompany us throughout the following demographic discussion.

The section that follows is based on selected demographic estimates of the Palestinian population around, or after, 1870. In the British document that is quoted above information is limited. Most researchers of the latter part of the century had also to resort, therefore, to methods that were not strictly based on official counts.

Late Nineteenth-Century Demographic Data: Approaches to Analysis

An interesting estimate by the British Foreign Service, based on official statistics dated approximately the same time, 1877-78 (H 1295),[28] is also not free of difficulties. The date of the census coincided with the Balkan war that ended with the Ottoman defeat and the loss of Bosnia-Montenegro and other areas. The British analysis, which in most cases included some estimation of the total population by using certain multipliers, provided no clues as to the method they used to arrive at the final demographic data of the Levant.[29] The population of Jerusalem, which was not in Syria, was estimated to be 390,000, a figure which is about 50,000 below McCarthy's estimate for the whole of Palestine (see above).[30] This estimate is, therefore, clearly exaggerated. If accepted, and if we add the combined population estimate of Acre and Nablus (about 208,000), the population of all of Palestine would be similar to that of 1908, that is, thirty years later.[31]

Gottheil Regional-Comparative Method

A method for filling the existing information gap was suggested by Fred Gottheil. Using Schumacher's 1886 data on Acre District (see above) he calculated the population of places outside of Acre and concluded that the rural population of Palestine was, in 1875, about 333,700 persons, while the total figure, for the entire country, including the urban zones and the Bedouin population, was 492,675.[32] Schölch considers this figure to be too large, but among other reservations, he also stated that it was unlikely that Gottheil's estimate for the Acre District (about 75,000) could be correct, because it is almost identical to Acre's official figure (73,253) according to the 1886 Yearbook (i.e., almost a decade later). It is more likely, however, that the exaggeration is to be blamed on Robinson and Smith, who quoted a figure equivalent to 72,140 for the same district more than three decades earlier than 1886 (c. 1850; see table 3.1) and as much as a quarter century before 1875.[33]

Despite these and other misgivings, a major one being his dependence on Schumacher (see below), Gottheil's method is fairly impressive. It shows how fairly close estimates can be arrived at when official figures are not available. The main difficulty is, however, that Gottheil, like other of his contemporary colleagues, ignored, or was not aware of, the existing official data. Even though he used a survey that had been initiated by the government, the information was based on the work of a Western researcher and not on any direct official count.

An additional criticism may be leveled at Gottheil's preference for a sample rather than full census data. Nevertheless, and despite these reservations, one must note that his estimate was not far from that of researchers who did use official data. According to McCarthy, the total population of Palestine in 1877-78 was 440,850 people,[34] but the Bedouin were not included, so that his estimate came closer to Gottheil's number for Palestine as a whole. The major contribution that Gottheil made was that he called our attention to the large differences among the various estimates.

Ben-Arieh's PEF-Based Method

Yehoshua Ben-Arieh suggested another resourceful method to contend with the problem of lacking sources of data. He relied on the use of various coefficients (multipliers) to arrive at an overall estimate of the population, on the basis of partial data relating only to males or to households. The selected coefficients were not uniform. Since they reflected the findings of studies that focused on different areas of the country, each one was specific to a different zone. They were suited to the assumed specific methodology employed in each area and to the problems faced by those who compiled the studies or the surveys to which Ben-Arieh had access.[35]

The coefficients that Ben-Arieh calculated could be applied to the Galilee (Acre District) and Judea (Jerusalem District), but there were no quantitative data with which to calculate the population of villages in the Samaria region (Nablus Sub-District).[36] Ben-Arieh, therefore, proposed an original solution based on substituting a numerical value for the qualitative (descriptive) information of the Memoirs of the Palestine Exploration Fund survey. This survey is the main source of information about the country during the 1870s. [37] Although it is an indispensable source of knowledge about the land, the archeology and its settlements during this period, it does not provide complete and uniform demographic information for all parts of the country. For most places the survey merely indicates the relative size of settlements at the roughest level (large, medium, or small). Ben-Arieh substituted these simple descriptive words with quantitative ones in order to fill in the missing information. Since Acre and Jerusalem districts had fairly reliable statistical data, it was necessary to use this method for Samaria only.[38]

Ben-Arieh's calculation led him to assess the total early 1870s population of Palestine at approximately 350,000 to 400,000. Since he reckoned that the lower figure applied to the settled population of the country and that the Bedouin numbered about 30,000, he concluded that the best approximation of the country's population was about 380,000. His upper figure is closer to those of other researchers, which will be discussed below. It was only slightly lower than the McCarthy estimate quoted above but was fairly similar to estimates of other contemporary scholars.

Like Ben-Arieh, I propose to add up the village data rather than start from the higher level of the settlement hierarchy. However, my approach differs from his in certain other respects. I chose to use the official Ottoman yearbooks rather than the surveys conducted by European scholars. As a result, I had to estimate the overall population from lists that did not provide complete population records, that is, household lists rather than single persons. My estimate of the total demographic figure was based therefore on multiplying the number of households by certain coefficients. The discussion of the proper multiplier and selected other methodological issues will be presented below.

McCarthy's Corrections Data

McCarthy's methodological research on the demography of Palestine and other Ottoman territories is broad in scope and coverage. This section is intended to provide a short summary of his methods and population estimate, but is not intended to cover his research comprehensively.

Unlike Ben-Arieh, McCarthy, in his Palestinian study, was not interested in consulting and utilizing the village level data. Nor does he make an effort to examine the population density or geographical distribution. His statistics deal almost exclusively with the macro data.[39] His statistical analysis suggests that during the last phase of Ottoman Middle Eastern administration, the rate of growth remained uniform. McCarthy himself believed, however, that his estimates were only close approximations.

According to McCarthy's estimate, the overall population of Palestine in 1877-78 (H 1295), was 440,850 (Jerusalem District - 232,645; Acre District - 79,675; Nablus Sub-District - 128,530).[40] This conclusion is based on amending the series starting from the Syrian Provincial Yearbooks (*Salname Vilayet Suriya*, see chapter 4) for H 1298 (1880-81). McCarthy presumes that the data presented by each yearbook were collected at least two years earlier.[41] He has provided no comparable data for the earlier decade, but according to the Syrian Yearbook of H 1288 (1871-72), whose data (see next chapter, chart. 4.1) refer to a decade or more before 1880, the population of Palestine was about 381,950 (the Bedouin not included). If these data are acceptable, they indicate that there was notable demographic growth between 1850 and 1878. But I feel that it is necessary to discuss in some depth the multiplier issue and its relevance to this and former estimation methods.

The Multiplier Issue: Discussion and Assessment

All the demographic data of the period preceding the eighth decade of the nineteenth century encountered the same fundamental problem: the data listed only households or males. Women were not counted. Karpat maintains that the term *hane* (household) is problematic because it can be interpreted in several ways, depending on the region being surveyed and the historic period in which counting took place. It is, therefore, difficult to present a comprehensive picture of the entire population based on the household figures.[42] Nevertheless, most researchers were able to identify the proper coefficient (multiplier) for any given region and to use it for estimating the overall population. The coefficients which were used by various researchers of Palestine range between 5 and 9. But in a study of reports relating to fourteen urban settlements in various regions or towns, Gerber found that the range varied between 3.1 and 7.2 (i.e., an average of approximately five family members per household). His study included, among other places, Jaffa (coefficient of 4.7), Nazareth (6.7), Safad (3.1) and Acre (4.9). However, neither the dates nor the sources for these data were uniform. They extended over a period of approximately one century (1816-1912) and included both official data and data collected from travelers who spent some period of time in the region.[43]

The method of calculating the coefficient in order to estimate overall population from household data has been the source of much controversy among demographers and other social scientists. After examining sources that contained both numbers of males and numbers of households, Schölch suggested, on the basis of certain Jaffa data, that a coefficient of 6 should be use for calculating the overall population provided by the Syrian Yearbook for the year H 1288 (1871-72).[44] This coefficient is lower than the coefficient 7 suggested by others.[45] The choice of the proper coefficient partly depends on various social or political considerations. For example, Karpat suggested to add between 8 and 15 percent to the estimates in order to compensate for population undercounts, for example, where evading the census is common because of the presumed linkage between it and taxation. A higher multiplier is particularly recommended in Ottoman areas populated by Muslims, since they suffered more than any other religious or ethnic community from military recruitment, exploitation by tax collectors, and various other impositions (see discussion in chapter 1). Therefore, they had a higher incentive than others to conceal the correct population figures.[46] Following Schölch, and also on the basis of my own investigation (see my findings in twenty-five villages of a mean household/males ratio of 2.86, chapter 4, section on mathematical problems). I preferred to use for my own analysis the 6 coefficient, but I have also considered the option of the 5 multiplier as a possible alternative, because even though it would appear that a coefficient of 6 fulfills the need for correcting the error noted by Karpat, where only household data are provided, it is possible that a coefficient of 5 would be even more suitable at least if tax evasion were not a significant problem. A multiplier of 5 is more appropriate also where there is a moderate population growth.

If mortality occurs among young adults, as happened among the Muslims of Ottoman Palestine, a coefficient of 4 is best suited. This coefficient is preferred for populations having zero growth. It is typical of populations if mortality and birth and rates cancel each other or during epidemics. These are clearly very crude approximations, but in the absence of adequate statistical data, particularly about the number of females, there is hardly any other way of enumerating the population.

The 7 coefficient, which is recommended by Schur and McCarthy for the demographic transition of the late nineteenth century, seems to be too high for the Moslem population and especially for the 1870s data.[47] Where adult males rather than households are counted, the multiplier should be 3 if only adult males are counted, but if all males are counted the best ratio is clearly 2.

A useful example is the following formula used by the German engineer Conrad Schick for estimating the demographic growth rate for a period of about twenty-five years (c.1868-1892). Schick was charged with the job of employing forced labor for constructing the Jerusalem-Jericho road. The work was apportioned out according to the population of each village (about one meter per person). He was handed, thus, a list of the recruited persons from the villages of the Sub-District of Jerusalem, and desired to use this list for estimating the population of the entire Jerusalem District by calculating the difference between his list and a parallel list, published by A. Socin in 1879. To arrive at this number he used a multiplier of 3, because he assumed that the recruits (males aged fourteen to sixty) accounted for one third of the total population. The whole population was thus three times that of the recruits. He used this formula for comparing the population of his own time with Socin's list of the Jerusalem District, which was compiled about twenty-five years earlier (c.1867). Unlike the Syrian H 1288 (1871-72) data, Socin's list (whose probable publication date was c.1870 or earlier) contained both households and males. Socin's list, however, included all males, and not only those of working age. For Socin's list, Schick assigned, therefore, a coefficient of 2 rather than 3.[48]

Schick's list was limited solely to the Jerusalem Sub-District, while Socin's included the whole district (i.e., including Gaza, Hebron, Lud [Lod, Lydda] and Jaffa Sub-Districts). To compute the rest of the people of his own time, he figured out that a factor of 2.5686 had to be added to the number of the recruits, in order to arrive at the sum that provides the desired figure for entire district. On this basis, Schick concluded that the rural population of the whole district (excluding Jerusalem) had grown in 1892 to 172,900.[49] The population rate of growth, calculated from his findings for about twenty-five years, was about 1 percent per annum. This is a fairly reasonable estimate, when compared with that calculated by McCarthy (1.24 per annum). It is possible that both Schick's and McCarthy's rates are accurate and the difference between the two reflects the rising rate of growth during the more recent years.

The significance of Schick's method is illustrated by the fact that Ben-Arieh used Schick's model to correct the findings reported by another engineer, Gottlieb Schumacher which was published in 1887.[50] Schumacher was also assigned, less than a decade earlier, to employ forced laborers for road construction in the Galilee (the Acre District). To estimate the total population from the number of the recruits he conducted a special survey in a small number of locations. His conclusion was that the number of the recruits (aged sixteen to sixty) had to be multiplied by 5. Ben-Arieh, quoting Schick, argued that Schumacher's multiplier factor cannot be correct. The proper factor must be 3, where solely adult males were counted and, in certain places, where all males were counted, it should be 2, but certainly not 5.

Unfortunately, other researchers who preceded Ben-Arieh were misled by Schumacher. V. Schwöbel, whose interesting study of the Galilee, published in 1904, intended to find the rate of population growth between Schumacher's 1887 study and his own time, was unaware of the mistake, and his conclusions about the region's population were clearly wrong. Despite this error, he contributed a new dimension to demographic knowledge. Rather than using the common administrative units, he divided the Galilee into ecological zones, and calculated their population by comparing them with those of Schumacher. He also added the calculation of differential growth rates among regions and by elevation above sea level. As a result, it was possible to find out, at the onset of the twentieth century, how the more remote or less accessible highland locations were affected by their relative inaccessibility and how the more attractive location (e.g., the Sea of Galilee coast) had fared.[51]

Socin, Schick, Schwöbel, and Schumacher were among the researchers who pioneered the study of Palestinian demography and geography. Some of the other contributors are mentioned or discussed in some depth in the next chapter, but most of the chapter will be devoted to an analysis of one source, the H 1288 Yearbook, whose data covered the whole country, the rural part dealing with the district of Jerusalem was first published and analyzed by M. Hartmann (see chapter 4).[52]

To conclude this discussion, we also have to focus on the coefficient suggested by McCarthy to solve the problem of the lack of registration of women and children. Women were registered from 1880, but this, too, was very problematic, because they were consistently under-reported.[53] He suggested correcting the official data by means of special coefficients based on the specific population composition of each province or district. His correction factors are:

Males x 2 x 1.1778 for Nablus and Acre districts, and
Males x 2 x 1.0463 for Jerusalem District.

This coefficient, unlike those mentioned above, was intended to correct official data that he believed to be faulty. According to his revised figures, the size of Palestine's population was, therefore, different from that recorded in some official publications. For example, there is a difference of more than 75,700 between the official figures for Palestine and his revised (and higher) estimates for the same country for 1911-12 (H 1330). The gap expands to more than 100,000 for 1914-15. It seems, thus, that his corrected estimates tend to overstate the demographic figures.[54]

These corrections are needed for improving the records that contain data on both sexes, because the distortions of the data tend to be high if women are also counted.[55] However, since the intra-territorial variations are fairly great, the coefficients produce no more than rough approximations.

Where only males or households are officially counted the problem differs. As was shown above, in this case it is how to estimate the values of data that are absent from the original source material.

Summary and Conclusions

As the Ottoman period drew to a close, the population of Palestine became a subject that occupied researchers, politicians and even laymen. Towards the end of the nineteenth century, as Jewish nationalism became more widespread, Jews also took great interest in it. The problem they all faced was the lack of reliable data, and a variety of measures were taken to find a solution. Some studies were deliberately biased for political, religious, or other reasons. It was only during the last fifty years of the Ottoman period that studies were published that allowed objective debate on the topic of demography. Most of the studies were carried out by European settlers, missionaries or scientific exploration teams who collected information about selected areas, usually the Galilee or Judea. Their published estimates were based partly on surveys derived from official lists (such as the lists of compulsory labor). However, the problem of a dearth of data and their questionable reliability, even those of the Ottoman censuses, was not satisfactorily solved.

It was only in the second half of the twentieth century that a significant change took place and all official data were re-evaluated, either because of the contribution of Turkish demographers or because research methods had improved. These approaches did not negate the information obtained from Ottoman sources, but attempted to correlate it with other sources in order to arrive at corrected or more accurate information. I will consider this approach further in the next chapter.

All the sources and all the researchers who studied them, regardless of their approach or the quality of their work, have considered people, in the physical sense of this word, and certainly did not confuse the numerical presence of people with any cultural traits or any other non-quantitative bias. Despite the varying methods, procedures and findings, there seems to be a fairly wide consensus that by the early 1870s the total population of Palestine was about 350,000. What is missing in the present chapter is an in-depth study of the regional data

Fig. 3.1
A page from the Syrian H 1288 Yearbook (1871/2)

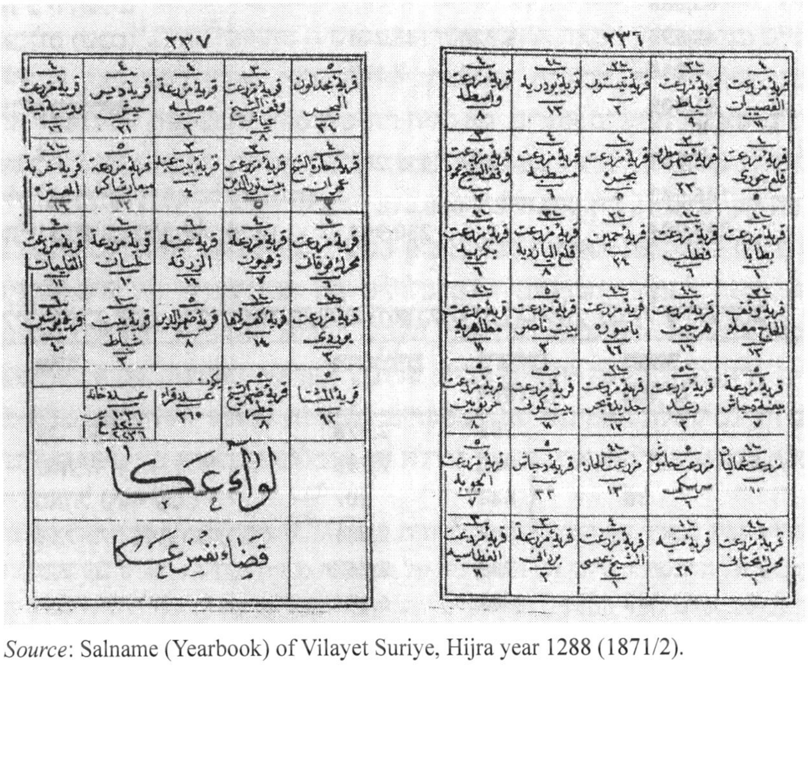

Source: Salname (Yearbook) of Vilayet Suriye, Hijra year 1288 (1871/2).

and, particularly, the significance of the inter-regional variations of the demographic densities.

This comment is not meant to suggest that the authors mentioned in this chapter ignored this issue. In-depth discussion of regional variations are included in many studies, either in specific regionally oriented treatises or in works devoted to various systematic discussions of the whole country. But as far as I know, none of them tackled the demographic issue methodologically in the manner that I intend to present in the next chapter, and by the use of the source that I selected for my intensive inter-regional study of density variations: the Syrian Provincial Yearbook for the year H 1288. Figure 3.1 illustrates the form of a page from this publication.

Notes

1. Doumani, "Rediscovering," p. 8.
2. A comprehensive discussion of the European mind-set may be found in Ben-Arieh, "Manners and Customs." See also CR, 1880, Willson, 4.10.1879, pp. 716-717. A few additional examples of authors who represent officials, academic researchers, novelists and the conceptions of the general Western public can be seen in: Kedem. "Gawler" and Bartal articles are in bibliography; Kedem, "Gawler"; Bartal, "Gawler's Plan"; Hollingsworth; Twain (Samuel L. Clemens); Pitrie.
3. This demographic "fact" was arrived at by subtracting from the total population not only the assumed number of all the nomads and non-Jewish migrants, but also all the Christians and other non-Moslems. See Frankenstein, pp. 115-131.
4. See Cuinet.
5. Peters, pp. 250-251.
6. Porath, *New York Review of Books*, March 27, 1986; Porath, "Letters from Readers," October, 1986, p. 5; see also Eric and Jean Isaac, *Commentary*, July 1986, pp. 29-37. He argued that the purchase of sparsely populated land by Jewish companies had nothing to do with the general Arab population distribution. The mostly pro-Peters Isaacs say that Peters "offers a generally sound thesis," but note that "she goes so far as to ignore evidence that does not bear out a specific point she wants to make even when [it] strengthens her general case." See special issues of *Commentary* July, 1986 and October, 1986 for Porath's, the Isaac's, and various other critiques on Peters' thesis.
7. Peters, p. 255.
8. Karpat, *Population*; Karpat, Demography and Social; McCarthy, *Palestine*; Schölch, *Transformation*. Details of their and other contributions are provided below.
9. McCarthy, "Fertile Crescent," p. 17 and note 43, p. 35, where a specific example of this procedure is cited. Karpat believed that Cuinet's data on Syria and Palestine were based on the census taken between 1882 and 1888, that is, on its publication. See Karpat, *Population*, p. 255. However, McCarthy found many differences between Cuinet's text and the official census, and his research led him to conclude that Cuinet's estimates for the Province of Sidon was based on the H 1308 (1890/91) Syrian Provincial Yearbook and not on data from 1882-1888, as Karpat stated.
10. See Karpat, Demography and Social, p. 10. See also Gerber, "Population," for a similar view.
11. Ben-Arieh, "Size and Composition"; Y. Porath, personal communication, 11 December, 1986.

12. McCarthy, *Palestine*, p. 12.
13. See Karpat, Demography and Social, p. 5. The word "count" is to be preferred, because most of the Ottoman statistics do not qualify for the word "census," according to the accepted definition of the term. But the non-official counts are often less helpful than those based on the official numbers.
14. Gottheil, "Population," p. 312. See Schumacher, Acre, and further discussion below.
15. Gerber, "Population," pp. 63-64. According to Gerber's calculations the growth rate of the population (the majority of which was Muslim) was 0.6 percent (6 to 1,000) a year for the years 1800 to 1836. The data for this last date were taken from Thomson. Thomsom was based in Beirut and had spent long periods in the area, but did not provide information on his source. His low growth rate estimates for that period are explained by occurrences of plagues, cholera and droughts in 1836-37, but such disasters had happened before that date also. It is difficult to explain why the growth rates declined just when sanitation measures and the campaign against the plagues were applied, Panzac, *La peste*, pp. 34-35.
16. Bahjat and Tamimi (Beirut, Vol. II) presented data from the year H 1331 (1912-13) for several sub-districts and cities in the Galilee. These data were probably used to calculate the gross birth and death rates. According to this source, the birth rate in the city of Safad reached 27 per thousand (0.27 percent), and in Nazareth 17 per thousand (0.17 percent). Parallel data for Acre and Tiberias are 0.15 percent and 0.1 percent, respectively. The birth rates for Acre and Tiberias are reasonable, but it is hard to know why the figure for Safad is so anomalous. It may be that the fertility was relatively high because of the Jewish population there, but this would be difficult to prove.
17. Doumani, *Nablus*, pp. 10-14.
18. Bowring, pp. 3-4.
19. Abir, p. 285, note 4. I was unable to obtain further information on the source of Abir's data.
20. See Schölch, *Transformation*, p. 29. Israel State Archives, DKJ, AIII, of September 1861.
21. See Bowring. The number of taxpayers in Syria and Palestine was estimated in Werry's report as 352,738, which was 1,253,830 people, using an average multiplier of 3.55. It was calculated on the basis of information that the Consuls had on the size of the average family in each area. Panzac, *La peste*, p. 272, gave an even higher result: 1,320,000, because he used a larger multiplier to estimate the total population. Other consuls who answered Bowring's inquiries offered even higher estimates. One even set the number at 1,800,000 (including 175,000 Jews). They did not supply numbers for territories smaller than the district.
22. The French report (from the Archive of the Commercial Consul, the French Foreign Office) is quoted by Schölch, *Transformation*, p. 29. The sub-districts of the Jerusalem District had the following numbers: Jerusalem 45,000; Gaza 40,500; Hebron, Jaffa, Lud and Ramla 63,500. Jerusalem contained 10,000 out of the 13,600 Jews counted. The data of the French document were probably also based on tax lists. The Prussian report was submitted to the ambassador in Istanbul by Consul Rosen, Israel State Archives, DKJ, AIII, of September 1861. The regional breakdown of the Prussian data is provided in chart 3.1.
23. There were numerous boundary shifts and other geographical changes. This makes it difficult to ascertain to which administrative unit a given territory belonged. Map 3.1 shows the boundaries of the district and sub-district shown on an official map dated H 1300 (the year that started on 11 Dec. 1882). But it does not represent the situation of 1850s. Maps that accompany official Ottoman publications are rare. The H 1300 one is an exception.

24. Robinson and Smith, *Later*, p. 629.
25. Robinson and Smith, *Later*, p. 629. The data were provided by J. Jamal, the United States consul in Beirut. The statistics for this region can be found in an appendix to the book. They listed only 7,642 Christians and Jews (citizens). The smallest unit counted was the *Nahiya* (village group). Haifa was the most populated (6,772 inhabitants in forty-two settlements, including Haifa itself).
26. The citizen population of Jerusalem and Nablus sub-districts included about 62,000 urban persons. The parallel number of other towns is unknown, because the only city for which there is a separate estimate is Acre itself. In order to calculate the size of the principal centers in the Acre District one may use the proportion of city to village for the District of Jerusalem. The number received is 78.8 percent, from which it may be concluded that almost 80 percent were rural inhabitants, and that the urban population of the District of Acre was almost 58,000 people. This allows us to conclude that city dwellers made up a fifth of the population of the country in the middle of the nineteenth century.
27. Schölch, *Transformation*, pp. 30-35. McCarthy, *Palestine*, p. 10, estimated the 1851 Palestine's population at 340,000. See also McCarthy, "Ottoman and British Mandate," where the overall population in the year 1860 was estimated as 411,000; see below chapter 4. Gilbar, pp. 45-46, quoted Schölch ("Demographic Development," p. 501), and wrote that the number 350,000 relates to 1870. But Schölch's data there (see table 15) relate to 1850-1865, and not to 1870.
28. BD/5, Documents 43-60, pp. 351-396.
29. BD/5, Documents 43-60, a note, p. 391, suggests that the original records were multiplied by 3. In this report the British attempted to assess the demographic changes by analyzing the smallest administrative units. These data cover the entire empire, but, unfortunately, the information on Palestine and on other parts of the Middle East was minimal.
30. BD/5, pp. 392-393. The Province of Syria, that had seven districts, two of them (Acre and part of Balqaa-Nablus) in Palestine, had altogether almost one million inhabitants (991,605), but the figure was not broken down to any unit lower than the provincial level. The tally for Lebanon and the District of Jerusalem were not included in the above figure.
31. Compare with McCarthy, *Palestine*, pp. 9-10. In BD/5, Doc. 60, p. 392, it is stated in parentheses that the Beirut District was not mentioned in the H 1295 (1877/8) Yearbook. In H 1296 (1878/9), its population consisted of 125,000 adult males (i.e., about 375,000 people). In 1864, fourteen/fifteen years earlier, the British themselves estimated the population of the Jerusalem District at 200,000 people. FO 195/808, Report on the Commerce of the Jerusalem District, May 1864; Hyamson, II, p. 331.
32. Hyamson, II, p. 331 and tables on pp. 314-316. For obtaining the data for the remainder of Palestine, Gottheil used a sample of thirty-one settlements for which information was available from various sources. The average population of his sample: 545 persons per settlement, was close enough to the parallel mean for the Acre area: 542. Gottheil's data for Safad (p. 315) seem to be overstated. The Bedouin were estimated to number 18,590 (see p. 216). The basis for this estimate is unclear. It conflicts with that of Ben-Arieh, who believes that they numbered about 30,000 (see below). It is also founded partly on Schumacher's survey, but no account was taken of the Negev Bedouin.
33. Schölch, "Demographic Development," p. 494.
34. McCarthy, *Palestine*, p. 11.
35. Ben-Arieh, "Size and Composition."

36. In 1887-88, as part of a major political reshuffling, Nablus became a separate district in the new Beirut Province. The rest of Palestine, with the exception of the Jerusalem District, was also transferred from Syria to the Beirut Province.
37. See Conder and Kitchener.
38. Ben-Arieh, "Size and Composition"; Ben-Arieh, "Sanjak Jerusalem; Ben-Arieh, "Sanjak Gaza"; Ben-Arieh and Oren, for additional information on rural Palestine during the 1870s. See also below the discussion and references for Socin, Schick, Schumacher, "Acca."
39. McCarthy's book contains tables that summarize data originally from the Syrian Yearbook and the Jerusalem District Vital Statistics lists (*nüfus*). Data of this nature only began to appear in Syria in H 1286 (the Moslem year that started on 13 March 1869); see also McCarthy, *Palestine*, pp. 6-10.
40. McCarthy, *Palestine*, pp. 7-10. The district of Balqaa included the Nablus Sub-District (S. D.). The Jenin S. D. seems to have been in the Hauran District, but its three Cis-Jordan (western) *nahiyas* were later detached from the Hauran. As I noted above (note to Map 3.1), I attached Jenin S. D. to Nablus S. D. to facilitate the discussion.
41. McCarthy, *Palestine*, pp. 6-11. The 1881-82 Syrian Provincial Yearbook covers Acre districts, Nablus Sub-District and the three Jenin's *nahiyas* of Cis-Jordan. The Jerusalem data are obtained by interpolation of census data of 1884-85 and 1885-86, and other sources.
42. Karpat, "Population."
43. Gerber, "Population,' pp. 61-62.
44. Schölch, *Transformation*, p. 26.
45. See, for example, Schur, "Change."
46. Karpat, "Population," p. 241. On p. 256, Karpat adds that the "margin of error in established communities located in relatively developed areas with reasonably good communication was ... between 2 and 5 percent [while] in remote areas [it] probably increased to 6-10 percent." This seems to refer to the Census that lasted from 1881 to1893, which he considered to be freer of errors than other counts.
47. See further discussion of this issue in chapter 4 and Schur, "Relationship" and Schur, "Change," for comprehensive data that were extracted from a variety of sources. The ratio of total population to males that he obtained was 4:1 or lower. He believed, however, that for the late nineteenth century the ratio should be 7:1 for the Muslim population (Schur, "Change," p. 252). A close scrutiny of some of the figures reveals, however, that the issue is more complex. To begin with, Schur does not distinguish between data that list males with those that consider households. The importance of this distinction is discussed below. Even so, in his Ratio, p. 104, Schur quotes Robinson and Smith (*Biblical Researches*, II, p. 85), where Jerusalem's Muslim Ratio was 4:1. However, Robinson and Smith stated there that the Muslims "are reckoned in the government books at 750 men." They considered this as an under-count and estimated the correct figure at 1,100. Multiplying by 4 and rounding it up, they arrived at a total of 4,500, that is, a ratio close to 6:1 between this figure and the official one. Robinson and Smith believed that the correct ratio should be 5:1, but because widespread tax evasion practices they preferred to use a 6:1 ratio. In the 1931 Census, the number of persons per house was stated to be 4.4 for Nablus and 4.7 for Nazareth; see Nadan, *Palestinian Peasant*, p. 210, note 110. This is not necessarily relevant for eighty years earlier.
48. See Schick. His formulation was based on the assumption that in the government lists published by Socin, the Jerusalem population referred to all males, not only those of work age. This assumption was adopted by Yehoshua Ben-Arieh and by

Uziel Schmelz, who, therefore, used a coefficient of 2 to estimate the total population. See Ben-Arieh, "Size and Composition." Schmelz, "Population," pp. 137-138. Schmelz, *Modern Jerusalem.*

49. Schick received from the government a list of males of the Jerusalem S. D. villages who were drafted for compulsory labor to pave the Jerusalem-Jericho road. Each village had to pave a section of the road, proportional to the size of its population. The sub-district population was calculated by using a coefficient of 3, based on the assumption that working-age males constituted two-thirds of all the males, who made up 50 percent of the population. He compared the figures with those of Socin, but this raised three issues: 1. Socin counted all males; 2. The time span between his and Socin's counts was assumed to be twenty-five years; 3. Socin's data refer to the whole district, while Schick's refer only the Jerusalem S. D. The first two issues were relatively simple. Socin's data were multiplied by 2 and his Jerusalem Sub-District population, by 3, arriving at 76,521 persons. This was found to be 2.5686 times higher than the equivalent Socin's data. The extra part (non-Jerusalem sub-districts) of Socin's list amounted to 37,523 persons. Thus, to calculate the equivalent figure for Schick's date, these extras had to be multiplied by 2.5686. The result was thus:

76.521 + (37,523 x 2.5686) = 172,902.6 (approximately 172,900).

The approximate growth since the late 1860s, as calculated by Schick, was, thus, approximately 2.260 percent over a period of twenty-five years, which is reasonable if we assume that the original population data only included males. See Schick, "Jerusalem"; Socin. The multipliers used by Socin when the data include males (multiply by 2) are validated by Davison, pp. 114-115.

50. Ben-Arieh, "Size and Composition"; see Shumacher, "Acca."
51. Schwöbel, map and tables I-IV. I did a somewhat similar, ecologically based, statistical analysis on the Samarian zone for 1922-1975 Israeli censuses. The correlation between land quality and population growth was positive and fairly high for the Mandate period, but negative and only partly significant for the later dates. See Grossman, "Population and Land Quality."
52. See Hartmann.
53. McCarthy found that in one of the counts conducted in Basra, Iraq, only fourteen women were registered. A somewhat similar case was reported by Schumacher in Safad, where the Ultra-Orthodox Jews refused to be counted. Such difficulties were not necessarily faced also among other religious Jews. See McCarthy, "Syria and Iraq," pp. 7-10; McCarthy, *Palestine*, p. 7. Schumacher, "'Acca."
54. Even larger gaps can be seen in the data that he did not select as the basis for his calculations; see also McCarthy, "Age and Family," pp. 317-320. His method of computation is based on using known data for certain base years and extrapolating them for years lacking in demographic data, assuming a uniform rate of growth for the period between censuses, presuming that there were no marked changes during the interim period; see McCarthy, *Palestine*, pp. 20-23. The official data cited by McCarthy are based on the Jerusalem *nüfus*. A comprehensive analysis of their quality can be found in Pagis' catalogue; see also Schmelz, *Jerusalem*, for a demographic study based on these data.
55. McCarthy, *Palestine*, pp. 7-11. http//www.palestineremembered.com/Acre/Palestine-Remembered/Story. 12/4/03.

4

Demographic Sources for the Years 1871-72 – 1922: Data and Comparative Analysis

The Syrian Yearbook for the Year H 1288 (1871-72)

The previous chapter reviewed the shortcomings of available Ottoman censuses and the various means of overcoming the paucity of demographic data. Despite the problems, a number of researchers have been able to derive useful information from them. In this chapter I examine and evaluate a single source of demographic information: the Syrian Provincial Yearbook of H 1288 (H = Hijra, i.e., "migration." The number refers to the Muslim calendar years that have passed since 622, when Muhammad "migrated" from Mecca to Medina. The Hijra lunar year has 354 days).

The first Syrian Provincial Yearbook (*Salname Vilayet Suriye*) was published in the year H 1286 that started on 13 April 1869. This and the following early yearbooks provided basic demographic information on the level of the *nahiya* (part of sub-district; the smallest administrative unit.). However, only in the yearbook of H 1288 (23 March 1871 to 11 March 1872 –henceforth: 1288 Yearbook) is the household the basic demographic unit. This is why I preferred to use this yearbook over the others for my present study.

The use of the household data presents some methodological problems, but, as shown in chapter 3, it helps to avoid under-reporting of females and children. It provides micro-level data that allows researchers to identify arithmetical or mathematical errors which, unfortunately, are frequent in the Ottoman statistical records.

The exact date of the actual counting on which the H 1288 data are based is not known. It may have been two years or more before the publication. The 1288 Yearbook, like other provincial yearbooks, contained many details that have no direct bearing on the size and composition of the population. There is a wealth of information on public officeholders and the central towns have lists of public buildings: schools, religious institutions, *khan* and the number of shops. Some of them (Yearbook H 1298, started on 4 December 1880 and H 1301, on 2 November 1883) include data on the extent of the cultivated land and the number of agricultural properties. I have made some use of the data contained in these yearbooks in order to gauge the degree of pressure on the land. A quantitative analysis of this nature requires a meticulous examination of the nature of the data and a comparison with other sources or periods.

The Syrian Yearbooks that were published after 1872 contain information on most of Palestine but not on the Jerusalem District (that became semi-independent). For the most part, the information they contain does not apply to the household (HH) level. In fact, rarely do we find information on the lowest territorial level, the *nahiya* or even on the *qadaa* (sub-district) level. On the *nahiya* level the data on the total household count of each village is missing. It is this information that is the basis for the following discussion and for this reason I selected to study the 1288 Yearbook.[1]

The section of the Syrian 1288 Yearbook that deals with the demography of the Jerusalem District (*sanjak*; also called *pashalik* or *liwaa*) was translated and analyzed by Professor M. Hartmann shortly after its publication.[2] Hartmann's stated intention was to compare the data on the Jerusalem District with a similar (but not identical) official publication on the same district that was already translated and edited by Professor A. Socin. Hartmann entitled this the "Syrian List," while Socin's, based on data published by the Jerusalem District's administration, was called the "Jerusalem List." Further analyses of these sources have been conducted recently by a number of scholars.[3]

Regional re-alignments like the one that detached the Jerusalem District from Syria were not unusual. During most of the Ottoman period the Galilee was under the administration of Sidon (later, of Acre), rather than of Damascus. Later, since 1887, all of it came under the newly formed Beirut Province. The borders of the lower administrative units were also repeatedly redrawn, a fact which makes demographic research quite arduous.[4] The advantage of the 1288 Yearbook is thus also that it is the only yearbook that includes all three districts of the country. For certain post-1872 years, the semi-independent Jerusalem data can be derived from census publications or from vital registration lists (*nüfus*), which are difficult to interpret.[5]

There are, however, added advantages to the use of single village records. The availability of data at village level is essential for mapping density, calculating settlement concentration, and understanding the factors underlying the population processes and rates of demographic change. The importance of these and other issues for a proper spatial analysis can be summarized by the following requisites:

1. To sub-divide the smallest administrative territories (*nahiya*) in order to isolate those regions that belonged to Jewish settlement areas after 1882 and the desert regions that were part of certain official administrative territories. The macro-method adopted by most researchers, based only on district or sub-district data, is not sufficiently refined for this purpose.

2. To cope with the repeated boundary changes that occurred at various times, in order to define fixed geographic units for purposes of comparison between censuses. This is necessary because, as already stated, the borders between districts, between sub-districts and within sub-districts were frequently altered by the government.[6] Boundary shifts were naturally more drastic when the ruling states or empires were changed. It is not surprising, therefore, that when, after 1917, the Ottoman Empire was replaced by the British administration, the new rulers decided to establish a different administrative system, and the boundary changes were quite drastic. Using single village territories rather than any larger territorial units facilitated the comparative process by fixing the 1288 Yearbook's *nahiya* boundaries, and using the same areas for analyzing the 1922 data.

3. To present quantitative material in statistical tables (unlike the present version, the Hebrew edition presents all statistics by tables) after findings, diagrams and maps for a geographic presentation of the findings. The relevant data for this purpose included the calculation of territorial settlement distribution, administrative size and demographic changes that occurred during the inter-enumeration periods. Some of the parameters required for a quantitative presentation (especially demographic change rate) are not area-dependent. Even in these cases, however, it is essential to define fixed areas and their distribution.

4. An in-depth examination of the village data uncovered a number of problems arising from the nature of the Ottoman bureaucratic sys-

tem. A detailed discussion of these problems has been omitted, but one cardinal problem had to be resolved: the dearth of maps. The Syrian Yearbooks for the years H 1300 (1882/83) and H 1310/11 (1893-94) contain maps whose scale is 1:1,000,000 showing approximate district borders. One of them was presented in chapter 3 (see map 3.1) but they had little value for the present analysis. The solution I found was to utilize maps containing 1945 data (i.e., about seventy-five years later than the 1288 records) on village territories.[7] My decision to use the1870s village territories is somewhat problematic. However, even if there were inter-village boundary changes during this period, the usefulness of this procedure is not seriously affected.

These 1945-46 data were used for plotting the boundaries on maps 4.3 (1288) and 4.4 (1922). The territorial boundaries were kept constant, despite the half century that separate them. The *nahiya* boundaries (or parts of them) were also fixed. The resulting territories are shown on map 4.1.

For illustrating the problem that results from boundary changes, I present an additional map (map 4.2) which is based on the Memoirs of the Palestine Exploration Fund (PEF).[8] A cursory examination of maps 4.1 and 4.2 reveals many significant differences, even though the date of the PEF survey was 1876, that is, just a few years after the 1288 publication.

The following maps, 4.3 and 4.4, are based on the demarcated administrative units of map 4.1. The two maps show the estimated population densities for the years 1871/72 (map 4.3) and 1922 (map 4.4) for groups of *nahiyas* or parts of them in these respective dates.

To complete this section it is necessary to explain why, in some cases, I chose parts of *nahiyas* rather than complete ones. I used this procedure for two main reasons: (a) for isolating the few Jewish settlement zones before 1948; (b) for isolating the dry lands, that is, those located outside the Mediterranean climatic zone. In both cases, these zones were mainly parts of certain other *nahiyas*. The isolation of the Jewish lands was performed by selecting from the 1945 Village Territories Map the areas marked as belonging to Jewish settlements. These areas were for the most part contiguous, and formed a fairly well defined N-shaped belt. The dry lands were more simply defined by following the village territories which bordered the banks of the Jordan River or the Dead Sea in areas whose annual precipitation averaged below 300 mm. As a result, the Negev dry zone was completely excluded from this analysis.

Map 4.1
Nahiyas (the lowest administrative units) and several sub-*nahiyas*

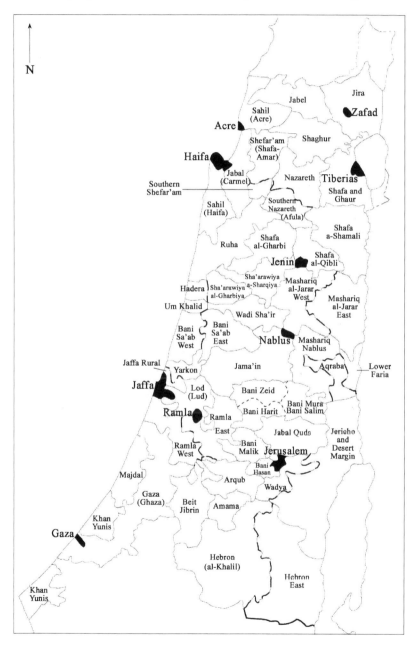

N

Jira

Jabel

Zafad

Sahil
(Acre)

Acre

Shefar'am
(Shafa-
Amar)

Shaghur

Haifa

Jabal
(Carmel)

Nazareth

Tiberias

Southern
Shefar'am

Shafa and
Ghaur

Sahil
(Haifa)

Southern
Nazareth
(Afula)

Shafa
a-Shamali

Ruha

Shafa
al-Gharbi

Shafa
al-Qibli

Jenin

Sha'arawiya
a-Sharqiya

Mashariq
al-Jarar
West

Hadera

Sha'arawiya
al-Gharbiya

Um Khalid

Mashariq
al-Jarar
East

Wadi Sha'ir

Bani
Sa'ab
West

Bani
Sa'ab
East

Nablus

Mashariq
Nablus

Jaffa Rural

Yarkon

Jama'in

Aqraba

Lower
Faria

Jaffa

Lod
(Lud)

Bani Zeid

Ramla

Bani Harit

Bani Mura
Bani Salim

Ramla
East

Jabal Quda

Jericho
and
Desert
Margin

Ramla
West

Bani
Malik

Jerusalem

Majdal

Bani
Hasan

Gaza
(Ghaza)

Beit
Jibrin

Arqub

Amama

Wadya

Khan
Yunis

Gaza

Hebron
(al-Khalil)

Hebron
East

Khan
Yunis

Map 4.2
Nahiyas according to the Palestine Exploration Fund, surveyed c.1875

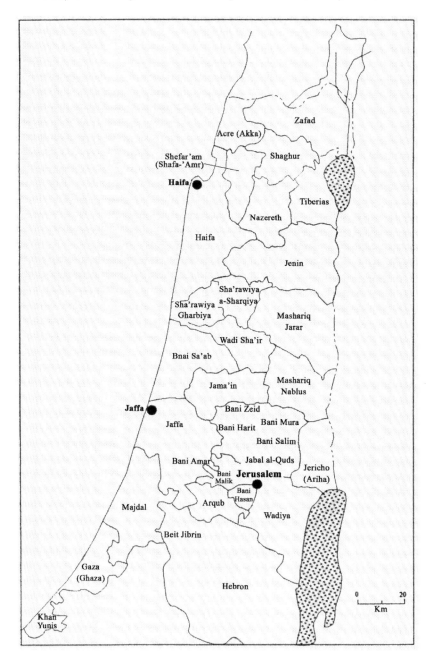

Map 4.3
Population density by *nahiyas* or sub-*nahiyas*

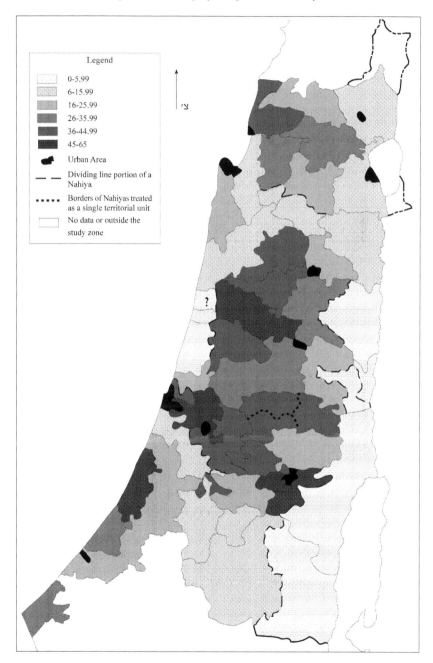

Map 4.4
Population density according to the 1922 Census.

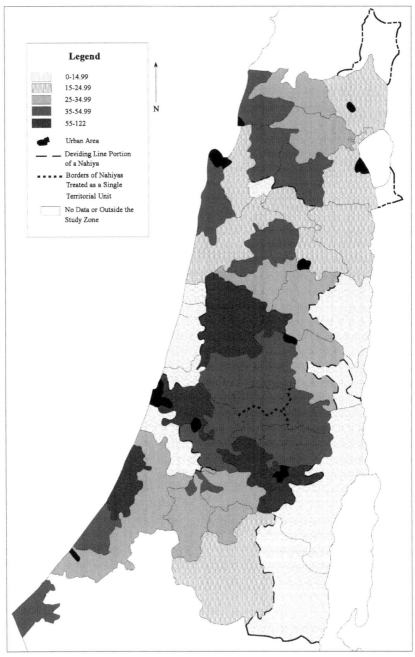

Population: Numbers and Distribution:
Findings of the H 1288 Data

Chart 4.1 presents the estimated population of three zones using two alternative coefficients (multipliers) that were used for estimating the population of each *nahiya* (or its parts):

A. Jerusalem District
B. Acre District
C. Nablus and Jenin Sub-Districts

Discussion and Interpretation:
The Distribution of Rural Population

Assuming that the counts were reasonably free of serious errors, and that they closely depict reality, rural Palestine, that is, the areas located outside the major towns (the centers of the districts and the sub-districts) had in1870 a total of 44,654 households (HH). I excluded from this figure, however, the households of two villages which were originally (in 1871-72) in the Acre District, but outside the territory that later became Palestine. On the other hand, all the northern Galilee that was outside Acre District was excluded from the study area (see map 4.1). Consequently, the number of rural HH c. 1870 (the approximate date that the counting published in 1871-72 was taken) was 44,601. If we assume that the average number of persons per HH was six, the total population of rural Palestine amounted to 267,606. These people resided in 654 villages, which had a mean size of 68.2 households, or a mean of 409.2 persons per village. The alternative assumption, that the average household had only five persons, reduces the estimated population to 223,005. The average population per village was thus 341. The population size (HH x 6) and the village distribution pattern are shown on map 4.5.[9]

The following discussion presents a selective account of the main features of the findings. Before proceeding, it should be stressed that the statistical data of chart 4.1 refer only to the citizens residing in rural *nahiyas*. They do not include non-citizens and the residents of the major towns.

We may now look at the population distribution pattern. The Jerusalem District, with a rural population of almost 100,000, was clearly the most populated zone while Acre was the least populated one. It is also notable that Gaza Sub-District (S.D.) was more populated than Jaffa S.D. Gaza town was indeed the most important economic center before the

Map 4.5
Estimated population growth during the 1871-1922 period

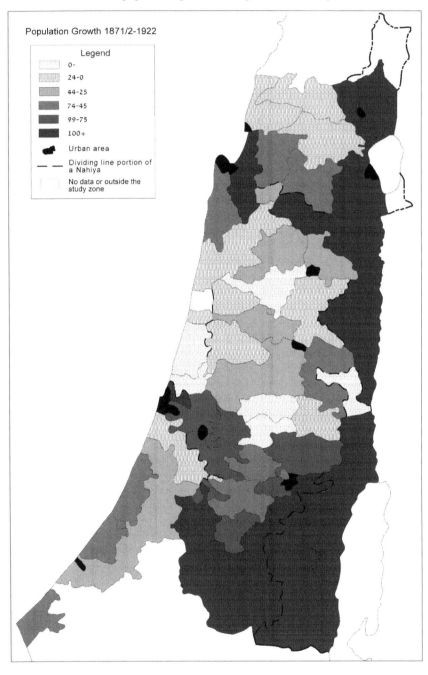

late nineteenth century, and was unrivaled by any other town for most of the Ottoman period. In the sixteenth century and, in fact, before the mid-seventeenth century, Jaffa was no more than an insignificant fishing hamlet, but since the late eighteenth century it gradually became a major economic center (figure 4.1).[10] Its eventual importance was the result of its function as the port of both Jerusalem and Nablus (which are approximately equidistant from it). Haifa was also a small village, whose population growth started even later than Jaffa's. Before the eighteenth century it served mainly as a trafficker and pirate haven.[11]

It is interesting to note, in addition, the relative size of the N-shaped zone (formed by the *nahiyas* of Safad, Tiberias, Ruha, the Carmel Jabal; the southern parts of the *nahiyas* of Shefar'am [Shafa-a'mar] and Nazareth, the Sharon and Ramla West; see map 4.1) that became the core of the Jewish rural settlement after 1882. It also coincided partly with the Bedouin-dominated zone. Without these (non-enumerated) nomadic tribes, the population of the N-shaped zone amounted to about 21,000-25,000, while the entire rural population numbered, as shown above, between 223,005 and 267,606, that is, it was close to one tenth of the total rural population.[12]

It should be recalled that McCarthy's estimate for the whole country, for 1877-78, was 400,850. Since the equivalent figure published in the

Fig. 4.1
Jaffa in 1836

Sources: W.H. Bartlett, *Jerusalem Revisited*, 1855. Reprinted in Kark, *Jaffa, A City in Evolution*, Jerusalem: Ariel Publishing House, 2003, p. 17, Courtesy of Ruth Kark and Ely Schiller, the publication rights holders.

Chart 4.1

Two estimates of Palestinian rural population circa 1871

A. Jerusalem District population

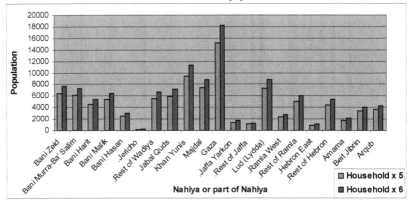

B. Acre District population

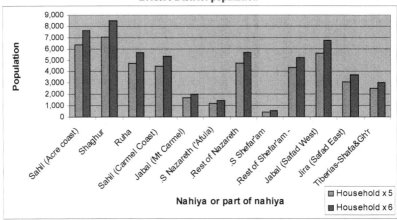

C. Nablus Sub-Deistrict and West Jenin population

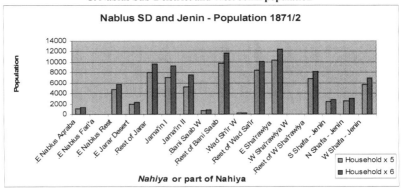

Chart 4.2
Two estimates of rural population densities circa 1871

A. Jerusalem District

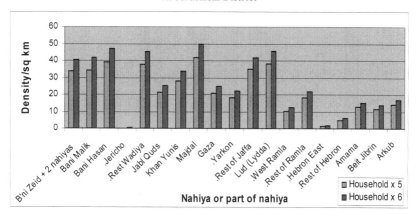

B. Acre District

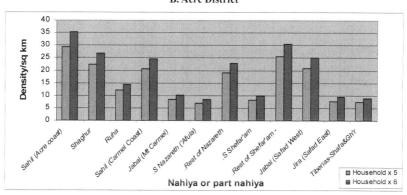

C. Nablus S.D. and part of Jenin S.D.

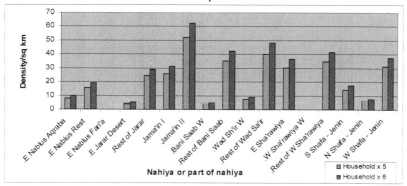

1288 Yearbook (approximately 381,000) relates to a census carried out several years earlier, McCarthy's findings do not contradict those in the 1288 Yearbook.[13] Even though the figures quoted here are not free of errors.

Except for some religious data that has already been discussed briefly in earlier chapters, the detailed ethnic and other population characteristics are omitted. The only additional analysis that I attempted was the calculation of the density per square kilometer. The following charts present the resulting densities (chart 4.2).

Discussion and Interpretation:
The Distribution of Rural Densities

Population density, which is one component of the relative pressure on the land, is discussed in a comprehensive and in-depth manner in chapter 6. The following pages are concerned with various other implications of the density issue. Charts 4.1 and 4.2 illustrate the relationships between people, size and density. As can be seen, while the absolute number of Arabs living in the N-shaped zone (called here Jewish Settlement zone; rural areas were still unsettled by Jews before 1882) is only a tenth of the total population, its density is about half of the mean overall density, and slightly larger than one third of the Arab density (table 4.1 and map 4.3). The rural density in the Nablus SD was clearly very high, especially in the northwestern *nuwah* (plural of *nahiya*). It was, in fact, the highest recorded in non-urban peripheries.

The difference between the Arab density in core zones and the rural Arab density of the area that eventually became the Jewish settled area was great, but not as great as it was perceived to be. However, a density of eight to ten persons per square kilometer is undeniably under-settled land. The sparse Arab population in the Jewish settlement zone is not

Table 4.1
Persons per square kilometer, c. 1870, in three rural Palestinian zones

Zones	HH x 5	HH x 6
Overall density	17.0	20.4
Arab villages: central mountains & hills	23.0	28.2
Jewish settlement area after 1882	8.3	10.0
Dry Jordan & Dead Sea	1.9	2.3

Source: Syrian Provincial Yearbook for H 1288

surprising, but its quantitatively low extent has not been known previously. There is, however, an even lower density in the desert-border zone that reaches the banks of the Jordan River. This and other parts of Palestine are discussed in the next chapter.

The 1288 Yearbook data have to be carefully examined and verified by comparisons with other contemporary statistical lists. The most important potential candidates for such comparisons have already been partly presented in chapter 3, but the subject has not been comprehensively treated, because the cardinal test for comparability is not only the reliability and validity of the source. An essential criterion, that has been repeatedly emphasized, is that the lowest statistical unit has to be the single village. This requirement severely limits the potential sources available for testing the 1288 Yearbook.

A selection of available yearbooks and other sources, including one that was discussed in chapter 3, are shown below, but all of them present only the Nablus S.D. (plus Jenin) and the Acre District. In fact, no source, including all the provincial yearbooks that I examined, fully met this criterion.[14] Despite the superior quality of the 1931 Census, I preferred to consult the earliest Mandate census taken in 1922. This census provides significant insights into the transition from Ottoman to British rule. It helps to evaluate at least one of the serious errors that stood in the way of understanding the 1288 population records. It is examined in the next section, but at least one of the errors located in the 1288 Yearbook, that raises serious doubts about this source's validity, has to have priority over other critical reviews.

The Mathematical Calculation Problem

To my knowledge, Victor Guérin's survey is the only one that provided some quantitative data on villages in Palestine for approximately the same period in which the H 1288 data was collected. This is especially significant for Samaria's statistical records which suffer from inadequate reporting.[15] But, unfortunately, his travels (in 1863 and 1875) did not cover the entire country, and the population data contained in his survey were rough estimates, based mostly on house counts. When compared with Guérin's survey, the 1288 Yearbook data seems quite reasonable.

A serious problem arose, however, from the figures that were recorded in the 1288 lists of seven *nahiyas* of western and northern Samaria. There is an arithmetical discrepancy between the official tally and those which I calculated for the household data. My summations were about three times as great as the officially quoted totals.

My hypothesis was that this absurd discrepancy resulted from confusing two parallel lists, that is, it occurred because the enumeration confused the two lists, one that counted all the males and the other, the official summation that referred to the households. If each household contained three males, the number of males in each HH should be three. It seems that the field enumerators counted the males, but the officers in charge of editing the results submitted the household lists. It is also possible that the confusion was caused by a misunderstanding of the original instructions. The result indicates, in any case, that the enumeration overseers were negligent.

To substantiate this hypothesis I searched the *nüfus* (literally, souls, i.e., vital registration statistics) of a *nahiya* neighboring western Samaria. The selected *nahiya* referred to 1876, that is, a date fairly close to the 1288 (1871-72). The data contained, indeed, lists of both households and males. The twenty-five villages listed in it had a total of 4,773 males and 1,669 households. The males/households ratio was thus 2.86, that is, very close to the mean ratio of the seven problematic *nahiyas* in the 1288 Yearbook whose seven *nahiya*'s mean was 2.92).[16] This result is close to similar ratios of other parallel HH/male lists.[17] I corrected the data for each household by dividing each of them by using each specific *nahiya*'s mean ratio. However, the villages belonging to the seven *nahiyas* had an unexpectedly large population even after their size was adjusted.[18]

These difficulties underline the need for careful examination of the Ottoman calculations. Fortunately, similar difficulties were not encountered in other lists. This was but one of methodological hurdles that had to be overcome during the course of the demographic research.

Evaluation of Various Official Records and Other Sources

The comparison between the 1288 Yearbook and the 1922 census suggests that the 1288 data do provide valuable information despite their shortcomings. Apart from the seven *nahiyas* of western Samaria, there are no glaring mistakes in this list, even though the records contain additional minor mathematical errors and other lacunae that result from inefficiency or negligence.

To obtain a better understanding of the 1871-72 data, I consulted four issues of the Central National Yearbooks which provided information on the imperial level during the period 1894-95–1908-09, that is, the last phase of Sultan 'Abd al-Hamid II's rule. Unfortunately, they were disappointing. Their statistical data, which referred to the number of settlements in each *nahiya,* appear to have been copied mostly without any updating for the entire fourteen-year period. The only changes that I encountered referred to Nazareth, where according to the 1906-7 Yearbook the number of its settlements declined from twenty-nine to twenty-eight. In the next yearbook (1908-09), the information on settlements in Nazareth was completely missing.

The provincial yearbooks that I examined do not seem to have similarly grave faults, but in some cases they also contained information that was evidently copied from previous publications. A case in point is the H 1289 Yearbook (the year beginning 11 March 1872), whose data were partly copied from the H 1288 that preceded it. During the 1880-1890 decade, however, there were a number of innovations. Females were first counted in 1881. The yearbook which was published in December 1880 (H 1298) listed farms and agricultural land (discussed in chapter 6). As was already stated, this information was included also in other yearbooks (H 1301; 2 November 1883). The information presented in the yearbooks of Beirut Province (that including Palestine after 1887-88)[19] was fairly static. This might be interpreted as an improvement over the previous administration. By 1892-93, according to the Beirut Yearbook for H 1311-2, the overall population figure (excluding Jerusalem District) stood at 204,212.[20] The 1900 Yearbook reported that the two districts north of Jerusalem already had close to 226,000 people. The following illustration (chart 4.3) provides a summary of the above Syrian and Lebanese yearbooks' data. It lists only males due to difficulty of including females.

The most interesting yearbook that helps to follow the changes that occurred in the rural areas of northern Palestine during the 1870s is the Syrian Yearbook of H 1299 (starting 23 November 1881). It contains a detailed list of all the villages in Acre and Nablus districts though, unfortunately, without any demographic information. This is, nevertheless,

Chart 4.3
Male citizens: selected years

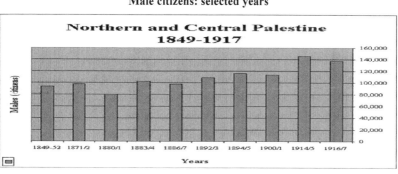

the only source that I encountered that provides some idea of regional settlement trends. By comparing it with the H 1288 list (1871-72), a picture emerges of the possible changes in the number of villages and other rural settlements. Its main advantage is that, unlike the list published a decade earlier, it also contains names of seasonal or temporary farms and Bedouin tribes.

By analyzing the data we learn that ten new villages were added in Tiberias and six others in Ruha. Two other *nahiyas* (Beisan, which was north Jenin, and Eastern Nablus*)* added five villages each. Nine other *nahiyas* registered between one and three additions, but there were also six *nahiyas* where former (1288) villages were missing. The list reveals that eight Tiberian Bedouin tribes which were missing from the 1288 list were added also.

Another rural settlement type is the "farm." It refers to thirty-six seasonal-temporary shelters and their fields. Of them, as many as twenty were in the eastern *nuwah* (plural of *nahiya*), while seven were in Jamain. *Nahiya* Ruha's four "farms" in Nablus northeastern periphery also belong to this cluster. Most of the Galilee, on the other hand, had only eight detached "farms" that were on the eastern, western, and northern margins of Nablus S.D. (including Beisan), northern Jezre'el Valley, western Galilee and the dry areas facing the Jordan basin. All of these zones have marginal resources. Overall, the fairly large number of the "farms" indicates that during the 1870s there was already a pronounced agricultural expansion in the Arab sector, which was particularly noticeable in the eastern fringes of the Galilee and Samaria.

Chart 4.4
Comparison of Arab settlements

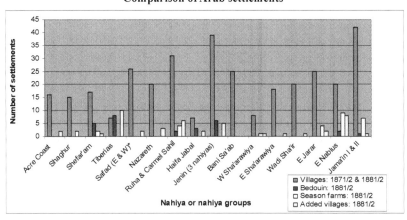

The number of "new" Bedouin tribes is not surprising. We already know that they were not counted in the 1871-72 yearbook. The Tiberias *nahiya* is, however, interesting. This is the area whose settled population was low in the 1871-72 yearbook. It appears that the Bedouin and the detached "farms" account for the low proportion of the official listing of 1871-72. Most temporary or seasonal shelters eventually evolved into recognized villages. The "farms" should be regarded, therefore, as incipient villages.

The differences between the 1288 and the 1299 yearbooks apply also to the Bedouin tribes that are completely missing in the earlier yearbook. It is not necessary to devote a special discussion to this issue, which is treated in some length in other parts of this volume.

A comparison of the reported villages in both provincial yearbooks is most significant for assessing the reliability of the 1288 data. It seems that villages were more numerous in 1881 than in 1871, but there were also a few opposite cases. It is not known when and why the additional villages were founded or registered, but my research verified that the trend of settlement expansion started in the late nineteenth century.[21] The total number of settlements (not including Bedouin tribes and temporary "farms") was 338 (77.35 percent of the total 435). There were, however, 45 (10.30 percent) villages which were not recorded in 1871/2. This suggests that settlement stability was not very high, but a look at the regional distribution of the difference is illuminating. The most outstanding zone is Tiberias *nahiya,* which in 1871/2 had only seven villages. In 1881/2 there were ten more villages. This is not surprising, because of the rehabilitation of Tiberias during this period. Beisan also took part in this change, though its share had to wait to 1905 when the link to Damascus and the Hijaz rail line was completed. There were some permanent villages, established partly by Egyptian settlers, or temporary "farms" that were fixed (see chapter 5).[22]

A useful source for the early twentieth century population data is that of two scholars, Muhammad Bahjat and Muhammad Tamimi, who were appointed by the Ottoman government to conduct a detailed survey of the Beirut Province. Their findings were published in two volumes. The first one, published in 1916-17 (H 1335), was devoted to the southern portion of Beirut province, which included the area that eventually became Palestine. The book contained a serious error concerning the Nablus District data in which about 20,000 persons were added to this area, but it was corrected in the second volume that treated the area north of Tyre. A few other statistical data were also altered. The overall population figure quoted by the second volume for Acre and Nablus districts was close to 295,000,[23] which was a large increase over former records.

To conclude this discussion it is necessary to add some comparative data about the Jerusalem District. McCarthy estimated, on the basis of the *nüfus* data, that the district's population for 1911-12 was about 366,742. According to both Ruppin and Schmelz, the population of the Jerusalem District in 1915 was slightly higher and approached 400,000.[24] It is, therefore, reasonable to assume that the entire population of Palestine numbered between 650,000 and 700,000 at the start of the First World War. There are differences of opinion regarding the number of Jews in the country at that time. It would appear that McCarthy was correct in his claim that Ruppin deliberately inflated the number of Jews. He did so, however, in order to arrive at a realistic figure, because official statistics consistently recorded only Ottoman citizens. Before the expulsion of Jews that was carried out during the World War, they apparently numbered 60,000.[25]

Demographic Trends: Circa 1870 and 1922

According to the 1922 census,[26] the entire non-Jewish population, apart from the Negev Bedouin, who were not properly counted, was 653,851.[27] This relatively low figure is largely explained by the loss of life incurred during the First World War. Compared with the estimates of the 1850s, however, the population of Palestine had almost doubled. The growth is the result of numerous social and economic factors: improved sanitation and health, increased opportunities for work in industry as well as in farming, transportation, and commerce. Another factor was the improved governance during the later decades of the Ottoman era (see chapter 1).

In this section I will focus on the demographic change of the rural Arab population. I will endeavor to analyze and explain the intra-zonal changes that occurred in the half century that preceded 1922. The formula for calculating the rate of demographic growth for the entire period is:

$$I = [(p1922 / p1871) - 1] \times 100$$
where: $I = 51$ year rate; $p =$ population.

However, we also want to know the mean annual rate of growth. The formula for calculating this rate is presented in a simplified form by the use of natural logarithms:

$$R = \ln \frac{(p1922/p1871)}{t} \times 100$$

where: ln = natural logarithms; p = population in a given year; t = time (in years)

The resulting rates for the whole period, which apply to the coefficient of 6 (HH x 6), are presented in map 4.6.

The inter-census interval chosen (t = 51) relates to the period between 1870-71 and 1922, in other words, one year before the initial (1288) records. I deducted one year only from the publication date of the 1288 Yearbook, but the actual count, whose exact date is not precisely given, might have been earlier. In any event, I assume that the difference in average growth rate between t51, t52 or t53 would not significantly affect the results.

The consequent calculations reveal marked geographical gaps in growth rates. The gaps were pronounced at all levels: inter-district, intra-district and sub-district. Some settlement zones even showed negative growth rates. A case that stands out is the Yarkon area just north of Jaffa, which had the highest negative rates. This was a malaria-infested zone, where those who raised water buffalo dwelt (see c\\hapter 2). Its residents also lost their former jobs in the water mills, which were gradually closed. The western Sharon plain also had high negative rates, though substantially lower than those of the Yarkon zone. Another possible explanation is that the population was reduced by malaria.

The negative growth rates west of Jenin most probably reflect the over-estimated count in c.1871 (see above), which was corrected by the 1922 census. The *nahiyas* to its north and south, which were also among those that were affected by the erroneous 1871-72 count, appear to have had low to moderate growth rates, but no negative ones. It is not likely that these rates represent real demographic trends.[28]

The impact of irrigation development since the late nineteenth century is pronounced throughout the Jordan Valley, where the extremely high growth rates reflect a condition of extremely low initial population. The highest rate is not evenly distributed. It represents the true trend only for the Jericho oases. For the same reason, the desert zone west of the Dead Sea fringing the Hebron Mountain core also registered an impressive growth rate. In fact, most of Hebron's territory lay along the settlement fringe, where the rural population was sparse during the Ottoman era. However, the area had many seasonally inhabited caves and ruins whose

Map 4.6
The distribution of settlements, by size, c. 1870

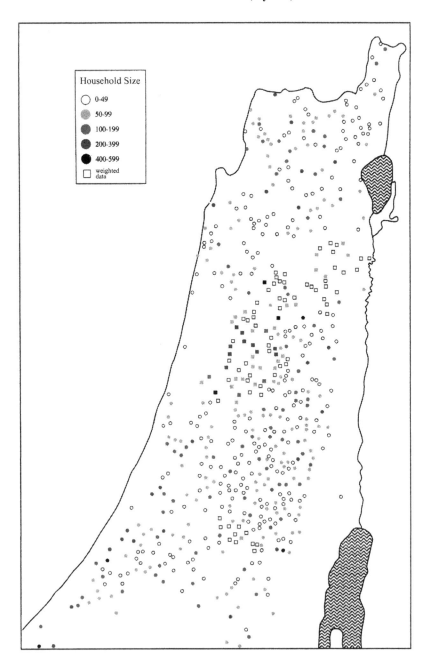

existence was not known to the government. There was, therefore, a large population under-count in the Hebron western and southern fringe. This will be discussed at some length in the next chapter. A pronounced exception is that of a sole eastern Samaria village, which was treated as a sub-*nahiya*, and was located on the uplands bordering the desert. But, in fact, its negative growth rate is not very different from that of its neighboring eastern Samaria villages that experienced high out-migration rates to the developing irrigated areas of the Jordan and its tributaries.

Mount Carmel also had unusually high growth rates reflecting the pacification that took place after 1860. The mountainous area had been practically empty before the sixteenth century. It was later inhabited by Druze families but they were subject to bloody conflicts with their Muslim neighbors. The inhabitants were also hard hit by Ibrahim Pasha and by their neighbors in the aftermath of his retreat.

The rest of the Galilee had mostly mild growth rates, but the eastern part (Safad and Tiberias) suffered from devastation and other disasters. The partial recovery took place only in the late Ottoman era when the towns Safad and Tiberias acted as growth poles for the local Arabs and especially for Jewish rural settlers. They later spread from these poles to the Beisan Basin, the Jezre'el Plain and the eastern Lower Galilee.

Summary and Conclusions

The rates of growth for the coefficient of 6 (HH x 6) were 0.79 percent on an annual basis and only 50 percent for the entire fifty-one years. Using the alternative coefficient (HH x 5), the average annual growth rate was 1.14 percent, which is fairly close to that suggested by McCarthy (1.24 percent; see above), for a similar period. During the entire 51-year period, the demographic growth was nearly 80 percent. The total rural population for 1871 was probably closer to 223,005 than 267,606 though it seems that the figure lies somewhere in between these two. The answer to this question depends on a further effort to scrutinize the data and cross-examining the information by additional comparative work. This task is taken up in the following pages.

This chapter was concerned with establishing demographic facts. Little room has been devoted to explaining the facts. This is the subject of the next chapter. But its main purpose is to provide added validation of the quantitative data by consulting non-quantitative information in the literature that deals with the various regions of the country, their resources and their cultural and historical geography. This regional-based approach is expected to provide the main facts on the human distribution and other demographical topics.

Notes

1. The demographic information in the 1288 Yearbook is unique. I am not aware of any yearbooks that relate specifically to the Jerusalem District, but some data about this district (al-Quds a Sharif) can be found in various statistical lists that appear in yearbooks of the National Ottoman Empire (*Salname Devlet Aliyah Osmaniya*). Among other things, these books list the names of government-appointed officehold-ers and statistical data relating to the number of settlements and *mazra'as* (cultivated plots or temporary shelters detached from the mother settlement) in each district and *nahiya*. On the basis of their examination we can conclude that in most cases the numbers were arbitrarily copied from one yearbook to the next. For example, the number of settlements listed in the State Yearbooks for the years 1312, 1314, 1324, and 1326 are almost identical, although there are some exceptions (notably for the year 1324, that began in February 1906).
2. Hartmann, "Jerusalem."
3. Ben-Arieh, "Sanjak Jerusalem," pp. 103-122. See also Schölch, "Demographic Development," pp. 485-488 and in Schölch, *Transformation*, pp. 20-25.
4. Compare map 4.1, which is based on Conder and Kitchener, and map 4.2 (based on 1288 Yearbook). For further explanation see below.
5. McCarthy, *Palestine*, pp. 7-10, based his estimates on these sources.
6. This subject is more extensively addressed by Kushnir, "The Districts."
7. Palestine Map, Index to Villages and Settlements, marks the boundaries of known villages throughout Palestine. The Village Statistic Sheets (henceforth Village Statistics) include demographic data and land use in all Palestinian villages. The edition presented here relates to 1 April 1945 and contains official data on the size of all Palestinian village lands in metric dunams, as well as the size of plots devoted to high-value agricultural crops.
8. Conder and Kitchener and PEF-based administrative map (map 4.2).
9. These two alternative estimates seem to be the most reasonable. The rationale for using these or other coefficients (multipliers) was discussed in chapter 3. The Jenin S. D. extended on both banks of the Jordan River, but only the three *nahiyas* that were located on the west bank (Palestine proper) are included. The same also ap-plies to the Tiberias S. D. where there was only one *nahiya* that was in the area that became Palestine. The three Jenin *nahiyas* were later transferred to the Nazareth S. D. (see map 3.1). In 1887, when the new Province of Beirut, which covered the west bank only, was created, Jenin's *nahiyas* were transferred to the new Nablus District.
10. Jaffa's port was occasionally revived when a ship landed in its waters, but the pas-sengers had to wait up to three days for the government's officials to arrive from Ramla (about ten kilometers to the east of Jaffa) before they could disembark. According to 1596-97 taxation records (see Hütteroth and Abdulfattah), its popu-lation consisted of fifteen taxpayers only (about seventy-five people). They were probably fishermen who used Jaffa's ruins as dwellings. Jaffa's growth restarted in the second half of the seventeenth-century (see Kark, *Jaffa*, and chapters 1 and 2).
11. Haifa's growth started after the first quarter of the eighteenth century. Its develop-ment is related to a function fairly similar to that of Jaffa. In Haifa's case it was its location that functioned as the main gateway to the holy town of Nazareth

that triggered its ascendancy. A main factor was the establishment of the Templer colony in 1868. However, its new town developed during the eighteenth century. See Cohen, "Coast of Palestine"; Kark, "Templer"; Ben-Arieh, "Twelve Major Settlements"; see also A. Carmel; Ben-Artzi, *Creation of the Carmel*.

12. These figures do not include the Negev (in the Mandatory borders of the Bir a-Saba' (Be'er-Sheva') Sub-District [S. D.]) which extended over 12,500 square kilometers, approximately half the total area of Palestine. By 1922 overall population density was thirty-two persons per square kilometer, but Arab population density in the area of Jewish settlement remained far lower than the average. A detailed comparative analysis of the 1871-72 figures and the 1922 Census appears later in this chapter.

13. As mentioned in the previous chapter, Schölch estimated that in the middle of the century the population of Palestine numbered about 350,000. McCarthy's estimate was somewhat lower: 340,000 (excluding Bedouin). For 1860-61, McCarthy put the figure at 369,000, but he did not provide data for 1870 or 1871. However, in a later publication ("Ottoman and British Mandate") McCarthy estimated the population of Palestine in 1860 at 411,000. By interpolating the data from 1860, and McCarthy's later figures, we can estimate the population of Palestine in the early 1870s at approximately 385,000. See McCarthy, *Palestine*, p. 10.

14. I compared the H1288 data with several additional Ottoman yearbooks. Selected data from these yearbooks were presented in Appendix 3 of the Hebrew edition of this book. Also included there is a selection from Cuinet's and Ruppin demographic data. Most of the selections refer to the district level, but in a few of them there is also sub-district data and, rarely, even *nahiya* level data. See also Appendix 4 of the Hebrew edition, pp. 270-277, for a discussion of the usefulness of several specific yearbooks published in the 1872-1912 period.

15. Crude statistical estimates on Samaria (based mainly on house counts) were reported by Guérin, Vols. IV and V. Conder and Kitchener, II, described the Samaria villages but did not offer statistical information.

16. See Jama'in a-Thani data in *Nüfus* book, Daftar 352, 1876-1890, but the calculations were performed only on the 1876 data.

17. An example is Socin's records of the Jerusalem District.

18. The multiplier was calculated by using the male/households mean ratio of the *nahiya* to which a given village belonged.

19. The boundary between Jerusalem (al-Quds) District and Nablus District remained, as previously, along a line connecting Wadi 'Auja (the Yarkon River) in the west to Wadi 'Auja (flowing to the Jordan River) in the east.

20. Because of the need to correlate between the Muslim calendar and the Gregorian calendar, this report covers the two years H 1311-1312.

21. See Grossman, *Expansion and Desertion*.

22. Most of the twenty-three Tiberias' upland villages were classified as intermittently settled, settled only in the late nineteenth century, or totally unsettled during the whole century. Only four existed throughout the century. These data are based on the Palestine Exploration Fund (PEF) and Guérin surveys and traveler reports. Bedouin tribes, which were undoubtedly present in this area, were not counted by Bitan.. See also Grossman, *Expansion and Desertion*.

23. According to Volume 2 of Bahjat and Tamimi's book, the data usually referred to a year that preceded the date of publication by a few years. This also applies to the 1335 Yearbook, whose latest recorded date is, thus, 1331 (corresponding to 1912-13).

24. The difference is attributed to the estimated number of 55,000 Bedouin that Ruppin added to the official figure. See Ruppin, Syria, pp. 8-9. See also Schmelz, "Review." McCarthy claims that Ruppin deliberately falsified the official figures

for 1914, the yearbook that, according to him, was the one that Ruppin used. The yearbook from which Ruppin quoted was, according to his own statement, the 1915 one. The difference between his figures and those of the official 1914 totaled only 17,667 after deducting the 55,000 Bedouin who were not included in the official data. Additional information that pertains to the Jerusalem District in 1905 was provided by Uziel Schmelz, *Demographic Evolution*, p. 18.

25. McCarthy, Palestine, pp. 17-23. See also Pagis for a comprehensive discussion of the *nüfus* (vital statistics) data. Some of the data of the yearbooks of *vilayets* of Syria and Beirut, which cover the 1870-1922 period, will be presented in a later section of this chapter, but for the comparative task, I had to slightly bend my requirement and turn to two non-official sources that partly meet the essential criteria, even though they cover only part of the country. Both apply to the same region –the Acre District (Galilee), and contain fairly complete records of the district's settlements, though only some demographic data.

26. See Government of Palestine, 1922 Census, introduction by J. B. Barron. There is no doubt that the census findings are inferior to those of the 1931 Census conducted nine years later, but no census, even when carried out under ideal conditions, is entirely free of omissions and mistakes. However, the 1922 Census was conducted shortly after the commencement of British rule in Palestine. This explains its greater value for the present study.

27. Gilbar, pp. 43-45.

28. A similar overestimation might be responsible for the registered decline in some *nahiyas* north of Ramallah (Bani Zeid and Bani Harit), but in this case there is no reason to doubt the 1871 records, because there was most probably a large out-migration from these peripheral areas either to Jerusalem or to Jaffa. It is likely that the pull of these towns was accompanied by just as strong a push factor, resulting from the increasing pressure on the agricultural land in these *nahiyas* whose meager resources were unable to meet the growing difficulty in eking out a livelihood.

5

Regional Patterns: Physiography and Historical Events

Introduction

Independent evidence is needed that can validate or refute the above data or any part of it. This purpose can be reached by studying the vast literature that deals with socio-economic and physiographic character-istics of Palestine and provides regional data on the impact of various events that influenced the demographic evolution in a given rural space. The following discussion focuses particularly on the areas that had rela-tively low densities during the late nineteenth century.

A glance at the regions reveals that there is a positive correlation be-tween the quality of their natural resources and population size. Almost all the regions that had low population densities according to the 1288 Yearbook had some natural deficiency. In the following discussion I illustrate this point by discussing the low-density territories in three successive north-south belts, first by looking at the physiographic impact and then by considering the effect of specific events, with specific focus on human factors.

The Safad Zone

According to the 1288 Yearbook, northeastern Safad (Jira *nahiya*) had a relatively low density. However, it had a rich settlement history that can be traced back to ancient times. The eastern margin of the *nahiya* was not free from problems of natural resources. Because of its steep slopes and its location in the rain shadow (i.e., low precipitation result-ing from being on the eastern flanks of the mountain ranges that are not exposed to moisture-bearing winds), it had a dry climate, though not extremely so. The basalt rocks between it and the Sea of Galilee (Lake Kinneret) were generally unsuited for farming, and most of the area was inhabited by Bedouin tribes. The few villages on these slopes were small and unstable. They and the hot, dry basin below them were the least settled part of the region.

The other parts of the *nahiya* had varied landscapes, but the best resources were in the basins and valleys that surrounded Safad town itself. The immediate vicinity of Safad had relatively deep, though limey soil and an abundance of water. The tall mountains were blessed with high precipitation that exceeded one thousand millimeters per annum. But much of the higher land consisted of rocky fields unfit for farming. Some of the most inhospitable sections were on the mountains surrounding the town, where patches of the shallow soils could be utilized only for rough grazing. A positive factor was the accessibility of Safad to the port of Acre to the west and to Damascus and Beirut on the east and north, respectively.

The major physical feature, which gave rise to its importance, was the rugged terrain that provided potential defensive qualities. The town was located in a small basin flanked by mountains, but it owed its prominence to a fortress that had been built by the Crusaders on a steep hill, surrounded on all sides by relatively flat (but narrow) terrain that the old city now occupies (figure 5.1). The fortress was reputed to be the strongest in Palestine during Crusader times. The city continued to prosper under the Muslims, after the Crusaders lost Jerusalem (1187). During the sixteenth century it was a leading commercial and industrial town that functioned as a spiritual center for the Jews who settled there after they (and the Muslims) were expelled from Spain in 1492. It subsequently served as a major transportation hub on the important Acre-Damascus axis and on the south-north Jerusalem-Sidon (*Saida*) routes.[1]

During the early seventeenth century there were a series of events that resulted in the almost complete annihilation of the formerly prosperous Jewish community, including epidemics, the decline of the weaving industry and, not least, raids of Bedouin and Druze. These natural and man-made disasters resulted in large-scale abandonment in the mid-seventeenth century. The Jewish community later recovered, but never succeeded in achieving its former position. These disasters, especially the Bedouin raids, also resulted in the decline of its rural Arab hinterland whose survival had depended on marketing their agricultural products in the town. The ruins of at least six villages which were settled in the late sixteenth century still provide visible evidence of the disasters.[2]

Fig. 5.1
Safad in 1918

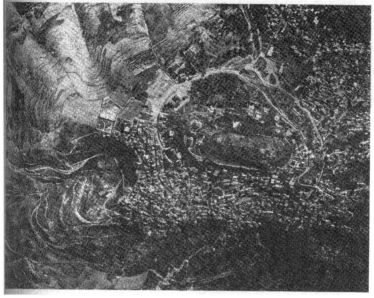

Source: German army Aerial photos, 1918, reprinted in: I. Damty, "Sites and places in Safad," *Ariel* 157-158, 2002, p. 143 (Hebrew). Courtesy Mr. Ely Schiller *Ariel* Editor, the publication rights holder.

Safad was badly damaged by the numerous earthquakes that occurred in the Galilee several times during its long history. Many parts of the town were almost completely destroyed during the 1837 earthquake when the hilltop fortress was practically demolished and the casualties amounted to several thousand.[3] In the surrounding countryside many villages were also damaged. Several villages, which were later given to Algerian refugees (see chapter 2), were most probably among the worst hit, and a few others were later re-occupied by poor Hauranian (south Syrian) migrants.[4] The town did not fully recover from the 1837 earthquake, which may explain why Safad registered the highest absolute population decline for the 320 years since the last known Ottoman tax record of 1596-97.[5] But, as already suggested, the downfall cannot be blamed solely on the rocks. Human-generated forces also played a part.[6]

Both instability sets were even more powerful in the adjacent Jordan Valley, which will be treated below. But in fact, Tiberias' settlement decline was more the result of human factors than of natural ones.

Tiberias and the Jordan Rift Valley

The Jordan Basin is part of the geologically unstable Syrian-African Rift Valley where earthquakes are more common than elsewhere in Palestine. The Jira (eastern Safad) *nahiya* extends into the upper Jordan Basin where population density is still very low. Compared with Safad, the physiographic pattern of Tiberias (Tveria) is reversed. The center of the Shafa *Nahiya* (in Tiberias zone) is in the Rift Valley while its western part is located mostly on plateau topography. Both parts are relatively dry. But the slopes facing the Sea of Galilee's narrow coastline are not as arid as the area further south where rainfall decreases gradually. Along the Dead Sea shores (c.110 km away), the mean annual precipitation drops to only about 100 mm, but this number is meaningless because the fluctuations are very pronounced and, therefore, even the scant rain is unreliable.

During most of the nineteenth century practically the whole length of the Jordanian Rift Valley was inhabited by Bedouin tribes. The area surrounding the Sea of Galilee had only a few permanent settlements, mostly of fishermen. The few farming settlements were intermittent or seasonal shelters of communities whose original villages were above the steep escarpment that marks the western limit of the Rift Valley.

Above the escarpment there are series of step-like tablelands. The northern ones are less arid than the southern ones. The valleys which dissect the tablelands offer good farmland and irrigation waters. The largest of these oases are in the Fari'a Wadi (which flows from its source north of Nablus to the Jordan), but much of its agricultural resources were developed only during the Mandate era.

This low-density area extended southward from Tiberias to Jericho. In the southern areas, the seasonal movement of farmers was also encountered above the escarpment, where precipitation was somewhat higher, though still insufficient for permanent settlement. In years of high precipitation, the inland mountain villagers migrated to the plateaus if the soil moisture, measured by inserting a stick into the ground, exceeded about 75-80 millimeters. Much of the eastern Lower Galilee and parts of the dry lands of eastern Samaria were used intermittently in this manner.[7]

The harsh climatic conditions, with their suffocating hot summers, were not always major drawbacks that impeded the permanent settlement of the area. The Tiberias zone was densely populated in ancient times. It gradually lost its attractiveness, and after the tenth century it slowly declined. During the sixteenth century it was still an important center, but on the banks of the lake the settlements were intermittent or seasonal. Their inhabitants were mostly fishermen. There was only one, which had a permanent population.

In the seventeenth century, Tiberias was apparently abandoned by most of its inhabitants. In 1669 no Jew was left in the town. Around 1740, a prominent Safad-based rabbi wrote that its Jewish population had dwindled to the point that no *minyan* (quorum of ten males for the core prayers) could be found in the town for ninety years.[8] A severe earthquake that destroyed the walls of Tiberias (whose building was completed in 1564) was a major event that contributed to the town's downfall. This could have been the trigger that generated the events that followed. The known fact is that during the seventeenth century conditions drastically worsened, and the city was depopulated.[9] Like Safad (only thirteen km away), Tiberias was hit by other severe earthquakes after1564 and was re-constructed in 1738. The repairs were completed, but it was again demolished by an earthquake in the mid-seventeenth century and in 1837 (figure 5.2).[10]

Tiberias's resettlement was resumed by a Bedouin sheik called Dahr al-'Umar, He repaired the damaged walls and fortified the town.[11] For reviving the town's settlement, he invited Rabbi Haim Abul'afia from Izmir to come with his students and assist in Tiberias's reconstruction.

Fig. 5.2
Tiberias in the 1870s

Source: S. Manning, *Those Holy Fields: Palestine Illustrated by Pen and Pencil.* Republished by Mr. Ely Schiller, 1976, p. 199. Courtesy of Ely Schiller, the publication rights holder.

The governor of Syria, who was the official ruler of Tiberias, attempted to prevent the initiative by bombarding the town, but he failed to stop the reconstruction. Dahr al-'Umar was, in fact, a charismatic person who held the post of *multazim* (tax farmer) and was never appointed to any higher position. He was able, nevertheless, to rule over the Galilee and gradually expanded the area under his control. For a short time, he extended his rule as far as Nablus and Jaffa. But he was more successful in the Galilee.[12] He fortified the southern border of the territory under his control (the northern Jezre'el Plain which was the official boundary between Sidon and Damascus territories). Acre and Haifa were fortified. One of the famous forts that he reconstructed was Jiddin, located northeast of Acre (figure 5.3).

This interesting case is an example of the impacts of the decentralized rule that prevailed before the last quarter of the nineteenth century. It also reveals that the impact of the local rulers was not necessarily negative. By the end of the eighteenth century the population of Tiberias had substantially increased. However, the area surrounding the town was only slightly affected by the improvement. Its rural hinterland remained underpopulated and was still inhabited mostly by Bedouin. As already noted above, Tiberias was hard hit by the 1837 earthquake, but because of the small size of the villages, the damage to the rural zone was minimal.

Fig. 5.3
Jiddin Fortress, situated in northeast of Acre Sub-District

Source: Photographed by David Grossman, October 2007.

The fate of the villages that did exist in the *nahiya*'s plateau zone was quite different. During the 1850s they were adversely affected by a violent battle that erupted between a local war lord and some Kurdish tribes. This event and the possible impact of severe droughts resulted in the abandonment of at least four villages, which were eventually resettled by refugees from Algeria and Circassia (see chapter 2).[13]

By the end of the nineteenth century Tiberias started to benefit from the economic potential of its warm winter climate. Persian Bahais found refuge there from Iranian persecution. A rich Bahai refugee bought land in a village located on the east bank of the lake, but the land was eventually sold to Jewish buyers. As a result of the attractive winter resorts and the initiatives of several foreign and local entrepreneurs, the number of populated villages in the *nahiya* constantly also increased around the Sea of Galilee.[14] The countryside surrounding the lake was also eventually revived, mainly by the development of tourism. A small seasonal fishing village located on the shores of the southern tip of the lake and another one next to the small Hula Lake (a few kilometers north of the Sea of Galilee) were given to Algerian refugees.

About thirty kilometers south of Tiberias, Beisan's experience was worse. The old Roman-Byzantine city with its monumental buildings was practically wiped out in the eighth century by a severe earthquake. In 1875 the site could not even be identified with certainty, and the hamlet close to the ruins was described as a "miserable" village, whose houses were partly demolished.[15] The unstable earth only partly accounts, however, for the fact that this city and practically the whole Jordan Valley were devoid of permanent settlements. The central Ottoman administration lost control over the provinces and the area faced political and economic crises that were accompanied by a deterioration of security. The people who took advantage of this condition were, of course, the Bedouin. They took over many parts of the marginal areas and their tribes controlled both sides of the Jordan Valley. [16]

Jericho and several minor Jordan Basin locations had a somewhat different history. Most of the area was also the domain of the Bedouin, but there was no town or permanently inhabited place throughout the whole region. The few oases that had benefited from the copious springs and streams during ancient times were in ruin. Some revival occurred in the Beisan Basin during the eighteenth century when water mills were restored during Dahr al-'Umar's rule, but most of the restoration works had to wait for 1905 when the railroad connecting Haifa and Damascus was completed. As a result of this development, a number of new permanent villages were settled in its vicinity. One of them, Hamidiya, was named in honor of the reigning sultan, 'Abd-al-Hamid II.[17]

In Jericho the only existing structure was the ruin of an ancient tower. There were also some makeshift huts. The settlement was repopulated only toward the end of the nineteenth century. Some of its ancient irrigation works were reconstructed a few years earlier, but the major rebuilding work was the result of the influx of Christian pilgrims (mainly Russians) who established hostels in the area and the rehabilitation of ancient irrigation works that were repaired and improved c.1880 by mountain villagers who descended into the Jordan Valley to cultivate their traditional seasonal fields.[18]

These developments explain why the Jordan Valley experienced very high rates of growth during the 1871-72-1922 period. The southern part of this belt, centered on the oasis of Jericho, registered phenomenal growth rates of 1,025.9 percent for multiplier of 5; and 838.2 percent if it is 6 (see map 4.5).[19] This growth started around 1880, i.e., at least a decade after the publication of the 1288 Yearbook. The rehabilitation of the ancient irrigation canals (fig. 5.4) carried the water from the copious local springs to Jericho and its surrounding fruit and vegetable gardens.[20]

Fig. 5.4
Ancient aqueduct near Jericho

Source: S. Manning, *Those Holy Fields: Palestine Illustrated by Pen and Pencil.* Republished by Mr. Ely Schiller, 1976, p. 81. Courtesy of Ely Schiller, the publication rights holder.

To sum up: The historical records confirm that the Safad and Tiberias regions, as well as the rest of the Jordan Rift Valley, had low population densities before the end of the nineteenth century. There is, thus, no reason to challenge the validity of the 1288 data. This conclusion does not necessarily mean, however, that there were no mistakes or inaccuracies in the enumeration process.

The Northwestern Mountains, Inland Basins and Coastal Plain

The greatest rural density in northern Palestine was found in the inland valleys and basins and on the coastal plain. These inter-mountain lowlands were mostly well drained, but one of the largest ones was poorly drained and, consequently, less populated. It was surrounded, however, by a ring of villages and seasonal hamlets which benefited from the receding waters after the winter, when the wet land could produce fruits and vegetables without extra irrigation (figures 5.5 and 5.6). Parts of the large Jezre'el Plain were also poorly drained. Before the 1930s, when its marshlands were dried up, it was practically unsettled, but despite the proximity of malaria-infested areas, the valley was flanked by several villages. The number of villages increased during the late nineteenth century when the absentee landowners established sharecropper settlements and a few Bedouin tribes replaced their tents by permanent houses.[21]

Fig. 5.5
Part of Beit Netofa poorly drained basin, winter season

Source: Photographed by David Grossman in the early 1990s.

Fig. 5.6
Part of Beit Netofa basin, summer season

Source: Photographed by David Grossman in the early 1990s.

The valleys of the Acre District's Jabal *nahiya* (the western Upper Galilee) were less hospitable than the other parts of the zone, but they contained several small valleys which were densely settled. Their main advantage was an abundant water supply. The surrounding ranges of this region have, in fact, the highest precipitation records of Palestine. The relative isolation of the mountains provided security, especially for the Druze villagers who sought protection from persecution by their neighbors. Between the Mediterranean and Jordan watershed, however, there were rocky grounds where farming was patchy. The relative medium to high population density in the 1288 Yearbook adequately represents the varied natural resources with which the area was endowed.

Samaria and Its Adjacent Areas

Samaria (Nablus and Jenin sub-districts) is quite similar to the Lower Galilee. In both, the internal valleys are relatively wide and their low, round hills are cultivatable on the whole. The most prevalent tree crop in both regions, the olive, is rain fed. Where the lime-rich soils of the hills are widespread, as in the ancient heart of Samaria (Sebastiya, originally Shomron), terracing near springs of these regions provided irrigation for the fruit orchards, though many of them grew well without watering.

Nablus, the central city of Samaria, is a typical pass-town, i.e., it occupies a narrow valley that opens to the east and the west, but is closed on the other sides by steep mountains. Most of the slopes surrounding the town are barely cultivable. Their slopes and most of the higher uplands are excessively rocky and have very thin soils. The valley that emerges from the site of ancient Shechem (Tel Balata), two kilometers east of the center of modern Nablus, was described by Robinson and Smith as "full of fountains, irrigating it most abundantly ... is rich, fertile and beautifully green ... so that the whole valley presents a more beautiful and inviting landscape than perhaps any part of Palestine."[22] These beautiful gardens are mostly gone by now. They have been replaced by buildings while the copious springs are used for providing potable water to the town's inhabitants.

The rocky central ranges that flank the narrow pass, where the town of Nablus is situated were, and still are, sparsely populated. The low density can be traced to the sixteenth century. It was accompanied by a negative demographic growth rate for a period of at least 320 years (1596-1922), but Safad *nahiya*'s negative rate was even more extreme.[23] Negative rates, though less pronounced, were also found in the northern Jenin zone and in the hills separating the Nablus and Jerusalem zones from the coastal plains. Like other parts of the country, Nablus experienced a great deal of violence and internecine warfare. Dahr al-'Umar's attempt to conquer the town resulted in the destruction of a number of villages near the city. Another village, located on a well fortified hilltop, survived several sieges but was destroyed by Ibrahim Pasha and remained in ruins until the early 1850s. Despite repeated acts of violence, the region, like its Galilee equivalent, benefited from the close ties between the rural *fallaheen* and the town-based leadership, which was the expression of the strong mutual economic interests (see chapter 1, the section on Urban-Rural Relationships). The Jerusalem countryside discussed below was less economically integrated with its central town.[24]

Judea: The Jerusalem and Hebron Mountains

The Jerusalem District (the Judean Mountains) is more varied. The valleys are narrower, but the slopes are mostly covered with olives. In the Hebron Mountains, the olives were planted mainly in the dryer, lower altitudes, while vineyards, which specialize in table grapes, covered the higher, cooler and moister places. The road and rail construction in this difficult terrain was somewhat facilitated by the east-west alignment of most ridges and valleys, but moving from one valley to the next was difficult and costly. The rail line was completely unable to move across the ridges. The line had and still has, therefore, numerous curves that double the travel time. The construction of costly bridges and tunnels has started only recently, but is still unfinished. The hard limestone required more laborious work for terracing than the hills of Samaria, but the level bedrocks and the alternating hard limestone and marl helped the farmer to construct terraces. [25]

The flanks of the Hebron Mountains have a much lower agricultural potential, because in addition to the sloping layers, the large rocky fields are also dry. These conditions are most pronounced on the slopes that face the Dead Sea, but even Hebron's more humid northern margin is inhospitable. It consists mostly of rocky fields except for a few patches of prime agricultural land that are small. Close to Bethlehem the length of the flat strips is only about three kilometers. The result is that permanent settlement was restricted to the core area while the settlements of the mountain's margins were characterized by seasonal or temporary habitation. The permanently settled zone was no more than an island in an unstable "sea" of seasonal or temporarily settled caves and ruins. Its inhabitants were pastoral nomads or farmers who occupied caves and ancient ruins (figure 5.7).[26] These shelters were occupied during the plowing and harvesting seasons, but some were used by Bedouin herders. These shelter-settlements were grouped in cluster-like patterns around the flanks of the valleys. Most of them were eventually fixed during the early decades of the twentieth century, but seasonal cave dwellings still persist in the southern and southwestern margins of the densely populated area of the Hebron Mountains.[27]

The existence of numerous ancient ruins in the margins of the Hebron Mountains testifies to the presence of resources that could support a much larger permanent population. More proof that this is possible is the recent expansion of agriculture even on Hebron's eastern and southern peripheries. Olive groves and fruit trees are now widespread there and many of these villages increasingly resemble their mountain-core mother villages (now mostly towns). Some of the ruins, especially those of the northern areas, were, however, clearly occupied during the late Ottoman period. The many ancient ruins and the recent developments testify that the main problem lies, at least partly, in man-made factors.[28]

The history of human settlement in the mountain zone is complex. It has been continuously settled for thousands of years by civilizations that left their mark on its landscape. Many villages were destroyed, and their

Fig. 5.7
Cave dwelling in S. Hebron

Source: Photographed by D. Grossman c. 1980.

population was altered by cycles of destruction and rebuilding. However, in the mountain core, the relative settlement stability is indicated by the many biblical names that have survived, though often in modified form, for several millennia. The core zone, along the divide between Mediter-ranean Sea and the Jordan-Dead Sea, is the most stable section. All the major cities of Palestine were located on, or close to, it. And almost all of them had biblical names.

Since the late nineteenth century, however, the human impact on the settlement pattern had experienced a process of redistribution. As noted in chapter 1, this happened mainly because of the rerouting of transpor-tation from the traditional inland orientation towards the Mediterranean coast. There was, in addition, some agricultural migration to supply the labor needs of the citrus groves and other products (see chapter 6). The main engine of the mobility was the growing population pressure in the former core.[29] The net result was a repopulation on the margin of the major cities. Among the urban interior cities, however, Jerusalem was a notable exception. Its attraction was based on religion and not on its locational advantages, but its position also benefited from its link with Jaffa and the railway line.

A related movement was associated with the fixation of former temporary or seasonal shelters and their eventual agglomeration into larger villages. One of the most important destinations was the western margins of the mountains, but the intensity of the process depended on a variety of causes, including the availability of land (very often only patches in rocky zones), the relative source-destination distance, accessibility (intervening obstacles) and, not least, the consent of the potential host to accept the new settlers. The consent was usually granted on the basis of clan or tribal affiliation, past neighborly experiences or lack of past grievances.[30]

During the later part of Ottoman rule, the mountain core population suffered from repeated periods of insecurity. They were intensified in the wake of Muhammad Ali's withdrawal. The chaotic situation ended, but not completely, in 1859, when the powerful warlord of a Jenin clan was finally subdued.[31] The inter-tribal Qais-Yaman conflicts probably started in the historical rivalry between the northern [Qais] and southern [Yaman] tribes of the Arabian Peninsula. In Hebron after Muhammad 'Ali's defeat, the Qaisiya (the eight permanent villages of Hebron) took over control of the sub-district and terrorized Hebron's Christians and Jewish communities.[32]

The Jerusalem Sub-District was also divided into factions of Qais and Yaman. Their territories coincided with the alignment of the east-west ridges. The area west of Jerusalem was against western al-Bira. (In the mid-nineteenth century Christian Ramallah was still a small village near al-Bira, which controlled the main highway from Jerusalem to Nablus.) The Bethlehem Christians and their allied Bedouin tribes campaigned against the Hebron Qaisiya. Several other coalitions (often assisted by Bedouin allies) also engaged in this type of petty warfare.[33]

The relationship between physiographic and human conflicts is the outcome of the cohesiveness that was formed by settlements located on each of the relatively flat inter-fluvial uplands. Another physiographic-conflict relationship was manifest in the rocky zone that marked the border between Bethlehem (Wadiya) and the Qaisiya. In northern Hebron there are several ruined villages that testify to the destruction caused by the inter-tribal wars that occurred during the eighteenth century.[34]

The Qais-Yaman conflicts of the 1840s and 1850s had relatively minor demographic impact. But the uprisings against the government such as the 1834 revolt during Ibrahim Pasha's reign and the earlier uprisings against the governor in 1825 were well documented. Both erupted because of taxation hikes, and both had strong demographic impacts. Villages were evacuated, some permanently, and in both cases the *fallaheen* lost the battle and had numerous casualties.[35]

Similar uprisings, mainly in reaction to military draft decrees, also occurred in the Gaza zone where they were more numerous and resulted in more permanent depopulation.[36] The outcomes were also similar. Bedouin raids were more evident in the Gaza District. Like the Jerusalem warfare, the Bedouin were engaged, in many cases, in alliances with *fallaheen* against similar opposing alliances. The Bedouin usually acted as mercenaries in these campaigns. As already pointed out, the role of the Bedouin could be positive. During droughts, the *fallaheen* suffered heavily from their raids, and their plight became a double-edged sword. But the Bedouin rarely attacked their neighboring allies, who paid them special *hawwa* dues (protection money).[37]

The main problem that emerges from this discussion is the low reliability of the records from the seven *nahiyas* of western and northern Samaria, but the Jerusalem and Hebron events do not reduce the credibility of the 1288 Yearbook because the cave and ruin dwellers were counted in their "mother" villages even in the 1931 census.

The Carmel and the Ruha (Menashe) Heights

The Carmel Ridge is unique. The ridge itself was very sparsely populated throughout most of the Ottoman period. An oral tradition of the Druze traces the origin of its settlement to refugees who escaped Muslim persecution in Lebanon. They led a semi-nomadic life in the Jezre'el Plain, but in the mid-fifteenth century they climbed the adjacent Carmel Mountain and after struggling with the tangled vegetation they reached a spring and a ruined village where they decided to settle. Other refugees came later (in the early eighteenth century) from the vicinity of Haleb (Aleppo) and established another village. From the time of their arrival they were repeatedly harassed and persecuted by their Muslim neighbors. The raids were intensified after Muhammad Ali's retreat, and as many as seventeen of their small offshoots (all of them have been traced) were deserted.[38]

This history suggests that the crest of the Carmel Ridge, probably because of its low accessibility and its narrow width, was shunned by most of the Muslim peasants. However, its rather repellant nature made it attractive to people who sought refuge from persecution. In the nineteenth century the Hauran Mountain of southern Syria was also selected as a Druze refuge, and since then has acquired the name Jabal Druze (Druze Mountain). The Carmel summit, however, is still almost exclusively inhabited by the Druze, but in one of the crest's two villages (now amalgamated into a single town) there is also a small Christian minority.

Formally, the Carmel *nahiya* (Jabal) extended into a marshland zone located northeast of Haifa, which was a Bedouin domain, but in the early 1870s two small hamlets with no more than thirty households each were recorded in it. The *nahiya* also contained three other villages on the mountain flanks. One of them was an offshoot of a summit village. Its inhabitants were sharecroppers of an absentee landlord's estate.

The Carmel Ridge is separated from eastern Samaria by the Ruha *nahiya* (or Bilad a-Ruha, the Ruha towns). This is a relatively low plateau, with an underlying poor, very thin soil and, therefore, was very sparsely populated. As already stated in chapter 2, this area attracted Egyptian settlers. It also functioned as a home base for Turkmen nomads who used the plateau and the part of the *nahiya* that is located below it for their seasonal migrations.[39] The latter zone was inhabited by various nomads and by marsh-dwellers, dark-skinned clans of various origins, who subsisted on raising water buffalos. This zone is part of the coastal plain, whose population and resource base is discussed below.

The Sharon, Gaza, and the Northern Coastal Plains

This section is treated here as a single geographical unit, even though it is composed of five clearly identifiable zones. This procedure is adopted because their physical and human impacts are closely intertwined, and this entanglement is better understood if it is treated as a single whole. The main focus is on the Sharon Plain, the largest and also the geographical center of the coastal plain. The region was shared by several *nahiyas* apparently because it had only a few scattered permanent settlements. It is usually defined as the plain located between the Yarkon (now northern Tel Aviv), and the southern edge of the Carmel Ridge. However, for the purpose of this discussion I am appending to it the section of the western part of the Ramla *nahiya,* which has a similar resource base (red sands and swamps). The added section is now part of the Tel Aviv conurbation, but before 1882 it was inhabited only by a few Bedouin clans.

Significantly, however, the trustworthy Volney, who traveled in Palestine in the late eighteenth century, described this region (that he equated with the district of Gaza) as extending from "Khan Younes [on the south] to the north, between Kaisaria and the rivulet of Yaffa."[40] This northern boundary definition suggests that the Sharon was, in Volney's time, a no-man's land where no significant settlement existed.

The Sharon is the area whose environmental/human dynamics require scrutiny to a greater extent than other zones. Climate played a relatively minor direct role in explaining the intra-zonal variance, because precipitation is fairly uniform over most of the zone (between 400 and 600 mm per annum), but significantly, the lowest precipitation is recorded where the highest Coastal Plain density was registered (the Gaza Sub-District) for most of the Ottoman period.

Human activity is one of the factors affecting the soil, climate, and water quality, but even though this is about the same everywhere, nowhere is it more obvious than in the Sharon Plain, where the region changed within a span of thirty years from a marginal, low-density grazing zone to the country's most densely populated and intensively cultivated space. The drainage of the malaria-infested swamps and the pumping of water from deep wells by machinery powered by fossil fuel revolutionized the area's economy.[41]

The equipment needed for this transition was unavailable in Palestine during the Ottoman era. This is why the 1871-72-1922 records do not reveal any drastic change in the Sharon's demography. Citrus was well established in the environs of Jaffa in the late eighteenth century,[42] but before the 1920s, when the change was initiated, the Sharon was dominated by poorly drained soils whose margins were cultivated only in the summer season when the water-logged swamps receded. In the 1920s the swamps were systematically surveyed (see map 5.1) and drained by the Mandate government with the participation of Arab and Jewish national institutions. The main Jewish efforts were made by employing Jewish settlers living in rural areas on land purchased by the Jewish National Fund.[43]

However, a more difficult problem was that of the over-drained red sandy soils that are widespread throughout the Sharon. The main agrotechnical problem was that these soils lose their moisture even after a short dry spell. Before the digging of deep wells that reached the groundwater level, usually at depths of hundreds of meters, the cultivation of a staple food crop such as wheat or barley was a risky business.[44] But the low price of these crops made their cultivation unprofitable by

Map 5.1
Swamps in Palestine, 1925

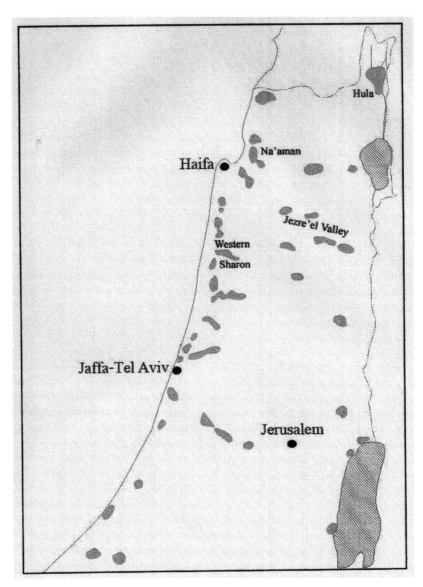

Source: The map was prepared for the annual report of the Mandate government to the League of Nations.

means of the expensive well irrigation. Only more profitable intensive crops, such as citrus that thrived on the sandy soils, were able to sustain the extra costs.

The other human-generated problem in the Ottoman era was insecurity, but it is difficult to tell if this was the cause or the effect of the Sharon's predicament. The Mediterranean coast had been considered by the local Palestinian Arabs as an unsafe war zone since the Crusader period. Its major coastal towns (including Caesarea and Jaffa) were deliberately demolished in the mid-fourteenth century in an effort to prevent their use as bases for a possible return of the Crusaders. The area later served pirates (especially in out-of-the-way locations such as Haifa) and invaders, the latest of whom was Napoleon (in 1799). The local Bedouin occasionally raided travelers and their weak neighbors. Travel through the Sharon was avoided also because there was nothing interesting to see there. It is difficult thus to conclude that insecurity alone was to blame for its low density.

A clear indication that resource quality played the central role prior to the technological revolution is the demographic contrast between the Sharon and the other parts of the coastal plain. These other coastal areas were also exposed to external threats and deliberate destruction. Acre was especially adversely affected by the Muslim conquest in 1291. Its Christians were massacred and the conquerors demolished the city, as they did to the other coastal towns, but it was too important to be left in ruins for long and, unlike Jaffa, which remained almost fully uninhabited until the mid-seventeenth century, Acre was not completely deserted. Its protected port was not the sole reason for its importance. It was also the gateway that served the fertile hinterland that produced valuable grain and cotton crops.

The other northern coastal section, the narrow Carmel coast, between the Sharon and Haifa, was also densely populated. Furthermore, the intervening areas fit for rain-fed farming, such as the wide Lud (Lod) Basin which separates the Sharon from Western Ramla, were continuously settled throughout all of known history. The same demographic stability is found in the Eastern Drain, the drain-shaped belt separating the low Sharon hills and Samaria. These soils, unlike those in the Sharon, were fit for wheat production, and did not need a technological revolution such as fossil fuel pumps.

Finally, the significance of southern Gaza was quite similar to that of Acre. Even though its seaport was less important than Acre, because it was less protected and located a few kilometers from the town, it functioned as the "port," for the "ships of the desert"—the camel caravans. It was the main gateway to Egypt, the pre-Ottoman ruler and a major commercial partner throughout the Ottoman era of Palestine. Like Acre, furthermore, it had a fertile hinterland which was continuously settled throughout known history.

These findings explain why there were only eight villages in the Sharon proper as late as 1922. Furthermore, three of them were on the Mediterranean coast, where they functioned as *minas* (harbors) for the long-shore watermelon trade with Egypt and with Syria. The watermelons were loaded from camels to sailing boats and, later, into larger steam ships. Seasonal markets developed in *minas* and some of them eventually evolved into permanent settlements.[45]

The southern Sharon villages that existed in 1871-72 were identical with those that were listed in 1922. By then, however, there were a few additional settlements, which functioned as seasonal or semi-permanent hamlets that sprang up mainly near the withdrawing seasonal pools and swamps.

A somewhat deeper scrutiny of the data reveals, however, that one of the largest and most important villages, located in the northern part of the plain that was listed in 1596 as the center of a *nahiya* called Qaqun, was missing from the 1288 list.[46] The "seven *nahiyas* problem" has thus surfaced again, though in a reverse form—this time, because of an omission rather than an addition. One way the mystery may be solved is by consulting a Palestine Exploration Fund (PEF) Survey, where the Memoirs, published about a decade after 1871-72, described Qaqun as large but "quite modern, having been built by a mixed population coming from the hill villages."[47] It seems thus that this village, as well as other Sharon settlements, was reconstructed after having been practically abandoned for a long time. In the 1870s it should have been populated, but the administration has either unaware of this change or ignored it. This error may suggest that the population survey was taken several years before 1870. One of the other villages, a-Tira, which had functioned as an important postal horse-relay station in pre-Ottoman times, was resettled in the mid-eighteenth century by villagers from villages of the Bani Sa'ab *nahiya*.[48]

Summary and Conclusions

The analysis of the 1288 Yearbook suggests that there is a vital need for verifying the data of the regional yearbooks. This was partly achieved here by consulting other yearbooks and several independent publications

of western researchers and trustworthy travelers that provided information on the spatial population distribution at the district and sub-district
or, rarely, even at the village level. However, even in the few cases
where the lowest administrative level is the *nahiya*, statistical data do
not allow a complete comparison with the 1288 data. For one thing, the
other official records also contain errors.[49]

Although there are some reservations about the accuracy and reliability of the Ottoman statistics, it would seem that modern Ottoman
demographers have not been very troubled by these defects. The leading
Turkish demographer, Kamal Karpat, who was cognizant of Ottoman
clerical efficiency and methods, maintained that the quality of the official censuses and the yearbook statistics based on them were fairly
satisfactory. This appraisal was also shared by non-Turkish scholars like
Schölch and McCarthy. Karpat believed, in any case, that the official
data are superior to those of western writers whose publications were
frequently deliberately biased.[50] Significantly, however, he added that
this holds only if we regard the official records as approximate data,
rather than as entirely accurate facts. He tells us, in other words, that
the alternative to the use of these sources leaves us empty handed. It is
better to use approximate data than none at all.

The short summary of the physiographic and man-made factors that
account for the three Palestinian belts discussed here, and particularly
the unique Sharon zone, are well documented. The main purpose of this
discussion was to utilize the non-quantitative information for testing the
validity of the 1288 records. The unqualified conclusion that emerges
from the comparative work is that this yearbook is reasonably reliable.
Even if some of the data, especially those that pertain to the seven
northern and western *nahiyas*, contain gross errors, most seem to closely
represent reality at their time, and their compilation can be of use for
demographic research. The need for consulting additional independent
sources, and of closely scrutinizing them, is irrefutable.

The findings of the present chapter added vital information to parts of
the previous chapters. They confirm that the 1288 information matches
the population density records. The focus of the following chapter, in
temporal and subject terms, differs from this one. It is concerned with
the British Mandate administration (1917-1948) rather than the Ottoman
era, and will deal with agricultural density and other aspects of land/man
relationships, rather than human density. Both density types are interrelated, but the material of the next chapter touches on a subject that
was, and still is, at the heart of the Arab/Israel conflict. It only scratches

the surface. But as in the former chapters, I have refrained from getting involved in the conflict itself.

Notes

1. Schur, *Safad*, provided useful accounts of the town's history since the Crusader era. For a short description of the ancient history of the town and its vicinity, see Stepansky.
2. Grossman, *Expansion and Desertion*, pp. 86-89 and map 6 on p. 80; see Hütteroth and Abdulfattah; Ben-Zvi, pp. 205-213; Avitzur, "Weaving," pp. 353-360.
3. See Schiller, pp. 106-112.
4. Conder and Kitchener, I, pp. 198-201, reported that one village was totally deserted and two others settled by Algerians. The deserted village also belonged to the Druze, and was granted to a Safad Jew by Ibrahim Pasha after its inhabitants fled to the Hauran, Yaari, *Memories*, pp. 144-145. Another Druze village, located west of Safad, had many vacant houses because many of its people fled to the Hauran to escape conscription, Guérin, VII, pp. 82-83. The real reason was, probably, that the inhabitants escaped from the vengeance of Ibrahim Pasha, following their raid and looting of Safad in 1834. See also Thomson, pp. 261, 267, on villages north of Safad and see Abbasi, pp. 45-46.
5. See the tax list in Hütteroth and Abdulfattah. Grossman, *Expansion and Desertion*, pp. 16-19. Several religiously oriented publications list sites around Safad that contain settlements or burial places of righteous persons. Many of them refer to former villages that were still inhabited in the sixteenth century.
6. Grossman, *Expansion and Desertion*, pp. 86-89; on the economic impact of the sixteenth century on the Jewish community, see Schur, *Safad*, pp. 107-130.
7. I am indebted to Mr. Uri Eliav of Kibbutz Tirat Zvi. Information on this seasonal migration is provided by Robinson and Smith, *Later*, p. 335.
8. Berav, p. 18. This long period of decline accounts for our scant knowledge about Tiberias between the mid-seventeenth and mid-eighteenth centuries.
9. Ben-Zvi, pp. 437-440.
10. Guérin, VII, pp. 250-263; Oliphant, pp. 151-158.
11. Oliphant, pp. 151-152, attributed the rebuilding of the walls to Uthman, the son of Dahr al-'Umar. It is possible that the walls needed repairs again, but Dahr could not have withstood the Syrian attack if the walls were still in ruins in 1740 (see below).
12. During his long rule (1735-1775) Dahr al-'Umar managed to fortify Acre and make it the capital of his territory. He also revived Haifa, which had previously functioned as a pirate haven. He built a number of fortresses, including a chain of fortifications along the Jezre'el Plain (the southern boundary of Acre District). One of his first actions was, naturally, to rebuild the walls of Tiberias, the central town of his birthplace *nahiya*. He was also credited for reconstructing the water supply of Beisan. These unusual achievements were accomplished despite the constant attempts by the Ottoman Sultan to depose him. This was finally accomplished in 1775 when he was killed. See among many other references, Heyd; Cohen, *Eighteenth Century*. See also Cohen, "Coast of Palestine," where he stated that contrary to the accepted notion, Haifa was relocated and reconstructed before Dahr al-'Umar assumed power.
13. A survey conducted during the early 1870s, known as the Sun [Exposed] Lands (see Shechter, pp. 151-152), found several deserted villages in this area. The desertion is also referred to by Guérin, VI, pp. 135-138.

14 See Ben-Arieh, *Jordan Valley*. The available statistics on the Jordan Valley reveal that, according to official records, there was a constant addition of inhabited villages between 1870 and 1945.
15 Guérin, IV, p. 285.
16 Volney's phrase that refers to the reluctance of Palestinian farmers to grow wheat "for fear of too much inviting the avarice of the Turkish governors, and the rapacity of the Arabs" [i.e., Bedouins], Volney, II, pp. 328-329, summed up the farmers' problem, as seen by many researchers. The comment was made as an introduction to the section that deals with Palestine. It is now considered by many scholars as a typical example of a white superiority bias, but some of the nineteenth century eyewitnesses tend to confirm it. An example of the Bedouin "avarice" is Tristram's account of the horrible scene of a massacre in Safieh (the southern shore of the Dead Sea) which was raided by a Bedouin tribe (Tristram, pp. 340-342). In another part of his book, Tristram reported on another Bedouin raid, this time on a village in the eastern part of the Tiberias *nahiya*. When the villagers complained about the damage done by a Bedouin raid they were sent soldiers for "protection [but this help] proved worse than none," because the poor villagers had to feed the soldiers for several days (Tristram, p 127). See also Schumacher, Acca, p. 186; Braslavi, I, pp. 376-377). A pioneer study of the Jordan Valley's Bedouin (and in its adjacent areas) is found in Burkhardt's diary. See Grossman, "Fallah and Bedouin," for a discussion of the nature of the Fallah-Bedouin relationships. For comprehensive studies of the Palestinian Bedouins see Marx; Ben-David; Meir, *As Nomadism Ends*.
17. The developments of the area are documented in Ben-Arieh, *Jordan Valley*; and by Nir, *Beth-She'an*.
18. See, for example, Robinson and Smith, *Later*, pp. 334-335, for a description of the Ghaur (the broad part of the Jordan valley) cultivation; see also Guérin, IV, pp. 222-232. Oliphant, pp. 429-437, provides excellent information on the ruins of some of the irrigation facilities of the Jericho zone.
19. In absolute terms it grew since 1871 from 170, if the multiplier was 5, or from 204 if it was 6. Whatever the mulitplier, the Jericho area's population had as many as 1914 people according to the 1922 Census. This means that during the fifty-one-year span (1871-1922) it grew more than eleven-fold if the mean household had five persons, or only about 9.4 times (if the mean household had six persons).
20. See Oliphant, pp. 409-428. Some crude irrigation facilities were reported south of Beisan by Robinson and Smith, *Later*, pp. 312-315.
21. Oliphant, pp. 73-74. See Grossman, "Population Growth and Land Quality"; and Grossman, *Expansion and Desertion*, pp. 71-78.
22. Robinson and Smith, *Biblical Researches*, III, p. 136.
23. Grossman, "Processes of Development and Retreat," pp. 305-310. Compare with Grossman, *Expansion and Desertion*, pp. 16-19.
24. See Hoexter; see Ron, "Terraces," note 38.
25. See Ron, "Terraces."
26. Grossman, "Fluctuations in Arab Settlement."
27. Grossman, "The Bunched Settlement"; Grossman, "Expansion of Settlement Frontier'; Grossman, *Expansion and Desertion*, pp. 213-231. Some of the caves are now occupied by young bachelors or homeless people.
28. Grossman, "Land Use Modifications." Amiran, "Dura," held that the insecurity generated by the adjacent Bedouin is responsible for this unique settlement pattern. The numerous archeological excavations conducted in this area since the 1920s have produced many interesting findings, particularly from the Roman-Byzantine periods.

29. See Brawer; Graham-Brown.
30. This process was only partly officially documented because the new shelters were not viewed as permanent villages. Even the 1931 Census counted their inhabitants in their home villages. Fortunately, however, it provided a list of most of the unofficial settlements (called *khirbas* = ruins). Some of them are listed, in fact, as independent villages in the 1922 Census.
31. Schölch, *Transformation*.
32. See chapter 9 of Finn's *Stirring Times* for a detailed account of these inter-clan rivalries.
33. Finn, *Stirring Times*; See among other publications Abir; Hoexter.
34. Grossman, "Fluctuations in Arab Settlement."
35. See Neophitos.
36. Cohen, *Palestine in the Eighteenth Century*; Grossman, "Processes of Development and Retreat."
37. More information on this subject is provided in Grossman, "The Fallah and the Bedouin."
38. See Tristram; pp. 113-114; Oliphant, p. 110; von Mülinen, pp. 142-149; Saleh, p. 193; Falah, "History of the Druze in Israel." See Grossman, *Expansion and Desertion*, pp. 162-169, for additional discussion and sources.
39. The instability of Ruha's settlements is evident from the survey reported by Shechter, p. 152.
40. Volney, II, p. 318.
41. The change process is documented in a number of publications. See Avitzur, *Daily Life*; Avitzur, *The Plow*. See also Kark, "Introduction of Modern Technology." See Dan and Raz for a comprehensive study of Israel's soils. The Sharon's soils are discussed in Dan and Yaalon.
42. Volney, II, p. 331.
43. The drainage of the main swamp was accomplished by a shared effort of Palestine's government (£7,500), a Jewish development company (£6,000), and the Waqf (Muslim Charitable Trust) (£4,500). See Royal Commission, p. 256. See also Nasr on the contribution of the Waqf.
44. Karmon, "Physiographic Conditions."
45. Avitzur, "Watermelons."
46. Hütteroth and Abdufattah, pp. 137-138.
47. Conder and Kitchener, II, *Memoirs*, pp. 152-153.
48. I am indebted to my former student, Walid Halabi, who lives in a-Tira for this information. He based it on the Bani Sa'ab clan's oral history.
49. For example, the data for 'Akka (Acre) District presented in the Beirut Salname of H 1318 (beginning 1 May 1900) were erroneously copied from the data that relate to the Nablus District. There are also several errors in the arithmetical calculations. Many yearbooks copied data from previous ones without making any attempt to update the information.
50. Karpat, Demographic and Social, p. 5.

6

Changing Land Pressure: Data, Concepts, and Processes

Introduction

This chapter focuses on agricultural density and its influence on the availability of land for the Palestinian peasants. It will attempt to quantify the agricultural density of the Arab farmers and assess the extent to which it deviated from the level required for obtaining minimal subsistence conditions. To accomplish this I begin with an overview of the issues that will be covered, and define, as far as possible, the concepts that need clarification. This discussion is accompanied by a short review of the research on *carrying capacity* and related terms that are essential for comprehending the Palestinian agrarian structure. These sections are followed by a short survey of the historical events and the policies that were adopted by the British Mandate administration to cope with the economic crises of the 1930s. This introduction leads to the core of this chapter: an attempt to measure the agricultural density in each of Palestine's zones for the period from c.1870 to 1945.

Clarifying and Defining the Main Issues

Four sets of interrelated questions are raised here:

- How did the agro-technical facilities available to the Arab cultivator affect land resources or land reserves?
- How did the traditional agricultural structure affect agricultural productivity?
- What was the impact of Jewish land purchases on land availability?
- What was the carrying capacity of the land and how was it calculated?

It is not easy to answer these questions. Human resource utilization and the factors that characterize it frustrate the attempts to define carrying capacity for any given area. This difficulty affects all the other questions posed above, and this subject will come up throughout the discussion that follows. Dynamism stands in the way of defining *carrying capacity.*

Spatial variability had a strong impact on the Arab rural areas, but the process of Jewish settlement and the methods that the Jews used for cultivating their plots of land were clearly not the only factors that impacted on the Arab cultivator or the nature of his farming. Despite the traditional agriculture that characterized the Arab peasants, land uses and their practices varied over space and time. The extent of this dynamism was not as obvious as that of the Jewish migrants (figure 6.1).

The methods for quantifying a given carrying capacity present a problem that is difficult to surmount. This difficulty has been the subject of numerous scientific studies.[1] The calculation depends on examining a certain static condition, in other words, on assuming that the system is immune to change. This was, in fact, the concept upon which much of the work of the commissions appointed by the mandatory government was based.

My own approach to the definition of this and related concepts did not overcome this difficulty. I calculated the extent of Arab land per person for a period that spanned about three full generations (c.1870-1945),

Fig. 6.1
Intensive irrigation close to Bethlehem, in an area of copious water springs

Source: Photographed by David Grossman, January 1985.

without giving much consideration to the changes that occurred during this long period of time, even though I noted that there had been some progress in agriculture during this period. My starting point for estimating the farmers' viable lot was the data of the official Village Statistics for 1945. The farm practices for this date also provided the yardstick for estimating the resource value of land reserves, which is based on two interrelated assumptions:

- The prevailing technology of the Arab staple crop cultivation in the 1940s was still fairly crude, and the use made of machines powered by fossil energy was rather exceptional.
- The Arab *fallah* produced his crops mainly for self-consumption. Most rural families practiced subsistence economy. Trade was no more than an auxiliary activity and much of it consisted of peddling in the nearby towns. For reasons that will be discussed below, the farmer had little comparative advantage over the global grain market.[2]

Agricultural Density and Carrying Capacity: A Review

The question of carrying capacity has concerned mankind ever since ancient times. The origin of this term can be found in the original biblical Hebrew text. It refers to the struggle between the shepherds of Abraham and his nephew, Lot.[3] In this context the term concerned the size of the area needed for the feeding of the flocks of two users and not for crops required to feed people. Measuring of land needed for sufficient pasture is relatively easy if one has good information on the quality of the resources, and, especially, on the available types of grasses and the size of the herds. But the measurement of carrying capacity for humans is far more complex. The literature on this subject is quite extensive, but there has not been a single agreed-upon method for arriving at quantitative estimates for explanation or planning.[4]

Reaching an agreed method for calculating the level of an area's carrying capacity for people has to include a variety of factors that consider life modes, economic practices, availability, gastronomy, cultural or religious codes and many others. The discovery of America added numerous plants and animals to our menu, but ever-changing technologies enabled mankind to embrace new resources and production means for increasing yields and the number of plant varieties in use and to extend the use of formerly marginal land.[5]

The changes affect not only regional carrying capacity, but also the ability of our planet to sustain human populations. Global warming resulting from a misuse of technology proves that our actions can have negative outcomes. Human requirements and priorities change rapidly, especially in the modern age. Therefore, it is difficult, if not impossible, to use formulae that relate only to physical factors.

Despite these problems, the question of carrying capacity became a central one during the British Mandate period. It increased in severity after the serious disturbances of 1929 when the British attempted to limit Zionist land purchases. In 1930 and the following years, several surveys and projects were carried out with the purpose of gaining more complete information about the *fallah* economy. I do not intend to dwell at length on the political questions that surfaced in that period. Even now, in the early twenty-first century, the core problems have not been resolved. A brief reference to the main issues is necessary.[6]

Palestine's Peasant Economy during the Mandate Era

The Mandate administration showed real concern over the presumed worsening conditions as a result of the declining per family agricultural land reserves, and, particularly, as a result of several consecutive drought seasons and other natural disasters that had occurred during the late 1920s and early 1930s. This period coincided with the Great Depression, but for the Arab peasants the local natural disasters were far more significant. Mandate officials were genuinely troubled by the *fallah*'s plight, but as is shown below, their policies were regarded by the Jewish sector as anti-Zionist.

The increasing pressure that was brought to bear by Arab nationalists, and the government's reaction to it, aggravated the situation. Ordinances which limited the ability of the Zionists to purchase land property were passed. The Arab Rebellion of 1936-1939 proved that the combination of worsening economic conditions for individual families and hard feelings generated by nationalistic incitement was extremely lethal.

John Hope-Simpson and other British officials who submitted their reports concerning the *fallah*'s hardships believed that assuring the Arabs a viable lot would quell the pressure and resolve the antagonism between the parties. They attempted, therefore, to calculate the amount of land that would be needed to sustain the average *fallah*'s family.[7] However, the possibility of reaching such a formula for the Arab customary economic systems by using modern economic analyses is questionable. A transition to commercial farming was beginning to be felt during the thirties, but the economy was only partly cash based.

The *fallah*'s economic system was part of an integrated way of life. Even artisans and service suppliers such as teachers and religious leaders spent a good deal of their time tilling their land in order to supply their families with food. Few stores could be found in rural areas, and the participation of individual farmers in the modern business economy was minimal. Many of the non-agricultural operations that the villagers were engaged in were also mostly parts of the primary sector: quarry operating, stone cutting, masonry, lime producing (in pits spread out in suitable limestone outcrops), charcoal making, and fishing and hunting. All these activities could supply vital sources of income, especially to those who lacked property. Many of these practices took place in or around the village and were either the major sources of family income or a form of supplemental income that provided some security for periods of stress. Certain villages were well known for a traditional crafts that concerned one of these specializations. An example is the village (now town) of Umm Al-Fahm (the mother of charcoal), whose location was adjacent to natural woodlands that provided the necessary raw materials for its and the surrounding hamlets' specialized occupation (charcoal making).

The difficulty in analyzing the *fallah*'s livelihood was accompanied by the lack of quantitative data. William J. Johnson and R. E. H. Crosbie headed a committee of ten persons that was appointed in April 1930 to study the *fallah*'s economic condition. They collected information on the local economy, and produced a report that included quantitative analysis of the annual budget of a *fallah*. They distributed a questionnaire in 104 villages, representing the major ecological zones, and collected information on agricultural crops, livestock, and tree crops. They also provided data on the yields and the values of the crops and described the methods of cultivation, including the length of the growing cycle and size of the cultivated areas. The report contained useful demographic data on the 104 surveyed villages (about 126,400 individuals in 21,066 families, i.e., an average of six persons per family). Their estimate of the *fallah*'s economy took into account the expenditure on rent payment, sales of crops, taxes, the problem of the *fallah*'s high indebtedness and a variety of other issues relating to households consumption and production.[8]

This comprehensive survey was a major contribution to a description of the prevalent economic structure and an evaluation of the performance of the rural Palestinian agrarian economy, but it took little notice of the non-monetary activities and the use of resources that could not be converted into monetary units. It is doubtful indeed whether it was at all possible to evaluate labor costs and other non-purchased production and service inputs in monetary units. Work of family members consisted of many activities that are difficult to break down into component parts. The family consumption and the farm yields were also measured by monetary values. Much of the household food came straight from the farm or the home garden and very little part of it reached the market. The surveyors' report made little attempt to assess the results by any form of non-money units.

The report noted that the *fallaheen* marketed only 3,807 tons of wheat, 1,295 tons of barley, 3,325 tons of durra (a sorghum variety) and 613,000 watermelons. They were unable to explain why the amounts of these marketed products were so low, and suggested that the *fallah* could not market his crops directly because he was forced to use the services of money-lending merchants to whom he was permanently indebted. The latter and the tax collectors took their share on the threshing floor, as the farmers were not allowed to carry home their harvest before the taxes were fully paid.

In most locations, the tax was still paid in-kind, and the tax-farmer himself also functioned as a merchant. He procured the crops from the *fallaheen* and sold them, thereby converting them into cash. This system was not substantially altered during the early Mandate period, even though the cash economy was gradually expanding into the rural areas.

Agricultural improvements and intensification practices that altered the resources were even less measurable in standard monetary units. It is almost impossible to distinguish between human capital and the natural state. This can be where man-made innovation is concerned in pre-technological societies. "Capital" expenditures were in pennies, for example, the farmer accumulated capital by building terraces, digging channels, or clearing the fields and using the stones for fencing and embankments, or for constructing small dams. In many cases these improvements were inherited from their ancestors, but they were useless if not properly maintained or if the farmer refrained from investing sufficient effort in repairing the terrace retaining walls or stone fences. The investments were not necessarily different from those of a modern farmer, but were not registered or counted in cash. It was clearly difficult thus to assign any monetary values to a plot where the changes amounted to no more than "reshuffling resources." Certain improvements were more visible but they were still based on human or animal "muscle energy" (figure 6.2).[9]

Apart from the problems mentioned above, there was the need to take into consideration the storage of parts of the yield as a form of insurance against the possibility of bad harvests. Research conducted in

Fig. 6.2
Plowing rough land, probably near Nablus

Source: Jacob Landau, *Eretz Israel in the days of Abdul Hamid,* Jerusalem: Carta, 1979 (Hebrew), p. 91. Courtesy of Professor Jacob Landau, who holds publication rights of this book.

Africa and elsewhere confirms that, despite pre-industrial technology, peasants are often capable of adjusting the use of their resources to their changing needs.[10]

The insufficient consideration of communal, family, and social or religious obligations, especially during religious holidays, also met with some criticism. The burden of the bride-price, especially if the number of sons and daughters in a family was not equal, was understated by Johnson-Crosbie report. In an anthropological study in the Bethlehem area in the 1930s, the bride-price was estimated to be around fifty Palestinian pounds. This sum was about 50 percent more than the average annual income of a *fallah,* as estimated by Johnson and Crosbie. The widespread practice of marriages of closely related individuals (often first cousins) was an attempt to ease this burden, but resulted, unfortunately, in a multiplicity of children with genetic defects. In addition to the bride-price, there were other expenditures for various family events. Johnson and Crosbie estimated at approximately one pound a year only.[11]

The weaknesses in their money-based economic model raised questions, therefore, about the validity of their estimate of the Palestinian carrying capacity. The criticism of the calculations of Johnson and Crosbie by Jewish scholars such as Isaac Elazari-Volcani (Vilkansky) related to specific omissions and mistaken estimates rather than to the investigation procedure or other methods that they had adopted. Elazari-Volcani also based his conclusions on similar cash-based criteria, and many of his own findings, for example, his estimate for the yields of wheat (600 to 1,000 kilograms per hectare, depending on resource quality) were not substantially different from those of the official commission.[12]

The main point of this survey is that even the best study could not overcome some of the methodological difficulties. But apart from the weaknesses reported above, the conclusions of Johnson and Crosbie concerning the minimum size of a viable agricultural lot failed to take account of the dynamic factor. The calculation of the viable lot size applied, at the most, to a static economic case, but even this purpose was only partly achieved. Despite the criticism, the contribution of Johnson and Crosbie's commission, both academically and practically, cannot be denied.

Estimating the Size of a Viable Lot on the Basis of Energy Units

An alternative method of estimating carrying capacity is based on energy units instead of monetary ones. This procedure particularly suits societies based on subsistence or near-subsistence economies in which commerce does not play a central role. However, it also has its faults. It does not solve the problem of the dynamic issue, nor does it succeed in circumventing the need for some cash to buy inputs and other production or consumption goods that had to be purchased. In spite of these limitations, I feel that it helps to comprehend the pre-industrial subsistence economy better than the monetary method.

A model for estimating carrying capacity based on energy was offered by Bayliss-Smith. The model consisted of an island whose total size was 150 hectares of which 100 ha (1 km²) were suitable for cultivation. He based his calculation on Colin Clark and Margaret Haswell's book (see below) that estimated the mean calorie needs reported in studies of peasants from China, Yugoslavia, and Nigeria. The Nigerian farmers' food consumption represented primarily roots and tubers as staple food, in Yugoslavia it was based on grains and in China on both. The work inputs and food outputs were calculated by energy units (million kilo-calories per hectare) and by work inputs (man-hours) for each of the parcels. The latter were equally apportioned to each of the three "countries," that is, each of the three was cultivated by the method used in the country that it represented. The resulting carrying capacity revealed that the island was capable of supporting a maximum population of 1,008 persons.[13]

Bayliss-Smith's method is unquestionably ingenious. It meticulously covered a subject in a way that is difficult to surpass. Even though Clark and Haswell's purpose was not identical to that of Bayliss-Smith who used their data, they preferred a simpler method for quantitatively tackling the problem of population pressure. For this purpose they used a standardized unit of *grain equivalent* (including rice and millet) and *wheat equivalent*. These units facilitated the measurement of the actual food needs by circumventing the need to measure caloric intake directly.

According to Clark and Haswell calculation, the "subsistence minimum," in kilograms of non-milled grains, required for obtaining the average annual energy needs per person is about 210 grain equivalents per person per year.[14] They also took into account various other non-food items. For example, the total agricultural wheat equivalents per person for circa 1960 in Egypt and Jordan were fairly identical (at 410 and 431 respectfully), but Egypt had an extra 119 non-food in wheat equivalent (WE) units derived from non-food items, while Jordan had only four non-food extra WE.[15]

The sources of most of Clark and Haswell's analyses date from the 1930s. Their findings are therefore very suitable for the present discussion of Palestine. In addition to agriculture, these authors calculated the grain equivalent levels needed for various non-food consumption items (clothing, building materials and medicines) and production inputs (draft animals, tools). They also considered higher than basic subsistence levels. Thus, when the personal grain equivalent rises to 400, the consumption items listed above can be purchased, but draft animals can be purchased only if it reaches at least the 500 WE level. Climatic conditions and various other local factors likely to affect the amount of the grain equivalent per person were also taken into account. The need for tax payment was also considered, but although not specifically measured in terms of grain equivalent units, they implied that it was not included in the "subsistence minimum" or in any level below 300.[16]

Clark and Haswell's Method Applied to the Palestinian Peasant Economy

The Palestinian *fallah* lived on subsistence level, but it is not likely that the level was as low as the "subsistence minimum" of yearly wheat equivalent (WE) units per person. I assume that the basic value was at least 300 WE per person if clothing, shoes, building materials and other basic consumption needs that the *fallah* required additional WEs and an extra 100 for draft animals and various farm implements. The tax payment added another 30 percent, bringing the sum to approximately 520 WE per person. Other miscellaneous expenditures bring the total to about 600 WEs.

The grain was mostly used for food, but the farmer had to allocate a sixth of it for seeds, which was part of his production cost. This portion, deducted from about 240 WE, can be estimated at 40 WE. However, the total WE for consumption included non-grain items such as vegetables, fruits, olives and some animal products (eggs, milk and some meat). The necessary daily protein needs could be derived largely from the wheat grains (which contain about 11 percent protein).

Animals did not require much additional land, since they could be raised on open grazing and other non-arable places and on arable plots during the fallow seasons. Rain-fed vegetables, grapes, olives, and most fruit trees (with some added well and cistern water) could be grown in gardens and yards as well as on empty village tracts that were unsuitable for crop growing. The grazing lands were, in most villages, communally held or open to general usage. In any case, the *fallah* did not have to choose between food crops for the use of good arable land.[17]

Draft animals were counted by Clark and Haswell among the production tools. They were more costly than those used for food, but they could have been bartered for other animals or crops. Added income could be obtained, in good years, also from the sale of surplus harvests that were not needed for feeding the family. Some purchases were indispensable for the *fallaheen* even if they were made by barter. But even if the major part of production and most of the inputs could be measured in WE units, it would have been impossible to avoid using some money for purchasing tools and for repairing them. Expenses such as transportation, bride-price, various family events, hosting relatives or other guests and, most important, keeping some surplus for security must also be added. Unforeseen expenses, including payments to letter writers for applications to the authorities, should also be considered. Education and health costs have to be included in this sum, but expenses such as fees for surveyors and lawyers were usually charged to the village community rather than to the *fallah*.

It is difficult to assess each and every item that the farmer needed, but it is likely that the *fallah* needed up to 600 WE per person. However, since the calculations were focused mainly on the farm unit, total expenditures should not be charged equally to all household members' who were consumers rather than producers. Their consumption costs were therefore closer to the basic 210 WE unit, but certainly not larger than 300. This makes a total of 1,050 WE for the remaining five family members. The correct sum is thus 600 + 1,500 = 2,100 WE.

The farmland that can supply these 2,100 WE has a mean wheat production level of about 600 kilograms per hectare (see above). For the *fallah's* 600 WEs the hectarage that was needed amounted to 2.1 ha. The other five family members required only an extra 2.5 ha. The whole household's total farm land subsisted, therefore, on 4.6 hectares. This is lower than the size of the 7.5 ha. that Johnson and Crosbie estimated.

The *agricultural density* per person (i.e., the reverse of the normal density formula)[18] would be 0.77 hectare per capita, when the means for the farmer and his family are averaged. This applies, however, only to owner-operated farmers or to holders of cultivation rights, that is, those who cultivate Palestinian *miri* (government domain) land. Share-croppers, who had to transfer part of the crop to the landowner, needed considerably larger lots. Johnson and Crosbie estimated it at double the size of the owner-operated farmland, that is, at 13 hectares. According to my calculation they needed an even larger farm size (4.6 x 4 = 18.4). This is because the agrarian system was based on the Islamic *Shari'a* (Koranic legal code) laws that allocated to each of the four inputs, labor, seeds, capital and land (which are legitimate according to the *Shari'a*), equal weight in partnership agreements. The compensation for labor was therefore identical to the three others—one fourth only.[19]

In Palestine, family-operated farms were the rule, but sharecropping increased substantially as a result of the 1858 land law (see chapter 1). In fact, the sharecropper had to pay taxes and additional costs such as corvée-like tasks. Their own share was thus, only one fifth of the yield, but they were not responsible for any part of the non-labor production costs. In comparison with the free farmers' costs, their total WE were therefore somewhat lower. The main additional fees were for social or religious expenses and other non-food consumption items.

The results of my calculations are not far from those of Johnson and Crosbie for an owner-operated farm, but they are much greater for the sharecropper. My estimates are designed to provide a yardstick for assessing the changing land pressure on the agricultural resources between c.1870 and 1948, which is the subject of the last section of this chapter.

I have not included in the above discussion an important subject: the economic impact of natural disasters that substantially reduced the food supply. Disasters force the farmers to use whatever surpluses they were able to raise. The initial response might have been to refrain from selling the remaining surplus, but eventually the *fallah* exhausted his entire surplus. His WE reached a critical point where the only alternative was out-migration, but the availability of food might have been even lower in his new location than what his family had experienced in their home village.

The next section focuses on a case where there was a series of natural disasters over several consecutive years. Such multiple problems had been responsible for many previous rebellions. The case of the Hauran was briefly mentioned above. The example that I will discuss here was responsible for even more serious outcomes. It involved the British rulers, but also the Jewish settlers. This was partly the cause of several Arab-Jewish confrontations that are still unresolved. The positive outcome of this difficult period was the formulation of a comprehensive tax reform.

The Natural Disasters of 1927-1934 and Their Consequences

The historical section presented here is vital for introducing the crises that led the Mandatory government to adopt a policy that amounted to a substantial reform of the rural fiscal policy during the early 1930s. As will be shown below, I used certain criteria that emanated from the reform as a basis for my analysis.

These crises of the 1930s reduced the total WE level of the *fallaheen* to well below that which was calculated above. The series of natural disasters started in 1927 with a severe earthquake that devastated mainly Nablus and other major Arab settlements in its vicinity, and caused numerous casualties. To add to these woes, the same year also saw adverse climactic conditions. Rainfall was low and the following years also sustained severe droughts. In 1929 there were disturbances that culminated in pogroms against the Jews in Hebron and other locations. The government reacted by appointing a Committee of Investigation, which was followed by a series of additional commissions. The years between 1929 and 1933 were hit by droughts or by other scourges that damaged the crops.

Although the situation eased somewhat in subsequent years, a seed shortage was felt until 1935. As a result of these crises, the land which was put on the market in exchange for sustenance and to pay off creditors increased. One solution, which rapidly became widespread, was to leave the village and join the workforce of unskilled laborers in the urban areas. These conditions fed the Arab's nationalistic spirit that eventually fired violent uprisings that lasted for three years.

A favorable result was that the Palestinian currency remained stable and there was no inflation in the ten years that ended in 1936. At the same time, however, the natural disasters and the government's slow response to the peasants' suffering significantly increased incitement against the government and the Jews. The government reacted with a series of ordinances, which limited the right of Jewish land acquisition for agricultural land. But this failed to appease the Arab leadership. The Arab Revolt, spearheaded by peasants, erupted shortly afterwards.[20]

The growing difficulty that the Jewish land purchasers met was also an indicator of increasing land scarcity. During the 1920s the shortage was not serious. The absentee landowners (*effendis*), who had obtained vast estates as a consequence of the 1858 Land Code, sold large parcels of what was often prime land. The largest purchase was the Jezre'el Plain where, in a deal that was completed in the early 1920s, the Jewish National Fund acquired 7,135.6 hectares.[21] But after the 1920s the supply gradually dwindled as large *effendi* estates were no longer offered for sale. At the same time the growing Arab pressure increased. The British authorities, trying to satisfy both ethnic groups, repeatedly claimed that the land reserves had substantially declined, and in 1930 the High Commissioner declared that all the arable land was already in use, and that no reserves were left for conventional agricultural development in Palestine.[22] Indeed, by around 1930 it became clear even to the Jewish leadership that they would have to shift their purchasing efforts to small landowners and even individual *fallaheen*.[23] However, the supply shortage does not explicitly prove that there was an absolute shortage of agricultural land. As was argued above, the shortage experienced by the Jewish population resulted from a combined effect of the dwindling supply of large blocks, a series of unforeseen natural disasters and rising nationalist hostility.

The Rural Tax Reform: Criteria and Land Classification System

The official ordinances that dealt with agricultural land testify to the importance that the Palestinian authorities attached to the plight of the *fallaheen*. The administration was genuinely interested in solving the crises, but it also insisted that "Palestine was meant to be self-sufficient and capable of operating on the basis of income from local taxes."[24] A similar fiscal policy was adopted, in fact, in all the British colonies. The Johnson-Crosbie Committee was appointed to investigate and "to examine the economic conditions of the agriculturalists and the fiscal measures of government in relation thereto."[25] This quotation leaves no doubt that "fiscal measures" are related to the "conditions of the agriculturalists" and the link between taxation and the state of the cultivators.

The first full-fledged effort to adopt an agricultural tax system that was a complete break with the Ottoman tithe system was passed in 1934. Previously there was a sort of "patchwork" formula that had been used between 1925 and 1934. The assessment in-kind, by a portion of the harvest, was translated at first into a monetary value (called the "commuted tithe"), but by 1934, when the report was submitted by a special committee assigned to study the issue, a totally new fiscal system was adopted.

The new tax was clearly progressive. The rates were determined by measuring the area's potential productivity rather than by harvest size or by the size of the farmland. The tax rate for all soil types was not a simple linear curve. It was considerably lower on poorer soils than on the better ones.[26]

The fiscal reform went into effect in April 1935. It was based on tax ordinances issued at the beginning of the same year. The basic apparatus was not significantly amended again, but, as will be shown below, the rates were later readjusted to changing conditions. In fact, compared with the previous systems, this reform substantially reduced the tax burden.

The new system also drew scathing criticism, particularly from the Arab agricultural experts.[27] Most of the criticism was directed to the methods adopted by the government for determining the soil grades and for measuring their productivity. However, at least one of the prominent Zionists, Avraham Granovsky, the head of the Jewish National Fund, favorably viewed the wide gap between the taxes rates imposed on the *fallaheen* as opposed to that on the citrus growers. Furthermore, he considered as too high even a tax of 5 percent of the *fallah*'s net income [28] Granovsky doubted, however, that the hasty surveys conducted by the government could establish meaningful land capability for use in evaluating the resource potential that was the basis for tax assessments.[29]

Prior to the implementation of the reform, each farm plot had to be graded for quality and potential yield. To this end the theoretical crop-yielding potential of each unit of land type had to be classified. As the critical comments of Granovsky and others suggest, the information collected, based on countrywide surveys, was fairly superficial. Nevertheless, the data were incorporated into fiscal maps at a scale of 1:10,000 and were published in a series called Village Statistics.[30]

The system that was finally adopted consisted of sixteen categories of soil grades that corresponded to the various tax rates. Later a seventeenth category, water bodies, was added. The data were not very precise, but they provided valuable quantitative information on land use and on the agricultural resources at the village level. The new land-tax assessment was also contingent upon type of crop and methods of cultivation.

The appraisal was highest for irrigated crops or on non-irrigated fruit tree orchards and for field crops grown on the best soils. The irrigated land and orchards were classified as categories 1-4. The other classes, which will be treated in some detail below, were concerned with various soil qualities and agrarian management systems that used non-mechanized cultivation of either staples or tree crops.

I do not include in my analysis (which is considered in the next section) the citrus orchards and banana plantations, even though these crops were considered the most profitable during the British Mandate era. My reason is that their cultivation was hardly present on rural farms prior to the 1930s, and later they belonged to the cash economy rather than to the semi-subsistence sector. Another reason was the difficulty of comparing the economic value of citrus fruits and bananas to the traditional food crops and fruit trees which I used for measuring changes in population pressure. It is difficult to evaluate the changes that took place from the 1870s to the 1930s. Citrus cultivation was also of low relevance to the carrying capacity question with which we are concerned. I did not ignore their economic significance entirely, however, and included some discussion of their contribution to the economy during the Mandate era.

Towards the end of the British Mandate the assessments were re-adjusted to changing market conditions, and the tax impositions were substantially altered. Citrus fruits, which were originally placed in the uppermost tax bracket, were fully exempt from taxes in 1945-46, because of the loss of marketing potential during the war, when shipping the fruit almost completely ceased.[31] The *fallaheen*, on the other hand, benefited from the rising demand for food during the war years, when large quantities grains were sold to feed the armies stationed in Palestine and adjacent countries. The war years thus turned the tables: the grain farmers were better off than the plantation owners, but these temporal adjustments did not alter the basic principles. There was a pronounced contrast, thus, between the proportional fiscal contribution of farmers during the British Mandate period and that of the Ottoman period, when farming had been the main source of fiscal income. Significantly during the Mandate era, the proportion of government income realized from the taxation of agriculture was inconsequential.[32]

As noted, the first categories (1-4) included only bananas, citrus and built-up village areas. The first categories that I considered belonged to the 5-8 classes. They include four successive grades of fruit plantations and crops grown on high grade soils. However, even those grown on relatively poor soils were included in this class if the fields were irrigated. The tax on these lands amounted to 2.226 times the level of the next land classifications (9-13). The latter consisted of a variety of lower-grade soils that were either irrigated or non-irrigated. The 9-13 categories were rather inhospitable. However, it seems that the government experts felt that they could still be productive if the cultivator invested in clearing them or provided them with irrigation works. They were taxed, therefore, at a reduced rate. Since many *fallaheen* spent a great deal of effort on tilling around rocks and other obstacles, these officials seem to be quite right. Since they had some, though marginal, value, I did not omit these areas from my analysis (figure 6.3).

The lowest tax assessment level (categories 14-16) applied to areas that had only limited farming potential or were lacking it altogether. Rocky areas or woodlands and patches of cropped fields on very poor soils belonged to this class. A special type, fish ponds, was also included, but it and the marginal 14-16 categories were not included in my analysis.

Analysis of the Diminishing Size of Farmland per Person, 1870-71-1945

The classification that was associated with the fiscal reforms provides the main tool for my analysis of the growing scarcity of agricultural

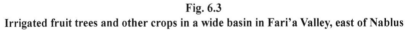

Fig. 6.3
Irrigated fruit trees and other crops in a wide basin in Fari'a Valley, east of Nablus

Source: Photographed by David Grossman in the late 1970s.

land. I have already noted this relationship in my comments on the link between the official criteria and my own selection system. In this section I intend to further explain the procedure that I adopted for measuring land pressure.

The main data base for my computations is the April 1945 Village Statistics, the last publication of this series. This publication provides a convenient yardstick for assessing the process of the change of agricultural land size that occurred between 1871 and 1945, that is, the gradual reduction of the farm size left to the *fallah* to sustain his household. It also serves as the only source for working with constant land units for the entire study period.

My calculations of the agricultural densities refer to the *nahiya* level (or to part of it). The rural areas purchased by the Jews at the beginning of the period under study (1871-1922) were small and had relatively low impact on the country's agricultural sector. Since the beginning of the Mandate period Jewish property gradually became more extensive. In order to evaluate the rising pressure on agricultural land by 1945, I utilized two data sets.[33]

Equation 1 used tax assessment to grant the higher soil grades an *adjusted hectarage* valuation that is high grades (categories). The higher soil grade (C) was multiplied by 2.226. This coefficient represents the tax rates imposed on 5-8 grades, which were assessed at 2.226 higher than those of the poorer (9-13 soil categories). This "enlargement" of the good categories (called "plantations" should reflect the assumed extra carrying capacity of the soils.

Equation 1:

$$A = [B + (2.226 \times C)] / Pt$$

Where:

A = Total adjusted land size (adjusted land) per person in a region or a village

B = Village or region area in metric dunams; (1 metric dunam = 0.1 ha), for 9 -13 categories

C = Village or region area in metric dunams (0.1 hectares), categories 5 - 8

Pt = Population in a given year

As stated above, the adjusted hectares per capita represent the agricultural density level. The comparison between the data from 1870-71 (one year before the publication of the H 1288 Yearbook) and those from the Mandate period show that with the exception of Gaza zone (the right part of the chart) in most areas the change in land/man relationships during the last half century of the Ottoman era (c.1870-71 to 1918) was minimal. The changes were more drastic in the shorter period, between 1922 and 1945 (see chart 6.1).

The following analysis is selective. It deals mainly with the extremes rather than with the normal cases. Its purpose is to direct the reader's attention to the marginal areas rather than to the center.

Chart 6.1 reveals that the greatest per capita agricultural declines occurred adjacent to the major cities. This is most obvious in Jaffa's (Lud *nahiya*) and Jerusalem's peripheries (Bani Hasan *nahiya* and part of Wadiya *nahiya*). Ramla's rural hinterland was mostly less agriculturally attractive (*raml* means sand) and was therefore more sparsely populated. The western part, Ramla West, was the most land-endowed zone in the Jerusalem District, but practically all of it was covered by infertile red sands. It is now part of the Tel Aviv conurbation and contains several Jewish towns. This zone had, initially, about 6.5 adjusted hectares, but this level was reduced, by 1945, to just 1.11.

The other area which had large land resources was the Hebron Sub-District. Three of its four *nahiyas* had an agricultural density of more than 3.5. These figures are, however, misleading because the numerous hamlets and cave dwellings that existed in this zone were not officially registered. Most of them were temporary or seasonal off-shoots of the largest settlement, Dura. In 1931 there were seventy places whose names had the prefix "Kh" (short for *khirba* = ruin or reconstructed ruin), referring to the ruins and caves that were resettled in recent time.

Chart 6.1
Adjusted hectares of agricultural land per person: Jerusalem District

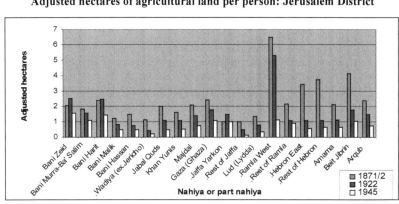

None of them had demographic data apparently because the population had been counted in Dura, their mother settlement. There were other villages which had numerous seasonal shelters. All of them developed into recognized villages (see chapter 5).

Arthur Ruppin, one of the Zionist leaders, noticed the low demographic record of this Hebron zone, and considered it, in a 1907 publication, as a potential for what he envisioned as a "Jewish autonomous territory." Similar ideas were also expressed by Haim Kalvarisky, who played a decisive role in purchasing the eastern Lower Galilee from the Algerian owners.[34] But like many others, Ruppin was misled by the under-reported official statistics.

The Acre District (chart 6.2) was distinctly better endowed with surplus land. The high quality areas, such as the *sahil* (plain) had high agricultural density and, consequently, low land reserves. Quantitatively, the highest levels of agricultural land per person were recorded in this district.

The Galilee mountain valleys were also densely settled, but Safad *nahiya* as well as the Carmel Mountain (Jabal *nahiya*) and Ruha *nahiya* had sparse populations. The attraction of Safad can be attributed to its role as the main center in the Galilee; the Carmel's case was due to the existence of a level area east of Haifa, which merges with the Jezre'el basin, while Ruha is a low plateau located south of the Carmel Ridge. It also borders on the Jezre'el Basin. The official *nahiya* also contains a section of the northern Sharon Plain.

Ruha had the lowest density. It had as much as 4.03 adjusted hectares according to the 1871/72 records, but only 1.03 in 1945. Since much of its uplands had very thin, unproductive soils, the area was clearly one

Chart 6.2
Adjusted hectares of agricultural land per person: Acre Rural Zones

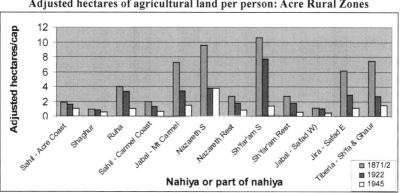

of the least favorable of the Acre zones. However, the northern Sharon section, which was part of this *nahiya*, was clearly different. Its soils are deep and fertile, but much of the land consisted of malaria-infested swamps. Only after the early 1920s, when the swamps were drained, did its fertile soil become a valuable asset (map 5.1).

The conditions were very different in the Nablus-Jenin zones, where Jewish real estate purchases were minimal. This was the area of highest land pressure. This record of farmland per capita dropped, in the case of eastern Bani Sa'ab *nahiya,* to only about 0.05 adjusted hectares per person.

The most valuable arable lands were in the Sharon's eastern margin, where the plain sloped gently from the low Samaria hills. These fertile soils also benefited from good drainage which prevented the formation of the swamps that plagued many other Sharon zones. The high agricultural density is consequently not a late phenomenon. It stands out clearly in the 1871-72 data (chart 6.3).

Many upland villages were close to the Sharon Plain, where the *fallaheen* had access to its abundant land reserves, but the productive quality of the non-swampy red sandy soils was very low. This proximity accounts for the villagers' ability to eke out a living despite the shortage of land on their upland farms. Even a greater advantage was its proximity to Jaffa (and later, Tel Aviv), where job opportunities were growing. Increasing opportunities for agricultural or non-agricultural employment could also be found in the Jewish sector elsewhere in the Sharon.

Chart 6.3
Adjusted hectares of agricultural land per person: Nablus Rural Zones

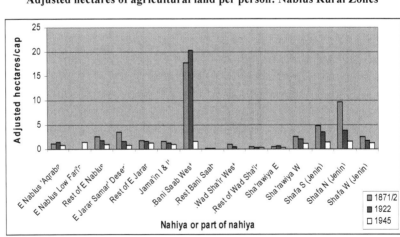

The rising land pressure in the hinterlands of Jaffa and Jerusalem was not repeated in the Nablus and Jenin urban areas. Nablus's hinterland, especially East (Mashariq) Nablus, had a low adjusted hectarage per capita, but it was not as low as the western Samaria zones (the chart's right side, except for the three Jenin *nahiyas*). This suggests that, in comparison with the coastal towns, Nablus was not strongly affected by modern urbanization.

The Nablus and the three Jenin *nahiyas,* however, were unique. They included large productive flatlands, such as the southern part of the Jezre'el and the Beisan basins. But parts of these areas were quite dry. The relatively sparse population accounted for the presence of extensive adjusted hectarage. The central town, Jenin, was no more than a small rural center and many of its inhabitants were themselves farmers. Its population according to the 1871/72 Yearbook was less than 6,000. The sub-district's *nahiya*s, located in the Hauran District, are excluded from this analysis.

A most unique case is that of the portion of Nablus *nahiya* that was located in the dry Jordan Valley at its confluence with the Fari'a tributary. This area was poorly drained, malaria-infested and subject to winter flooding. It was originally inhabited only by nomadic Bedouin who lived there, along other sections of the Jordan Basin and in other dry areas. The basin and its tributaries' flood plains were practically devoid of permanent settlements. The Mandate authorities encouraged its rehabilitation and constructed irrigation schemes for the Bedouin as well as for settlers from neighboring villages.[35] As a result, many small hamlets and estates sprang up along the new canals (figure 6.3). But the total agricultural area available to the Nablus Sub-District residents was low. The average for Nablus and the better endowed Jenin *nahiyas* was, in 1945, 0.99 adjusted hectares.

The Impact of Jewish Settlements on Arab Agricultural Holdings

The second set of data, designed to assess the influence of Jewish land acquisitions on Arab holdings at the end of the Mandate period, is presented in chart 6.4. The chart refers only to the zones that were affected by the Jewish purchases, but for comparative purposes, some territories that were not affected have also been included. It shows that the size of the holdings that remained in Arab hands varied widely.

The zones of this chart are not identical with the three previous ones. The Sharon and Beisan are treated as single territories even though each of them covers several parts of or complete *nahiyas*. The areas with

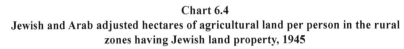

Chart 6.4
Jewish and Arab adjusted hectares of agricultural land per person in the rural
zones having Jewish land property, 1945

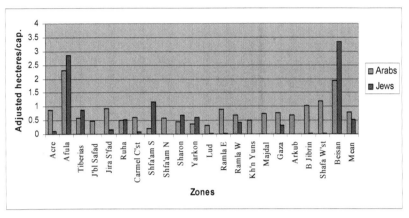

the most per capita adjusted hectares were in the zones that were later amalgamated into the Beisan Sub-District, while the least per capita Arab land was found in Southern Shefar'am (in the northwestern part of the Jezre'el Plain), where only 0.116 adjusted hectares per person was left in Arab possession, but much of the sub-*nahiya* consisted of poor rocky land which was extensively used for Bedouin grazing (figure 6.4). In the neighboring 'Afula zone, which was one of the most affected by Jewish settlement, the Arabs in 1945 still held more than 2.2 adjusted hectares per person. The zone still retained, in fact, the greatest per capita amount of Arab land in Palestine. Both of these areas (S. Shefar'am and 'Afula) contained, however, relatively large zones of marginal resources (dry climate or rockiness).

The peri-urban zones, as the cases of Jerusalem and other major cities, illustrate the highest agricultural density levels. The dense Lud zone, about ten kilometers from Jaffa-Tel Aviv, had low Arab agricultural land per person, but the agricultural areas that the Arabs retained in the periphery of Gaza were more extensive. In these areas Jewish rural property was either low or totally non-existent.

In the zones that were most affected by Jewish settlement, outside the Jezre'el and Beisan basins, already covered above, the impact on Arab agricultural density appears to have been only moderate. In Tiberias, Ruha and the coastal plain zones (Sharon, Yarkon, and western Ramla), the Jewish impact was quite pronounced, but a number of the non-Jewish settlement zones had even lower agricultural densities. Safad town had

Fig. 6.4
Low grade soils on a rocky hill in southern Shefar'am

Source: Photographed by David Grossman, December 1990.

many Jews, but in Safad's rural zones (Jira *nahiya)*, the Jewish settlement started in 1878 by some town residents, and in 1870 the existing
Arab density was lower than the Safad S.D.'s western neighbor (Jabal),
where post-1878 Jewish population was practically nil.[36]

A look at the preceding charts provides additional information about
areas which were omitted from chart 6.4 because they had no Jewish
settlement. Many *nahiyas* had lower Arab density than any of the zones
that were reviewed here. Outstanding were western Nablus and the Jerusalem periphery. Like Jaffa-Tel Aviv, Jerusalem was surrounded by
nahiyas that had very high agricultural density (small lots). This was
also found in the Jerusalem periphery. Haifa's periphery is less obvious because of the Carmel Mountains and the relatively inhospitable
plains north of it. The only clear effect is in the narrow Coastal Plain
to its south, where Arab agricultural density was very high. However,
the Galilee inland valleys, with the exception of one (see above figures
5.5 and 5.6), which was often waterlogged in the winter, also recorded
high agricultural density.

The charts discussed above do not contain information about the
important cash crops that provided a crucial source of livelihood for
the densely settled zones. The most widespread were citrus fruits, but
in some places, especially in the Jordan Rift Valley, bananas and some
other crops were also grown. These were intensively cultivated under

irrigation and demanded large amounts of water. There were, however, many other intensive crops, which were usually rain fed. The most widespread were grapevines (on the slopes and in the valleys of Hebron) and olives (in the hills of Samaria and Galilee). These were also commercially grown, but their products were mostly sold locally or exported to neighboring countries. Vegetables were also grown for local consumption, generally in the house compounds or on other empty lots in the village. Intensive irrigation was applied only near springs or, on the coastal plain, near wells.

The Yarkon region, the site of 1879 Jewish pioneer citrus cultivation, and the adjacent Sharon and most of the West Ramla zone, evolved as citrus-growing areas. This was preceded, on the Jewish farms, by the cultivation of vineyards and other fruits, but after a period of trial and error, including losses of vineyards from disease, citrus proved to have the highest comparative advantage. The Arab citrus orchards preceded those of the Jews, but were initially confined to the outskirts of Jaffa where groundwater was fairly close to the surface.

As already noted, the Sharon's citrus industry depended on the utilization of mechanized pumps. By the early Mandate era, the Jewish Sharon's citrus cultivation was more extensive than the Arab's, but in 1945 the Arab sector was larger than the Jewish.[37] Even though both ethnic groups grew the same crop, their settlement patterns were very different. The Jews lived in villages (called *moshavot* or *moshavim*). The Arabs, on the other hand, preferred to reside in dispersed settlements which contained estate structures within their groves. The houses contained their own and the permanent staff's quarters and a pumping machine.[38]

Summary and Conclusions

Chart 6.4 suggests that the influence of Jewish land purchases on Arab land reserves towards the end of the Mandate era was relatively small. Only in one zone (Southern Shefar'am, in the northern Jezre'el Plain) did the Arab agricultural land decline substantially below five adjusted hectares per person. In the other Jewish-dominated rural areas, influence on the Arab agricultural land reserves was quite limited, though there were several zones where the Arab reserves were lower than that of the Jews. There were no Jewish purchases, there was an even greater decline in unused Arab agricultural land, as a glance at the preceding charts show.

The declining holding size in the peri-urban areas was most pronounced, but this was not necessarily related only to Jewish acquisitions.

In fact, the general Jewish impact on the Arab economy was rather beneficial, because it generated employment that provided opportunities for relatively high income jobs. The critical demographic factor was the Moslem's high growth rate (2.65 percent), especially in the Mandate era. Clearly, this had no relation to any Jewish activity in Palestine. Demographically, the ethnic factor was significant. This is evident particularly when the 1922 census figures are compared with the later estimates.[39]

To the *fallah*'s strategy of abandoning agriculture and migrating to the city, there was an additional alternative: the possibility of finding work in the flourishing citrus industry. This alternative offered an attractive economic means of leaving the rural home without abandoning agriculture altogether. But in order to acquire land suitable for citrus cultivation the *fallah* had to sell off his family lands. The usual means of accomplishing this was to sell the family land to the Jews. The best areas for irrigated citrus growing were in the Sharon or western Ramla. Both were not too far from Nablus or Jerusalem. However, most of the *fallaheen* did not take part in this process because of the low level of their capital resources. The large scale of their indebtedness also made major investment unfeasible.[40]

In spite of the agricultural development and the alternative economic opportunities, the life of the *fallah* was not substantially changed during the British Mandate period. The balance between man and resources actually worsened. The rural population growth rate exceeded, as the Malthusian model predicted, the resources growth rate, which failed to match it both in terms of the farmed land and capital investment. The population rose from 1922 to 1946 by 113.5 percent while the farmland (both irrigated and non-irrigated) increased from 1922 to 1946 by only 40 percent.[41]

The outcome of the large demographic increase was not related only to the people/ resource ratio. What worsened it was the changing dependency ratio. The wide-base of the age pyramid meant that the dependency ratio was too high. The main economic problem was the inability of those who stayed on their ancestral farms to make the transition from subsistence to commercial agriculture. Experts like Johnson and Crosbie understood that the *fallah* could not compete with the American farmer on the world market. In their chapter that deals with the need to limit the purchasing of wheat they note that:

> [it] may be asked why the Arab farmer does not increase his wheat cultivation so as to eliminate the need for foreign imports. First, allowance must be made for the fact that whatever the local supply might be, a certain quantity of foreign white flour,

estimated at 12,000–15,000 tons per annum, would be imported to make bread of fine quality and confectionery [produced in] large scale cultivation in the great wheat centers of the world.... this additional quantity could be raised only by increasing the area under cultivation or by more intensive cultivation. [But] Palestine is not a large country containing large tracts of land suitable for economical mass production of cereals.[42]

It was clear to these experts that Palestine could not match the resources of the United States and other "bread basket" countries. In other words, since growing grain in Palestine had no comparative advantage, it would be a mistake to encourage the *fallah* to engage in wheat and barley production on small farms. The continuation of this traditional cropping system can be justified only in subsistence agriculture. The implication was that the price for continuing traditional farming methods would lead to foregoing any agricultural development.

The policy of the Mandate government that favored the *fallah*'s subsistence agriculture would have led to continued, and even worsening, poverty. Other factors that contributed to the policy were the growing tensions that preceded and followed the Second World War. These were clearly beneficial to the *fallaheen*, but they fed the rising prices and led to the postponement of any attempt to improve the cultivators' condition.[43]

In a historic perspective, the crisis of the late 1930s was just a passing episode, but it could also be regarded as a forerunner to the greater problems that faced the Palestinians a decade later. The Arab Revolt of the late 1930s was partly the result of the frustration caused by economic conditions, but, like other events discussed here, it had other causes. It may also be partly viewed as a traditional pattern of behavior that was shaped by earlier experiences with the Ottoman government. The most well known of such uprisings was the 1834 revolt against Ibrahim Pasha and the similar outbreaks that had occurred in the Jerusalem zone about ten years earlier during the Crimean War and again about a decade later. However, the nationalistic factor that played a major role in the revolt of the late 1930s was more of a pre-playing the future than a traditional event.

This chapter has focused attention on the agrarian factors and other socio-economic aspects of the revolt that are less well known than the nationalistic ones. From the present perspective, in retrospect, it is doubtful if the revolt was justified because, as demonstrated in this chapter, the Mandate government was genuinely interested in easing the tax burden that had been the main cause of most previous outbreaks.

The insistence of the Mandate administration on using the concept of *carrying capacity* as a central policy pillar can retrospectively be viewed as a short-sighted and misdirected policy because it stood in the way of wider long-term goals of enhancing agricultural development. However, despite its presumed short-sightedness, the policy was not without advantages. It was probably quite suitable for the economic conditions of Palestine during the inter-war period. The basic supposition of the British officials was that the process of transition from traditional to modern agriculture would eventually come about, but that it would be very long and slow. Therefore, they insisted on finding solutions for the interim periods.

Some onus can also be placed on the Jewish population that did not pay enough attention to the *fallah*'s plight during the early 1930s. It should be noted, however, that Avraham Granovsky (Granot), Arthur Ruppin and other Jewish leaders were aware of these needs, and suggested that the government increase its investment in the rural Arab economy. But most Jews were concerned with the need to employ the large number of Jewish *olim* (immigrants) and particularly the refugees from Nazi horrors who were denied entrance to the United States and most other Western countries. Another difficulty that strained Jewish-Arab relationships was the ideological principle, especially among kibbutz members and other rural settlers who insisted on strict self-employment and self-management of their farms. This ruling was written into the contracts that the settlers had to sign. The settlers were criticized for refusing to employ Arabs. In retrospect, a greater concern for the *fallah*'s plight might have improved Jewish-Arab relations also in the political realm.

Notes

1. See Bayliss-Smith for a very useful and detailed survey of this issue. See also, among others, Notestein; Porter.
2. Kark and Oren-Nordheim provided a detailed description of the economy of Jerusalem's periphery during the Mandate period. See especially pp. 286-293.
3. Genesis 13:6. The English translations vary in the wordings they use for conveying this concept.
4. See Bayliss-Smith. Allan suggested the use of an ecological criterion for measuring carrying capacity, that is, finding the point that the yields of a given land area start to decline. This approach negates that of Boserup (see below), and has not been adopted by demographers or other Social Studies researchers.
5. Galbraith summed up this point in the following manner: "Changing technology … alters progressively and radically what can be obtained from a given supply of factors. But there is no way by which this intelligence can be developed at length in a text book. So economic instruction concedes the important, and then discusses the unimportant." Galbraith, note on p. 46.

6. The most relevant can be found in Hope-Simpson; Johnson and Crosbie; French.
7. Hope-Simpson.
8. Great Britain, Colonial Office, 733/185/77072 Johnson and Crosbie Report, pp. 6-39. The demographic data reported here are based on the official vital statistics. However, some of the interviewed villagers quoted figures that were about 9 percent higher.
9. See Schultz, pp. 90-94, on "Penny Capitalism." See also Nadan, *Palestinian Peasant*, e.g., pp. 187-188.
10. Porter, and see Netting, p. 300, whose research is based on the "Peasantry Theory" developed by Chayanov; Boserup; and see also Elazari-Volcani, *Transition*; and Ruppin, *The Jews*, for analyses similar to Netting's. The ability of peasants to adjust their methods to their needs is still controversial. Like industrial technology, it has a limit, as global warming and various ecological disasters have recently demonstrated.
11. See Graham-Brown, p. 146. Johnson and Crosbie based their estimate on the principle of yearly deductions, but the assumption that the *fallah* was used to setting aside yearly funds for this purpose cannot be substantiated. See also Nadan, *Palestinian Peasant*, introduction and pp. 176-188, for a systematic discussion and criticism of Johnson and Crosbie's proposals.
12. Elazari-Volcani (Vilkansky), *Fallah's Farm*, and see Nadan, *Palestine Peasant*, pp.196-200.
13. Bayliss-Smith, pp. 65-68, also calculated the total population that could be sustained if the islanders decided to spend lesser energy on production and devote more time to enjoying leisure or on other activities rather than on production for subsistence alone. Another assumption that was tested was that the islanders wanted to spend a certain amount of their time for maintaining a surplus production (that varies from 10 to 150 percent above the subsistence needs), either for security against crop failure, for paying various taxes or other impositions, and for exchanging part of their crops for various non-essential goods and services. The various welfare expenditures would clearly result in reducing the population far below the maximum carrying capacity.
14. Clark and Haswell, pp. 58-59.
15. Clark and Haswell, pp. 77-78.
16. Clark and Haswell, pp. 62-68.
17. According to the 1858 Ottoman Land Law, which was also in effect during the Mandate period, such areas were defined as *mawat* (dead land). They were either rocky areas or too remote from the settlement (where a loud human voice could not be heard in the village). The villages also held a land type called *matruka* (public areas), which were available for the grazing of animals and for other purposes. At any rate, most animal husbandry did not compete with cultivated land. Baer, *Agrarian Relations*; Poliak; Granovsky, *Fiscal System*.
18. *Land per person* rather than *Person per land*. The denominator is *person* , because the purpose is to calculate the amount of land per person, not vice versa as in the more common formula which refers to the number of persons in a given land unit.
19. Firestone, "Crop Sharing."
20. A prominent rebellion leader was 'Azz a-Din al-Qasam (whose name was given about a half century later to a Hamas fighting unit). Although most of the Mandate's ordinances (the first was issued in 1920) proved to be ineffective, the government continued its efforts to limit the sales to the Zionists in order to protect the rights of the sharecroppers. To this end the Transfer of Agricultural Land Bill was issued

in 1929, followed one year later by Passfield's White Paper. However, the most sweeping prohibition on land purchase was the White Paper of 1939 which prohibited Jewish purchases in most regions of Palestine. The paper was postponed from 1936 to 1939 because of the Arab Revolt of 1936-1939. See: Ofer, pp. 291-292; Porath, *Rebellion*, p. 129; see also Stein, "Rights of Sharecroppers," pp. 69-70; Stein, *The Land Question*; Stein, "Rural Change," pp. 154, 163. Relevant reports on this subject include: Palestine, Administrative Report, 1922, pp. 42, 47, 73-75; Files of the Great Britain Colonial Office: C.O. 733/224/97270/1, Chancellor to Shakesborough, Document Paper 1, 4.2.1930; C.O. 733/192/77304, Chancellor to Passfield, 29.3.1930; C.O. 733/207/87275, Telegram from the High Commissioner to the Settlement Secretary, 25.5.1931; C.O. 722/224/97270, Telegram from the High Commissioner to the Settlement Secretary, 10.8.1932.

21. Deed of Sale between Najib Bey Sursouk and Yehoshua Hankin, signed on November 30, 1929, in Ein-Harod-Tel-Yosef Museum.

22. Great Britain, Colonial Office, 733/185/77072. In the opinion of the report's authors, hardly any uncultivated land remained in Palestine other than in the Beer-Sheva region, the Jordan Valley and the Hula Basin. They felt that agricultural development of the remaining cultivable areas would require too much capital investment, since it would entail a large investment to improve water sources and to conduct the water over large distances, in order to convert rain-fed farming to artificially irrigated agriculture. The British government downplayed the peasants' ability to adopt intensive farming methods. See Johnson and Crosbie, Report, pp. 57-58; Report of the Royal Commission (Peel Report), p. 255; Reichman, Katz and Paz. To these factors, the growth of Arab nationalism that succeeded in thwarting land purchases and even pressured the British government to legislate against the sale of land, should be added.

23. Kimmerling, table on p. 23. The Jewish leadership claimed that these assertions were attributable to the hostile attitude of British government officials towards Zionism, but even Arthur Ruppin, who was in charge of Zionist land acquisition, acknowledged in January 1930, in his letter to Chaim Weizmann, the president of the World Zionist Organization, that it had become extremely difficult to obtain uncultivated or unused land reserves in the country.

24. Biger, p. 75.

25. Johnson and Crosbie, Report, C.O. 733/185/77072, title page.

26. Johnson and Crosbie argued that before the reform the peasants paid higher taxes than city residents. To rectify this distortion it was recommended that the tax on winter harvests be reduced by 10 to 5 percent. Horowitz, *The Economy*, pp. 170-171; Abramowitz and Gelfat, pp. 40-43; Horowitz and Hinden, pp. 204-206; also Stein, "Political Implication," pp. 145-149; see also C.O. 733/267/37560, Report of Committee for Tax Reform, Paper 3, 14.5.1934; Draft of tax reform signed by the General Advocate, 8.12.1934, pp. 1215-1240 and other documents in this file.

27. Hadawi, pp. 48-50.

28. Granovsky, *Tax System*, p. 347. The 5 percent rate was adopted by the government.

29. Granovsky, *Fiscal System*, p. 189; Gross and Metzer, pp. 193-197, 203, 307; Reuveni, pp. 79-84; Gavish, p. 193.

30. Palestine, Village Statistics, 1945. This publication is extensively used below.

31. According to the Village Statistics, 1945, Sheet 3, Arabs and Jews devoted approximately the same amount of land to citrus cultivation. Jewish Agency data indicate that the majority of Arab orchards were planted by the villagers themselves rather than by wealthy landowners. Jewish Agency for Palestine, Memorandum; Giladi, p.

401. Changes in citrus cultivation during the British Mandate have been discussed in several studies, for example Tolkovski; Rokach; Horin.

32. Information on the Palestinian economy in the inter-war period is found in: Horowitz, pp. 170-171; Abromowitz and Gelfat, pp. 40-43; Stein, "Rural Change," pp. 145-149. See also Kamen.

33. Village Statistics, 1945; Due to the vast time difference between 1871 and 1945 (approximately seventy-five years), it is quite possible that the process outlined here was not gradual or continuous. One of sets compared the data for 1945 with those of 1871 and 1922. It referred to per capita remaining farmland and its uses.

   This analysis dealt exclusively with the Arab data. Another table focused on Arab and Jewish properties in a separate table for 1945 that compared Arab and Jewish per capita farmland.

34. Ruppin, *Thirty*, pp.1-8; reprinted in Reichman, *Foothold*, pp. 138-144. See also Amit, Project; Amit, Creator, where we read that a similar idea was suggested for the eastern Lower Galilee by Kalvariski. The unusual settlement pattern of the Dura area was largely the result of its semi-arid environment that separated the core highland settlement from its satellites.

35. The Ottoman government had also attempted to develop this area by declaring it *jiftlik* (estate) and the Sultan took it over as his own estate until 1908 (when the Young Turks deposed him). The Ottomans, however, did nothing to change this area's conditions.

36. See Nadan, *Palestinian Peasant*, pp. 83-86, for an analysis based on specific crops. He concluded that the Jewish impact was greater. He also states, however, that there is a difference between actual land use and potential yields.

37. Citrus orchards in the Arab sector should be the subject of a separate discussion, but according to Village Statistics data from 1945, sheet 3, Arabs and Jews devoted approximately the same amount of land to citrus farming. In 1946, before the establishment of the State, Arab orchard areas outnumbered those of the Jews. The Arabs had 13,000 ha compared to the Jewish 12,800 ha. See Giladi, p. 401. Changes in citrus farming during the British Mandate are discussed in several studies, e.g., Horin.

38. For further information see Grossman, "Arab Settlement Process in Ottoman Times."

39. The Arab natural growth rate in 1935 was 26.5 per 1000, Boneh, p. 25; See Johnson and Crosbie, pp. 57-58; Ruppin, *Thirty*, p. 381.

40. Porath, *Rebellion*, pp. 52-53.

41. Porath, *Rebellion*, pp. 52-53.

42. Johnson and Crosbie, pp. 57-58.

43. See Kamen, pp. 41-56.

7

Conclusions and Summary of the Main Issues

The *Fallah* and the Jewish Rural Settlement

Palestine was clearly not entirely empty during the nineteenth century. Except for the southern Negev no location was totally devoid of inhabitants. Population density, however, was far from uniform. The purpose of this book was to evaluate the density of each of the regions as accurately as possible, to check the reliability of the source material and to explain the background of disparities among the regions. The conclusion drawn from this analysis is that the disparity between the sparsely inhabited regions and those more densely populated was a larger than expected.

Demographically, the 1871-72 rural Arab population was estimated to be between 223,005 and 267,606. The higher estimate refers to the total household data multiplied by six, and to the lower one, when it is multiplied by five. It is reasonable that the number lies somewhere between these two results (i.e., between 223,005 and 267,606). The mean between the two, 245,305, may be selected, but the higher estimate is more likely, because my study of neighboring villages and studies of other researchers preferred it over any other multiplier, where the number of households and the number of their members (or only males) were directly counted.

The demographic processes that account for the population distribution and for the regional demographic differences are rooted in a complex array of factors. Natural and man-made circumstances occasionally led to unexpected disasters or to devastating hostilities. The impact of daily life, the socio-economic system, and agrarian practices also contributed to the conditions that prevailed during the nineteenth and the early twentieth centuries. These subjects were discussed in chapter 1, though they cropped up again in other parts of the book. One of the main findings of the introductory chapter is that population instability was largely the result of recurring combinations of natural and man-made disasters. The most vulnerable regions were those where sparse population and erratic settlement were endemic.

The demographic analysis reveals that there was a rising rate of population growth in the late nineteenth century. This was partly the result of migration, but it was also made possible by the introduction of modern sanitation and the establishment of health and welfare facilities. Despite these improvements, the economic situation of most of the rural population did not change materially. Heavy reliance on agriculture brought about an expansion of land under cultivation,

There are differences of opinion regarding the timing of the turnaround in economic development. However, by the last quarter of the nineteenth century Palestine was involved in international trade, and diverse businesses and commercial banks in Jerusalem and the coastal towns had been established. Even though the development enriched some urban dwellers, especially those who were in any case members of the upper economic classes, the modernization process hardly touched the *fallah* (peasant, literally tiller). In fact, the peasants' condition actually deteriorated because of the 1858 Land Code that resulted in transferring the title to the land to urban merchants and other absentee landowners. These people were able to exploit the ignorance of the *fallaheen* who gave up their right to register the land because they were fearful that registration would entail increased taxation. Some of the landlords used more "sophisticated" methods like offering to free the farmers' children from military service in return for the land title, or simply force and deception.

The Jewish settlers ultimately gained from this situation because it afforded them the opportunity to purchase considerable blocks of property from absentee landlords. The purchases, however, were usually followed by evicting sharecroppers who lived on the land. Despite the fact that the evicted sharecroppers were compensated, this became a thorny issue during the British Mandate.

In some areas the low prices offered for the land reflected the soils' low quality, rockiness or other inadequate resources. Additional factors that accounted for the relative attractiveness of the land were financial crises that forced some landlords to sell their properties, and clearly, the increasing opportunities for profit.

The changing political climate eventually complicated the economic equation, but the early Jewish settlement pattern that was established during the First and Second *Aliyot* (migration waves), between 1882 and 1914, lasted throughout the British Mandate era, and eventually emerged as the backbone of Israel's territory.

The *Fallah* and the Bedouin

The book's focus was on the *fallaheen*. The Bedouin were not thoroughly discussed, but their involvement in various aspects of Palestinian life was often mentioned. Naturally, the correlation between the presence of Bedouin and the low-density of *fallaheen* population seems to be quite rational, but it has to be stressed that this was related to the nature of the Bedouin survival strategy. They did not need extensive land areas for their flocks.

There is no question that the Bedouin-government relations were fraught with many difficulties: violence, disobedience, refusal to pay taxes, and even outright rebellion, but the impact of this tension on the settled rural people was more complex. The prevailing opinion that this involved "one way" violence and had solely negative impacts on the farmers is subject to dispute.

The effect of resource marginality cannot be completely isolated. There was also a certain symbiosis rather than competition between the *fallaheen* and the Bedouin. True, the Bedouin raids on their neighbors were well documented in the nineteenth century by scholars and certain travelers. The damage they inflicted was often devastating. During periods of drought, the farm population was impoverished. To alleviate their own suffering, the Bedouin would attack their neighbors, thereby intensifying the hardship of the *fallaheen*. The Bedouin were blamed for the insecure conditions and their instability.

Since the Bedouin were left out of the population counts during the 1870s, the calculation regarding the population geography that is the basis of the 1871/72 Yearbook is not complete and must be so treated. The policy of the British Mandate was completely different from that which had preceded it. The most conspicuous example of a "pro-Bedouin" approach was in 1921, when the *jiftlik* (Sultan's estates) lands that had been taken from the Bedouin, were returned to them. But a serious attempt to count them had to wait for the 1931 census. Even so, most of Bedouin pastures in the Negev were excluded from title registration project conducted by the Mandate authorities. Consequently the legal status of their holdings remained unclear.

Mobility and low population density were perhaps the most important causes for the failure of the Ottoman government to cope with the Bedouin and for their failure to include them in the official demographic reports. The statistical publications from the end of the Ottoman period gradually began to include partial data on the Bedouin, but the Negev population was still largely unrecorded.

Moslem Migrants and Jewish Settlement Expansion

The Egyptian migration and their settlement model were not very different from the Jewish one. They were the most numerous Muslim group. There were, in fact, several waves of their migrations. Some were the consequence of the political situation, when refuge was sought from harsh rulers—rising taxes, forced labor or conscription—and some were the consequence of poverty or natural disasters, such as hunger and epidemics. One of the most striking events in this series occurred at the close of the eighteenth century, when famine in Egypt brought about a vast migration wave to Palestine.

But the wave that left its greatest demographic mark on Palestine was the one that occurred between 1829 and 1841, during the rule of Muhammad Ali and his son Ibrahim Pasha, whom he appointed as governor of Syria and Palestine. The total number, comprised of Egyptian army deserters, refugees and various displaced persons, reached altogether tens of thousands. After the Egyptian retreat of 1840/41, the Egyptian migrants settled in areas of the Negev, the Sharon Plain and the hilly area that linked it to the Jezre'el Plain, and other parts of Palestine. These areas were more sparsely populated before 1870. It can reasonably be assumed that this wave reduced, to some extent, the disparity in density between the Palestinian heartland and the rest of the country.

Other waves of immigration from various Muslim countries brought many refugees to the area, especially between 1855 and 1885. They were mainly Caucasians (Circassians), Bosnians and Algerians who were refugees from France or other European powers. Unlike the Egyptians, who had to make do with "leftovers," they were granted land in the Lower Galilee and the northern Sharon, though their demographic influence on western Palestine was limited in comparison with that of the Egyptian migrants. Before the onset of the Jewish rural settlement the low-density areas had been settled mainly as a result of internal and external migrations. Migrations of this kind, whether as a result of government persecution or economic concerns, are not unique to Palestine. The information obtained from the variety of sources corroborates the

1288 Yearbook data about the existence of regional disparities, especially between the crowded mountainous zones and the sparsely populated plains. This generalization overlooks, however, several prominent outstanding exceptions. The Gaza (Philistia), the Acre and the Carmel coasts were included among the densely settled zones, while some mountain zones (parts of the Hebron and Carmel mountains) had temporary or intermittent settlements that functioned only as seasonal shelters. Like the areas of the Jewish N-shaped zone, they attracted some migrants. Their population composition was, therefore, unstable and the land tended to change hands at a faster rate than in other areas.

The Bosnians, Circassians, and Algerians somewhat reduced the supply of potential land available for Jewish rural settlement, but not as much as the Egyptian settlers did. The Jewish post-1882 rural expansion followed, broadly, the Egyptian model. Like them they had to satisfy themselves with the marginal lands that were still available. But, unlike the Egyptian settlements, the Jewish settlements were mostly planned. Accessibility to the main Jewish towns and, later, security and contiguity with already existing Jewish territories were important considerations for site and location. A conspicuous outcome of this policy is the Ruha Heights which were settled by Jews after the 1937 revolt to provide a "bridge" between Jewish holdings in the Sharon with Ruha and the Jezre'el Plain.

The legal status of the potential settlement sites was also closely examined. Large-scale purchases of potentially fertile land, as in the case of the Jezre'el Plain, were available in the 1920s, but their supply was an exception rather than the rule. Such purchases were made possible mainly because the existing absentee landowners experienced financial difficulties. The model was described by a leading land purchaser of the Jewish National Fund (JNF) as an oil blot that spread from a pole. This model is similar to "growth pole" theory.[1]

The second chapter reviews some of the major migrations that took place in the nineteenth century, but excludes the Jewish ones. The Jews had four towns that had been recognized as Jewish holy places for many centuries: Safad, Tiberias, Hebron, and Jerusalem. Each of them had an important Jewish community, but during the nineteenth century only two of them functioned as growth poles for the young people whose motive was the revival of agriculture. The other two were replaced by two other towns: Jaffa and Haifa. This "replacement" also changed the original attracting factor: economy rather than religion. Both poles established the foundation of rural settlements in areas that had a fairly high land supply but low population. Hebron and Jerusalem faced an opposite condition: low supply and high Arab density, but the reasons were actually more complex; and these two areas were left out of the spreading Jewish footholds. Jaffa became the leading center because of its port and because it provided the best highway to Jerusalem. The immediate vicinity of Jerusalem was consequently purchased by Jews mostly for residential purposes.

The fate of Hebron Jews was tragic. The Jewish population was relatively small and isolated from the protection of European consular missions and other modern facilities. In 1929, its Jewish community was attacked and most of its members were massacred by an incited mob. This pogrom brought an end to Hebron's old Jewish community. This attack was followed by a growth of animosity that culminated in the late 1930s by the Arab rebellion and by the White Paper of 1939.

The Demographic Factors and Their Impacts

The demographic development of Palestine was influenced by natural disasters, some of which were particularly destructive. One of the worst ones was the earthquake of January 1837 that destroyed Galilee villages and claimed thousands of lives in Safad and Tiberias. High mortality was also endemic during years of heavy droughts, pests and disease. Other natural calamities (swarms of locusts, ground mice, plagues, cholera and other epidemics) occurred frequently.

Man-made disasters only exacerbated the natural ones: wars, insecurity of men and material, abusive taxation policies and forced military conscription targeted family food security. The economic and demographic consequences of this situation were grave, not only because of direct damage from invasion or war losses, but also because of the dearth of capable young workers and destruction of crop yields. Crops and farm animals were neglected, leaving impoverished *fallaheen* devoid of the most vital food supplies. The wars in the Crimea, the Balkans and World War I decimated the population and increased the subsistence pressure on the *fallah* economy.

The persistent correlation between man-made and natural disasters, especially in the arid and semi-arid areas where sharp fluctuations in precipitation were normal, doubled the harsh food instability and was exacerbated by incursions of nomadic tribes that took advantage of government weakness.

The *fallaheen* were not always the victims of violence. They used force against the government and against their *fallaheen* opponents, and in many cases they formed alliances with their Bedouin neighbors to fight against other *fallaheen.*

Local wars were fought over vital resources such as water and cropland. But the widespread series of violence known as the *Qais-Yaman* wars were mostly of local nature, which resulted from inter- or intra-village struggles for family dominance. Their origin is obscure, but was probably rooted in historical tribal conflicts that began in the Arabian Desert.

The factors influencing population distribution and density were quite varied, but the agricultural resources were a major factor. The areas of Palestine most susceptible to droughts were in the Negev, but the Jordan Valley and the plateaus of the eastern Lower Galilee were also affected. In these areas, only near the few copious springs and streams was it possible to cultivate the land. Such areas were found in Jericho and Beisan (Beit She'an), but even there the major land use was pastoral herding.

The other resource-deficient areas were the rocky fields of many parts of the mountains, the swamps, the dunes and the poor red sands of the Sharon. These areas were usually sparsely populated and settled mostly by nomadic tribes. In the Sharon, as in the Jezre'el Plain, there were many poorly drained, swampy zones. But much of the Sharon also had many excessively drained sandy soils, which yielded low grain crops and where crop failure was common after short dry spells. The solution came only when, in the early 1920s, petroleum-powered pumps allowed the use of irrigation, and the low-yielding wheat and barley fields were replaced by citrus groves. This revolutionized land use converted the formerly sparsely settled Bedouin areas into densely settled land that eventually became the rural core of Israel.

The Agrarian System and Man/Land Relationships

Another question addressed in this book, primarily in chapter 6, was: To what extent did the Jewish settlement during the British Mandate period have a negative effect on the *fallah*'s means of livelihood? In order to answer this question, the discussion was based principally on an analysis of population distribution at the beginning and at the end of the Mandate, correlated with land utilization data. The Village Statistics for April 1945 provided the necessary basic geographic and demographic data for this purpose. The population data which were published in 1871-72 and those of 1922 were then charted. The analysis of these data indicates that the per capita agricultural land was drastically reduced during the seventy-five years that elapsed from 1870 to 1945, but the main areas of land shortage were in the densely settled Arab mountain zones, though a pronounced reduction was also encountered in the Sharon and part of the northern Jezre'el Plain. These findings do not confirm the view that the Jewish purchases were responsible for depriving the local Arabs of their vital land resources.

The regional variation in carrying capacity is a function of various added factors, such as access to urban centers, special local resources or local customs and religion. Most regions share the same factors, though religious affiliation affected the exposure to Western life modes and to education, both of which affect economic opportunity.

Common to all, or almost so, was the historical heritage—the Ottoman and the British reigns and their cultural impacts. The taxation systems had a profound effect on rural life, and may also have been partly responsible for the anti-Jewish disturbances during the Mandate period. The fiscal policy was also inseparable from specific land tenure practices and the land use systems. The negative impact of the 1858 Land Code on the *fallaheen* and on the Bedouin has also been linked in a variety of ways to the taxation policy. The most obvious example was the way the *effendis* utilized the *fallaheen*'s fear that registration was linked to tax hikes. Exploiting this apprehension, the absentee landowners convinced the farmers to transfer their land rights to them.

The rules and the practices that govern land use rights cannot be considered merely in legal terms. Even though in Palestine, as in many other peasant systems, the rules were anchored in tradition and religious law, they were an integral part of the communal and socio-economic system that evolved to manage the community's subsistence agriculture even though the path of the specific evolutionary process is often obscure. Such is the Palestinian communal land possession (*musha' al-balad*; literally: town or village commons) system. Its exact origin and relation to demography is uncertain, but there are a number of indications that it was the result, and not the cause, of the sparse population that accompanied the endemic instability of rural Palestine during most of Ottoman rule. There is also a hypothesis that it was linked to the prevailing taxation system that was imposed collectively on the village communities, forcing the farmers to organize in order to cope with it. The village-based *musha'* system facilitated the job of the tax farmers, who bought the right of collection by pre-paying an agreed amount.

Whatever the origin of the *musha'* there is general agreement that its purpose was functional and certainly not religious. It provided answers to pressing needs such as cooperating for vital financial purposes or for redistributing vacated land that had been left unused. It could also have been used to coordinate farm tasks in order to ensure that the harvest would not be overrun by Bedouin. Those who hold a positive view about it acknowledge that it no longer fulfilled its original functional role, but its exact original purpose is also subject to disagreement. The official policies of the Ottoman and the British alike were, however, clearly anti-*musha'*. The 1858 Land Code did not recognize collective rights, a fact generally interpreted as intended to promote land privatization. Even so, the *musha'* system continued to exist well into the post-Ottoman period.

A less controversial question pertains to the influence of the absentee landlords and their impact on the sharecroppers that the former employed on their estates. In keeping with *Shari'a* law, the landlords were entitled to three quarters of the harvested crops, but they also imposed added charges and forced services (including the taxation fees) that reduced their tenants' shares to no more than one fifth of the harvest. Its negative impact on the carrying capacity is thus undisputed.

The sharecroppers' economic condition deteriorated during the early 1930s at least in part as a result of a series of droughts and pest infestations. The Arab nationalists blamed their plight on the Jews and the British government, although the latter had persistently attempted to improve the sharecroppers' lot. The small landholders were also affected by the deteriorating economic conditions, and by 1936 the situation led to a revolt that lasted for three years. The Jewish position was that *fallah* migration to the city would solve the economic problem of their displacement. An analysis of the agrarian situation, and the relatively small number of persons who had been found eligible for a government-sponsored resettlement project, gave credence to this claim. The Arabs were obviously unconvinced, and their anti-Zionist drive eventually led, as the Second World War approached, to a government prohibition on Jewish land acquisition in most of Palestine, and to a drastic limitation of the Jewish immigration quota. The Arab plight was thus assuaged by a policy that shifted the problem, with dire consequences, to the Jews who were trying to escape from the Nazi slaughterhouse and death factories. The war actually benefited the *fallaheen* because of the rising demand for their food products.

An analysis of the temporal changes in the agricultural land reserves since about 1870 presents a clear picture: the declining size of the *fallaheen*'s per capita plots can be explained mainly by rapid and accelerating population growth. This process was accompanied by an intensification of agricultural production. The distribution of agricultural land per person reinforces this conclusion. It shows that the influence of Jewish settlement on the supply of *fallaheen* land was relatively minor. It was most clearly in evidence in the margins of the Jezre'el Plain and the Sharon Plain, both formerly inhabited mainly by Bedouin. Their most notable per capita declines were in the mountainous areas, especially in western and northern Samaria.

Methodological Issues

It became apparent during the research that despite the methodological problems, a comparison between the quantitative regional data and the data based on non-quantitative studies was sufficiently conclusive to give credence to population records of the official government reports. The descriptive sources were, for the most part, written by well known and reputable researchers, and they present accurate information on many essential facts regarding Palestinian regions, communities, and historical background. Most researchers, and even many less professional travelers' itinerary diaries and reports, were able to present important facts regarding agricultural resources and their use.

A comparison of these sources with various other official ones offered valuable material for a verification of the quality of the 1288 records. The most valuable were specific surveys conducted in the 1870s, such as the British Palestine Exploration Fund (PEF) survey that was conducted during the 1870s and the Ottoman survey of the Sun Lands (i.e., uncultivated or neglected lands exposed to the sun), that were also conducted around the same time (the early 1870s). The Schumacher survey of the mid-1880s and the Schick survey of the early 1890s (see chapter 3) were also helpful. A later government-sponsored, country-wide survey published in the years 1915-1917 by Bahjat and Tamimi also proved fairly reliable, though of lesser comparative value because of its late publication date. It contained mostly descriptive information but also some quantitative data and discussion pertaining to the last phase of Ottoman rule in Palestine. Much of the other official data were, however, of lesser value for the specific needs of the present study.

The attempt to quantify density data for the early 1870s in different parts of Palestine required me to relate extensively to methodological issues arising from the character of these sources. I therefore devoted considerable space throughout this book (especially chapters 3 and 4) to this end. My purpose was to define the spatial distribution of the rural population, delineate the different areas of density, and map them according to the Syrian Yearbook published in H 1288 (1871-72). The effort that I devoted to mapping and recording village by village data made it possible to compare the 1871-72 records with those of the 1922 census. However, it was necessary to adopt constant (fixed) geographical boundaries in order to match the two sources. This was done by adjusting the 1922 boundaries to those of 1871-72.

The results of this comparison reveal that there was a fairly high link to sparsely-populated regions and the Jewish rural settlement zone (which is customarily described as a continuous N-shaped territory). This positive correlation tends to verify the H 1288 Yearbook's data that showed that the areas later settled by Jews had a low rural Arab population. The density of this area was found to be, at most (assuming six persons per household c.1870), only ten persons per square kilometer compared with an average population density of about twenty-nine persons per square kilometer in the major Arab-inhabited areas. This exercise, and comparisons with other nineteenth century sources, provided convincing evidence that the quality of the H 1288 Yearbook's data is acceptable.

Final Observations

My findings reveal that approximately ten years before the First *Aliyah* most regions which comprised the area that later became the Jewish settlement zone were sparsely populated. My analysis of the agricultural density levels lead to another important conclusion: There is no concrete proof that Jewish land purchases were the main cause for the growing agricultural pressure on the Arab settlement zones. The reduced per capita cultivable land reserves have to be attributed, rather, mainly to the high demographic growth rate that was partly achieved by migration and settlement of non-Jews. Thirdly, the question posed in the opening sentences of chapter 3, whether the emptiness of Palestine referred to uncivilized people or the absence of actual people may be answered by stating that part of Palestine was sparsely populated, but certainly not empty. The nineteenth-century European travelers and the Zionists did not distort reality by describing Palestine the way they did. They wrote what they saw, without any cultural or other purpose in mind.

The conclusion that Jewish settlement turned to areas of low rather than dense population fits George Kingsley Zipf's "Principle of Least Effort."[2] As the principle implies, the Zionist settlement process was characterized by moving into places where there was the least resistance. As is true of other models, some details may not precisely fit the principle, but for the general outlines of the low density, N-shaped zone,

Jewish settlement closely followed the least effort principle, or the least resistance pattern.

Finally, some practical implications of the process are also called for. On the basis of remarks made by prominent members of the Zionist movement, it is clear that they understood the geographical consequences of the purchases, even during the phases that preceded the establishment of formal settling institutions. Their policies were manifest in the adoption of an approach that largely conformed to the Principle of Least Effort. It is hard to attribute any definite political planning to the settlers of the First *Aliyah*, but though they lacked even the most basic information with which to choose between alternatives, they were the creators of the incipient settled Jewish territory and even determined the broad perimeters of the Jewish settlement zone that in time became the State of Israel.

This has an additional important ramification: It is logical to assume that the rational path charted by Ruppin, Kalvarisky and other early Jewish leaders should also be followed today. These initial land purchasing leaders understood that only a geographically compact territory could provide the necessary conditions for establishment of a national home that would have a chance to have a Jewish majority. Ruppin's objective seems to have been attainable under conditions existing in the early twentieth century, since the settlements were then concentrated in areas of low population density.

Although today's demographic situation is different, there is still a logical basis for settlement based on consolidated blocks rather than scattered fragments lacking both demographic strength and proper security.[3] The outcome of the present day settlement process, however, is the reverse of what Ruppin had in mind a century ago. Instead of a coherent, well defined territory, the present-day settlers have advocated a pattern that is "gerrymandered," devoid of clearly defined borders, and located in the densest non-Jewish parts of the area that was called Palestine. The ideologues of our generation, who pretend to be the present-day Zionists, should acquaint themselves with genuine Zionist values and with the real historical-demographic processes that shaped the Jewish N-shaped territory of Israel. It is not enough to make do with a selective and superficial imitation of ideas.

In conclusion, casting its shadow over this entire book is the significance of current demographic processes for the Arabs of Palestine. The question of the distribution and its causes was discussed here in some detail, but the spatial pattern has many ramifications also for the future. Even if the questions presented at the opening of chapter 1 were not unequivocally answered, it appears that demography provides not only the most logical answers to the issues presented in this book, but also describes the frustrations that are likely to be the portent for the future. During the nineteenth century the difficulties experienced by the rural population were a result of slow population growth and the consequent low population density in substantial parts of the Palestine. The economic and political difficulties of the early twenty-first century stem from rapid natural increase and consequent high population density. Under such conditions the Arab population throughout Palestine is incapable of supporting itself independently. The ensuing frustration is usually vented in anti-government and anti-Zionist attitudes, but it must be recognized that it is rooted in the internal structure of the Palestinian people. Their economic prosperity cannot be achieved without proper family planning that allows each household to invest sufficient resources in educating and training the coming generation for their proper place in the dynamic society of the new century. There is no alternative route for achieving this goal.

Notes

1. Weitz; as is widely known, a fairly similar model was published by F. Perroux about a half century later.
2. See Zipf.
3. The twenty first century's Israeli public is apparently not familiar with Ruppin's writings. During a recent radio broadcast, a well known journalist, identified with the modern settlement movement in Judea and Samaria, "quoted" Ruppin as if his opinion were the opposite of what has been set out here.

Bibliography

Books, Articles, and Unpublished Papers

Abbasi, Mustafa, "From Algeria to Palestine: The Algerian Community in the Galilee from the Late Ottoman Period until 1948," *Magreb Review* 28 (2003), pp. 41-59.

Abir, Mordechai, "Local Leadership and Early Reforms in Palestine," Moshe Ma'oz (ed.), *Studies on Palestine during the Ottoman Period,* Jerusalem: Magnes Press, 1975, pp. 284-310.

Abramowitz, Z. and Gelfat, Y., *The Arab Economy in Palestine and in the Countries of the Middle East,* Ein Harod: Hakibbutz Hameuhad, 1943/44 (Hebrew).

Abramson, Albert, "An Aspect of Village Life in Palestine," *Palestine Post,* 6.7.1937.

Agmon, Iris, "Foreign Trade as a Catalyst of Change in the Arab Economy in Palestine (1897-1914)," *Cathedra* 41 (1986), pp. 107-132 (Hebrew).

Aktan, Resat, "Agricultural Policy of Turkey," Charles Issawi (ed.), *The Economic History of the Middle East 1800-1914: A Book of Readings*, Chicago: University of Chicago Press, 1966, pp. 108-113.

Amiran, David H.K., "Dura: A Portrait of the Settlements on the Bedouin Frontier," *Bulletin of the Society for Research of Eretz-Israel and Its Antiquities* 14 (1948/49), pp. 29-37 (Hebrew).

Amit, Irit, "Projects for the Settlement of Jews in the Sanjak of Acre (1902-1903)," *Cathedra* 49 (1988), pp. 103-116 (Hebrew with English abstract).

Amit, Irit, "Creator of Jewish Settlement in the Eastern Lower Galilee," *Yahadut Zemanenu (Contemporary Jewry)* 5 (1989), pp. 137-152 (Hebrew).

al-'Araf, 'Araf, *Bedouin Tribes in the Beer-Sheba District*, Trans. from Arabic to Hebrew by Menahem Kapliuk, Tel Aviv: Bustani, 1935 (Hebrew).

Asaf, Michael, *The History of the Awakening of the Arabs in Palestine and Their Desertion*, Tel Aviv: Dvir, 1967 (Hebrew).

Ashkenazi, Tuvia, *The Tents of Kedar, From the Yarkon to the Carmel*, London: Kedem, 1932 (Hebrew).

Atran, Scott, "Hamula Organization and Musha'a Tenure in Palestine," *Man* 21 (1986), pp. 271-295.

Avitzur, Shmuel, *The Palestinian Plow, Its History and Development*, Tel Aviv: Hasadeh, 1964/65 (Hebrew).

Avitzur, Shmuel, "Watermelons in the Economy of Palestine until the Establishment of the State," *Moravia* 1 (1974/75), pp. 80-91 (Hebrew).

Avitzur, Shmuel, *Daily Life in Palestine in the Nineteenth Century*, Jerusalem: Rubenstein, 1975/76 (Hebrew).

Avitzur, Shmuel, *Man and his Work, Historical Atlas of Tools & Workshops in the Holy Land*, Jerusalem: Carta, 1976 (Hebrew).

Avitzur, Shmuel, *Changes in the Agriculture of Palestine, 1875-1975*, Tel Aviv: Milo, 1977 (Hebrew).

Avitzur, Shmuel, *The Banks of the Yarkon River (1947)*, Tel Aviv: Dvir, 1980.

Avitzur, Shmuel, "The Wool Weaving Industry in Safad and its Termination," Avshalom Shmueli, Arnon Soffer and Nurit Kliot (eds.), *The Lands of Galilee*, 2 vols., Haifa: University of Haifa, 1983, I, pp. 353-360 (Hebrew).

Avitzur, Shmuel and Shavit, Ya'akov, "The Face of Palestine and Its Population, Settlements and Economy," Ya'akov Shavit (ed.), Vol. VIII of *The History of Eretz Israel*, Yehoshua Ben-Arieh and Yisrael Bartal (eds.), *The Last Phase of Ottoman Rule (1799-1917)*, Jerusalem: Keter, 1983, pp. 48-67 (Hebrew).

Avneri, Arieh L., *Jewish Settlement and the Assertion of Eviction* (1878-1978), Tel Aviv: Hakibbutz Hameuhad, 1979/80 (Hebrew).

Baer, Gabriel, *The History of Agrarian Relations in the Middle East, 1800-1970*, Tel Aviv: Hakibbutz Hameuhad, 1971 (Hebrew).

Baer, Gabriel, *Fallah and Townsman in the Middle East*, London: Frank Cass, 1982.

Bahjat, Muhammad B. and Tamimi, Muhammad R., *Vilayet Beirut,* (a) *The Southern Part,* Beirut: Vilayet Matba'a (Turkish ed.), H 1335 (1916/17); (b) *The Northern Part, Beirut:* Vilayet Matba'a (Turkish ed.), H 1336 (1917/18).

Bailey, Clinton, "The Negev in the Nineteenth Century: Reconstructing History from Bedouin Oral Traditions," *Asian and African Studies* 14 (1980), pp. 35-80.

Baldensperger, Phillip J., "The Immovable East," *Palestine Exploration Fund Quarterly Statement* 1906, pp. 190-197.

Baldensperger, Phillip J., *The Immovable East: Studies of the People and Customs of Palestine,* London: Pitman, 1913.

Bartal, Yisrael, *Travel Diary and Letters from Palestine from the 1830s*, Jerusalem: Yad Izhak Ben-Zvi, 1973/74 (Hebrew).

Bartal, Yisrael, "The Rise of the Old Community and Its Settlement Distribution," Ya'akov Shavit (ed.), , Vol. VIII of *The History of Eretz Israel*, Yehoshua Ben-Arieh and Yisrael Bartal (eds.), *The Last Phase of Ottoman Rule (1799-1917)*, Jerusalem: Keter, 1983, pp. 197-218 (Hebrew).

Bartal, Yisrael, "George Gawler's Plan for Jewish Settlement in the 1840s: The Geographical Perspective," Ruth Kark (ed.), *Redemption of the Land of Eretz-Israel*, Jerusalem: Yad Izhak Ben-Zvi, 1990, pp. 51-63 (Hebrew).

Bayliss-Smith, T. P., "Population Pressure, Resources and Welfare: Towards a More Realistic Measure of Carrying Capacity," H. C. Brookfield (ed.), *Population-Environment Relations in Tropical Islands: The Case of Fiji*, Canberra: UNESCO/UNFPA, 1980, pp. 61-91.

Ben-Arieh, Yehoshua, *The Central Jordan Valley: A Regional Geography of the Central Jordan Valley in Israel*, Tel Aviv: Hakibbutz Hameuchad, 1965 (Hebrew).

Ben-Arieh, Yehoshua, "The Population of the Large Towns in Palestine dur-
ing the First Eighty Years of the Nineteenth Century According to Western
Sources," Moshe Maoz, (ed.), *Studies on Palestine during the Ottoman
Period*, Jerusalem: Magnes Press, 1975, pp. 49-69.
Ben-Arieh, Yehoshua, "The Uniqueness of the Samarian Settlement System,"
Avshalom Shmueli, David Grossman and Rechavam Zeevy (eds.), *Judea
and Samaria, Studies in Settlement Geography*, II vols., Jerusalem: Canaan,
1977. II, pp. 383-387 (Hebrew).
Ben-Arieh, Yehoshua, "The Sanjak of Jerusalem in the 1870s," *Cathedra* 36,
(1985), pp. 73-122 (Hebrew).
Ben-Arieh, Yehoshua, "Size and Composition of the Population of Eretz-Israel:
Palestine in the 1870s," Paper presented at a colloquium on Palestine 1840-
1948: Population and Immigration, University of Haifa, 9-11., 1986.
Ben-Arieh, Yehoshua, "The Sanjak of Gaza (Including Jaffa and Ramla) in the
1870s," *Shalem* 5 (1986/87), pp. 139-187 (Hebrew).
Ben-Arieh, Yehoshua, "Manners and Custom s in Palestine as Perceived and Stud-
ied during the Nineteenth Century and until 1948," Yehoshua Ben-Arieh and
Elchanan Reiner (eds.), *Studies in the History of Eretz-Israel Presented to Yehuda
Ben-Porath*, Jerusalem: Yad Izhak Ben-Zvi, 2003, pp. 451-493 (Hebrew).
Ben-Arieh, Yehoshua and Oren, Amiram, "Settlements of the Galilee Prior to
Jewish Settlement Projects," Avshalom Shmueli, Arnon Sofer and Nurit Kliot
(eds.), *The Lands of Galilee*, II vols., Haifa: University of Haifa , 1983, I,
pp. 315-352 (Hebrew).
Ben-Artzi, Yossi, *The Creation of the Carmel as a Segregated Jewish Residential
Space in Haifa, 1918-1948,* Jerusalem: Magnes Press, 2004 (Hebrew).
Ben-Artzi, Yossi, and Biger, Gideon, "Transitions in the Settlement Landscape
of the Upper Galilee during the Mandate Period," Avshalom Shmueli, Arnon
Soffer and Nurit Kliot (eds.), *The Lands of Galilee*, II vols., Haifa: University
of Haifa, 1983, I, pp. 443-460 (Hebrew).
Ben-David, Joseph, *The Bedouins in Israel—Land Conflicts and Social Is-
sues,* Jerusalem: Institute for the Study of Land Policy and Land Use, 2004
(Hebrew).
Ben-Shemesh, Aaron, *Land Laws in the State of Israel*, Tel Aviv: Massada,
1953 (Hebrew).
Ben-Zvi, Izhak, *Eretz-Israel under Ottoman Rule: Four Centuries of History,*
Jerusalem: Bialik Institute, 1954/55 (Hebrew).
Berav, Ya'akov, "The Choice Fruits of the Land" (quoted in *Good Sights*, Jeru-
salem: 1974, pp. 14-36 (originally published in Mantova: 1745, Hebrew).
Bergheim, Samuel, Land Tenure in Palestine, *Palestine Exploration Fund
Quarterly Statement* (1894), pp. 191-199.
Biger, Gideon, *An Empire in the Holy Land: Historical Geography of the Brit-
ish Administration in Palestine, 1917-1929,* New York and Jerusalem: St.
Martin's Press and Magnes Press, 1994.
Bitan, Arieh, *Settlement Changes in the Eastern Lower Galilee, 1800-1978,*
Jerusalem: Yad Izhak Ben-Zvi, 1982 (Hebrew).
Boneh, Alfred, *Eretz-Israel: Land and Economy*, Tel Aviv: Dvir, 1937/38
(Hebrew).

Boserup, Ester, *The Conditions of Agricultural Growth: The Economics of Agrarian Change under Population Pressure*, Chicago: Aldine, 1965.

Braslavi (Braslavski), Yosef, *Do You Know the Land?*, IV vols. I: *The Galilee and Northern Valleys*, II: *Land of the Negev (The Northern Negev)*, Tel Aviv: Kibbutz Hameuhad, 1955 (Hebrew).

Braudel, Fernand, *The Perspective of the World*, III vols.,Vol. III: *Civilization and Capitalism*, *15th-18th Century*, trans. Sian Raynolds, New York: Harper and Row, 1984.

Brawer, Moshe, "Migration as a Factor in the Growth of the Arab Village of Palestine," *Merhavim* B (1974/75), pp. 72-81 (Hebrew).

Brawer, Moshe, "The Supply to Jerusalem from its Rural Environment during the Late Nineteenth and Early Twentieth Centuries," *Eretz-Israel* 22 (1991), pp. 45-51. (Hebrew with English abstract).

Burkhardt, John L., *Notes on the Bedouin and the Wahbis Collected during His Travel in the East,* London: Colburn Bently, 1831.

Carmel, Alex, "The Formation, Growth, and Significance of the German Protestant Community in Palestine 1840-1914," Paper presented at a colloquium on Palestine, 1840-1948: Population and Immigration, University of Haifa, 9-11.6.1986.

Clark, Colin and Haswell, Margaret, *The Economics of Subsistence Agriculture,* London: Macmillan, 1970.

Clark, Edward C., "The Ottoman Industrial Revolution," *International Journal of Middle East Studies* 5 (1974), pp. 65-76.

Clay, Christopher, "The Financial Collapse of the Ottoman State 1863-1875," Daniel Panzac (ed.), *Economic and Social History of the Ottoman-Empire and Turkey (1326-1960)*: Proceedings of the Sixth International Conference Held in Aix-en-Provence, 1-4.7.1992, Paris: Peeters, pp. 165-176.

Cohen, Aaron, *The Arab East*, Merhavia: Hakibbutz Haartzi Hashomer HaTsair, 1955 (Hebrew).

Cohen, Amnon, *Palestine in the Eighteenth Century: Patterns of Government and Administration,* Jerusalem: Magnes Press, 1973.

Cohen, Amnon, "Ottoman Rule and the Re-emergence of the Coast of Palestine," *Cathedra* 34 (1985), pp. 55-74 (Hebrew).

Commentary, July and October 1986.

Conder Claud, R. and Kitchener, Horatio H., *The Survey of Western Palestine, Memoirs,* III vols., London: Palestine Exploration Fund, 1881-1883. See also Maps of Palestine, 26 sheets, Palestine Exploration Fund, Scale 1 inch to 1 mile.

Cuinet, Vital, *Syrie, Liban et Palestine: Géographie, administrative, statistique, descriptive et raisonnée*, Paris: Leroux, 1896.

Damty, Immanuel, "Sites and Places in Safad," in *Ariel* 157-158 (2002), pp. 141-145.

Dan, Yoel and Raz, Zvi, *The Soil Association Map of Israel,* Rehovot: Israel, Ministry of Agriculture, 1970 (Hebrew with English abstract).

Dan, Yoel, and Yaalon, Dan H., "The Formation of Soils in the Sharon in Relation to Landscape Characteristics," David Grossman, Avi Degani and Avshalom Shmueli (eds.), *Hasharon Between Yarkon and Karmel*, Tel Aviv: Eretz, 1990, pp. 83-97 (Hebrew).

Davison, Roderic H., *Reform in the Ottoman Empire 1856-1876*, Princeton, NJ: Princeton University Press, 1963.

Deed of Sale between Najib Bey Sursouk and Yehosua Hankin, signed on November 30, 1929 (typescript, Hebrew).

De Haas, Jacob, *History of Palestine: The Last Two Thousand Years*, New York: Macmillan, 1934.

De Planhol, Xavier, "Demographic Pressure and Mountain Life with Special Reference to Alpine-Himalayan Belt," Wilbur Zelinsky, Leszek A. Kosinski and R. Mansell Prothero (eds.), *Geography in a Changing World*, New York: Oxford University Press, 1970, pp. 235-248.

Doumani, Bashara, "Rediscovering Ottoman Palestine: Writing Palestinians into History," *Journal of Middle East Studies* 21 (1992), pp. 5-26.

Doumani, Bashara, "The Political Economy of Population Counts in Ottoman Palestine: Nablus circa 1850," *Journal of Middle East Studies* 36 (1994), pp. 1-17.

Doumani, Bashara, *Rediscovering Palestine: Merchants and Peasants in Jabal Nablus 1700-1900*, Berkeley: University of California Press, 1995.

Duran, Binyamin, "The Ottoman Agriculture 1880–1917," Daniel Panzac (ed.), *Economic and Social History of the Ottoman Empire and Turkey (1326-1960):* Proceedings of the Sixth International Conference Held in Aix-en-Provence, 1-4.7.1992, Paris: Peeters, pp. 165-176.

Efrat, Elisha, "The Population of Safad," *Ariel* 157-158 (2002), pp. 23-24 (Hebrew).

Elazari-Volcani, Isaac, *The Transition from Primitive to Modern Agriculture in Palestine,* Tel Aviv: Hapoel Hazair, 1925 (Hebrew).

Elazari-Volcani, Isaac, *The Fallah's Farm*, Tel Aviv: Jewish Agency for Palestine, Institute of Agriculture and National History, Agricultural Experiment Station, 1930.

Falah, Salman, *History of the Druze in Israel*, Jerusalem: Office of the Advisor on Arab Affairs, 1974/75 (Hebrew).

Falah, Salman, "History of Druze Settlement in Eretz-Israel," Nissim Dana (ed.), *The Druze*, Ramat Gan: Bar-Ilan University, 1997/98, pp. 171-185 (Hebrew).

Finn, James, *Stirring Times or Records from Jerusalem Consular Chronicles of 1853 to 1856*, 2 vols., London: C. Kegan Paul, 1878.

Firestone, Ya'acov, "Land Equalization and Factor Scarcities: Holding Size and the Burden of Imposition in Imperial Russia and the Late Ottoman Levant," *Journal of Economic History* 41 (1981), pp. 813-833.

Firestone, Ya'acov, "Crop Sharing Economics in Mandatory Palestine," Elie Kedouri and Sylvia G. Haim (eds.), *Palestine and Israel in the 19th and 20th Centuries*, II vols., London: Frank Cass, 1982, I, pp. 153-173, II, pp. 175-194.

Firestone, Ya'acov, "The Land Equalizing Mushā' Village: A Reassessment," Gad Gilbar (ed.), *Ottoman Palestine 1840-1948: Studies in Economic and Social History*, Leiden: Brill, 1990, pp. 91-129.

Firro, Kais, "Silk and Socio-Economic Changes in Lebanon 1860-1919," Elie Kedouri and Sylvia G. Haim (eds.), *Essays on the Economic History of the Middle East*, London: Frank Cass, 1988, pp. 20-25.

Firro, Kais, *A History of the Druzes*, Leiden: Brill, 1992.

Frankenstein, Ernst, *Justice for My People*, New York: Dial Press, 1944.

Galbraith, John Kenneth, *The New Industrial State*, Boston: Houghton Mifflin, 1966.

Gavish, Dov, "Land Settlement during the British Mandate Period," Ruth Kark (ed.), *Redemption of the Land of Eretz-Israel*, Jerusalem: Yad Izhak Ben-Zvi, 1990, pp. 185-198 (Hebrew with English abstract).

Gerber, Haim, "The Ottoman Administration of the Sanjaq of Jerusalem 1890-1908," *Asian and African Studies* 12 (1978), pp. 33-76.

Gerber, Haim, "The Population of Syria and Palestine in the Nineteenth Century," *Asian and African Studies* 13 (1979), pp. 58-80.

Giladi, Dan, "Citrus Growing in the Sharon–A Lever to Settlement and Regional Development," David Grossman, Avi Degani and Avshalom Shmueli (eds.), *Hasharon Between Yarkon and Karmel*, Tel Aviv: Eretz, 1990, pp. 397-408 (Hebrew).

Gilbar, Gad G., "Trends in the Demographic Developments of the Palestinian Arabs, 1870-1948," *Cathedra* 45 (1987), pp. 42-56 (Hebrew with English abstract).

Golany, Gideon, "The Settlement Geography of the 'Iron ('Ara) Valley," unpublished Ph.D. dissertation, Hebrew University Jerusalem, 1966 (Hebrew with English abstract).

Golany, Gideon, "The Settlement Geography of a Traditional Village: The Example of Taibeh," Haifa: The Technion, Faculty of Architecture, 1967 (Hebrew, mimeographed).

Golany, Gideon, "The Development of the Human Landscape of the Iron Valley (Wadi 'Ara)," *The New East* 18 (1968), pp. 42-63 (Hebrew with English abstract).

Gorkin, Michael, *Days of Honey Days of Onion: The Story of a Palestinian Family in Israel*, Boston: Beacon Press, 1991.

Gottheil, Fred M., "The Population of Palestine, circa 1875," *Middle Eastern Studies* 15 (1979), pp. 310-321.

Gottheil, Fred M., "Arab Immigration into Pre-State Israel, 1922-1931," Elie Kedouri and Sylvia G. Haim (eds.), *Palestine and Israel in the 19th and 20th Centuries*, II vols., London: Frank Cass, 1982, I, pp. 143-152.

Graham-Brown, Sarah, "The Political Economy of Jabal Nablus 1920-1948," Roger Owen (ed.), *Studies in the Economic and Social History of Palestine in the Nineteenth and Twentieth Centuries*, Carbondale: Illinois University Press, 1982, pp. 88-176.

Granovsky, Abraham, *The Tax System in Eretz-Israel*, Jerusalem: Economic Department of the Jewish Agency for Palestine, 1932/33 (Hebrew).

Granovsky (Granott) Abraham, *The Fiscal System of Palestine*, Jerusalem: Mishar ve-Ta'asia, 1935.

Gross, Nachum T., "Economic Transitions in Palestine at the End of the Ottoman Period," *Cathedra* 2 (1976), pp.111-125 (Hebrew).

Gross, Nachum T., *Not by Spirit Alone, Studies in the Economic History of Modern Palestine and Israel*, Jerusalem: Magnes Press and Yad Izhak Ben-Zvi Press, 1999 (Hebrew).

Gross, Nachum T., and Metzer, Jacob, "Public Finance in Interwar Palestine," Jerusalem: The Maurice Falk Institute, The Institute of Contemporary Jewry, The Hebrew University of Jerusalem, Discussion Paper No. 776, 1977.

Grossman, David, "The Bunched Settlement Pattern: Western Samaria and the Hebron Mountains," *Transactions of the Institute of British Geographers*, New Series, 6 (1981), pp. 491-505.

Grossman, David, "Population Growth in Reference to Land Quality: The Case of Samaria 1922-1975," *Geographical Journal* 147, part 2 (1981), pp. 188-200.

Grossman, David, "The Expansion of the Settlement Frontier on Hebron's Western and Southern Fringes," *Geography Research Forum* 5 (1982), pp. 57-63.

Grossman, David, "The Development of Rural Settlements between the Yarkon and the Ayalon from the Sixteenth to Twentieth Centuries," David Grossman (ed.), *Between Yarkon and Ayalon, Studies on the Tel Aviv Metropolitan Area*, Ramat-Gan: Bar-Ilan University Press, 1983, pp. 87-103 (Hebrew).

Grossman, David, "Land Use Modifications and Population Growth in the Southern Hebron Mountains," Roser Majoral and Francesc Lopez (eds.), *Rural Life and the Exploitation of Natural Resources in Highlands and High-Latitude Zones*, Barcelona: Department of Geography, University of Barcelona, 1984, pp. 153-162.

Grossman, David, "Spatial Analysis of Historical Migration in Samaria," *Geo-Journal* 9, 1984, pp. 393-406.

Grossman, David, "Processes of Development and Retreat in the Rural Settlement of Samaria and Judea during the Ottoman Period," Shimon Dar and Zeev Safrai (eds.), *Shomron Studies*, Tel Aviv: Hakibbutz Hameuchad, 1986, pp. 303-388 (Hebrew).

Grossman, David, "Rural Settlement in the Southern Coastal Plain and the Shefelah, 1835-1945," *Cathedra* 45 (1987), pp. 57-86 (Hebrew with English abstract).

Grossman, David, "Fluctuations in Arab Settlement in the Hebron Mountains as Background for Jewish Land Purchases," Ruth Kark (ed.), *Redemption of the Land of Eretz-Israel*, Jerusalem: Yad Izhak Ben-Zvi, 1990, pp. 218-244 (Hebrew with English abstract).

Grossman, David, "The Implications of Settlement Expansion and Fixation: The Mountains and Their Fringes in Israel and the West Bank," Walter Leimgruber (ed.), *Spatial Dynamics and Ecological Problems in Highlands and High-Latitude Areas*, Fribourg: Institute of Geography, 1990, pp. 65-80.

Grossman, David, "The Arab Settlement Process in Ottoman Times," David Grossman, Avi Degani and Avshalom Shmueli (eds.), *Hasharon Between Yarkon and Karmel*, Tel Aviv: Eretz, 1990, pp. 263-277 (Hebrew).

Grossman, David, *Rural Process-Pattern Relationships, Nomadization, Sedentarization, and Settlement Fixation*, New York: Praeger, 1992.

Grossman, David, "Arab Agriculture in Eretz-Israel Palestine at the End of the Nineteenth Century and the First Decades of the Twentieth Century," Research Report Submitted to The Institute of Land Use Studies, 1993/94 (Hebrew).

Grossman, David, *Expansion and Desertion, The Arab Village and its Offshoots in Ottoman Palestine*, Jerusalem: Yad Izhak Ben-Zvi, 1994 (Hebrew).

Grossman, David, "The Fallah and the Bedouin at the Desert Fringe, Relationships and Subsistence Strategies," David Grossman and Avinoam Meir (eds.), *The Arabs in Israel, Geographical Dynamics*, Ramat Gan: Bar-Ilan University Press, 1994, pp. 21-47 (Hebrew).

Grossman, David, Goldshlager, Naftali, and Bar-Cohen, Anat, "Arab and Druze Settlements in the Carmel and Ramat Menashe Zones," Research Report No. 34, Submitted to the Institute of Land Use Studies, 1994 (Hebrew).

Grossman, David and Kark, Ruth, "Communal Holdings and the Economic Impact of Land Privatization," Walter Leimgruber, Roser Majoral, Chul-Woo Lee (eds.), *Policies and Strategies in Marginal Regions*, Aldergate: Ashgate, 2003, pp. 20-34.

Grossman, David and Kark, Ruth, "Common Pool Management: Implications for Israeli Settlements," *Horizons in Geography* 60-61 (2004), pp. 99-107 (Hebrew).

Guérin, Victor, *Description Géographique, Historique et Archéologique de La Palestine, Accompagnée de Cartes Détaillées,* VII vols., Amsterdam: Oriental Press, 1969 (Reprint of 1880 Paris edition).

Hadawi, Sami, *Palestinian Rights and Losses in 1948: A Comprehensive Study*, London: Saqi Books, 1998.

Hapoel Hatzair, Tishri (September-October), 1908, No.1.

Hartmann, M., "Die Ortschaftliste des Liwa Jerusalem in dem Türkischen Staatkalender für Syrien auf das Jahr 1288 der Flucht (1871)," *Zeitschrift des Deutschen Palästina-Vereins* 6 (1883), pp. 102-149.

Hershlag, Zvi, *Introduction to the Historical Geography of the Modern Middle East*, Jerusalem: Kiryat Sefer, 1964/65 (Hebrew).

Heyd, Uriel, *Dahar el 'Umar, A Ruler of the Galilee in the Eighteenth Century, His Life and Works*, Jerusalem: Reuven Mass, 1942 (Hebrew).

Hoexter, Miriam, "The Role of Qais and Yaman Factions in Local Political Divisions," *Asian and African Studies* 9 (1973), pp. 249-312.

Hofman, Yitzhak, "Muhammed Ali in Syria," unpublished Ph.D. thesis, The Hebrew University of Jerusalem, 1963 (Hebrew).

Holingsworth, A. G. H., *Remarks upon the Present Condition and Future Prospects of the Jews in Palestine,* London: Seeleys, 1852.

Horin, Yehuda, "A Century of Jewish Agriculture," *Economic Quarterly* 113 (1982), pp. 213-218 (Hebrew).

Horowitz, David, *The Development of the Economy of Eretz-Israel*, Tel Aviv: Dvir, 1947/48 (Hebrew).

Horowitz, David and Hinden, Rita, *Economic Survey of Palestine*, Tel Aviv: Economics Research Institute, 1938.

Hütteroth, Wolf D. and Abdulfattah, Kamal, *Historical Geography of Palestine and Southern Syria in the Late Sixteenth Century,* Erlangen: Palm & Enke, 1977.

Ilan, Zvi, "Turkmen, Circassians and Bosnians in the Northern Sharon," David Grossman, Avi Degani and Avshalom Shmueli (eds.), *Hasharon Between Yarkon and Karmel*, Tel Aviv: Eretz, 1990, pp. 279-287 (Hebrew).

Inalcik, Halil, "Military and Fiscal Transformation in the Ottoman Empire 1600-1700," *Archivum Ottomanicum* 6 (1980), pp. 283-337.

Inalcik, Halil and Quataert, Donald (eds.), *An Economic and Social History of the Ottoman Empire 1300-1914*, Cambridge: Cambridge University Press, 1994.

Isaac, Eric and Jean, "Whose Palestine?" *Commentary, July 1986,* pp. 29-37.

Issawi, Charles, *The Fertile Crescent 1800-1914: A Documentary Economic History*, New York: Oxford University Press, 1988.

Izraelit, Elimelekh, *Kastina, A Colony in the South of Eretz-Israel, Conditions and Future*, Jerusalem: (n. p.) 1912 (Hebrew).

al Jaludi, Alian, and al Bakhyat, Muhamad Adnan, *Ajdlun Sub-District during the Ottoman Tanzimat Period,* Amman: Manshirat Lajnat Tarikh al-Urdun, 1992 (Arabic).

Kamen, Charles S., *Little Common Ground: Arab Agriculture and Jewish Settlement, 1920-1948*, Pittsburgh: University of Pittsburgh Press, 1991.

Kark, Ruth, "Jaffa – From Village to Town: Changes in the Urban Structure." David Grssman (ed.), Between *Yarkon and Ayalon, Studies on the Tel Aviv Metropolitan Area*, Ramat-Gan: Bar-Ilan University Press, 1983, pp. 105-124 (Hebrew).

Kark, Ruth, "Agricultural Land and Plans to its Cultivation by Jews during the Early Ottoman Period," *Cathedra* 33 (1984), pp. 57-92 (Hebrew).

Kark, Ruth, "Land Acquisition in Emeq Hefer," David Grossman, Avi Degani and Avshalom Shmueli (eds.), *Hasharon Between Yarkon and Karmel*, Tel Aviv: Eretz, 1990, pp. 345-362 (Hebrew).

Kark, Ruth (ed.), *Redemption of the Land of Eretz-Israel*, Jerusalem: Yad Izhak Ben-Zvi, 1990 (Hebrew with English abstracts).

Kark, Ruth, "Land Purchase and Registration by German-American Templers in Nineteenth-Century Haifa," *International Journal of Turkish Studies* 5 (1990/91), pp. 71-82.

Kark, Ruth, "Land-God-Man: Concepts of Land Ownership in Traditional Cultures in Eretz-Israel," A.R.H. Boker and Gideon Biger (eds.), *Ideology and Landscape in Historical Perspective*, Cambridge: Cambridge University Press, 1992, pp. 63-83.

Kark, Ruth, *American Consuls in the Holy Land 1832-1914*, Jerusalem and Detroit: Magnes Press and Wayne State University Press, 1994.

Kark, Ruth, "The Introduction of Modern Technology into the Holy Land (1800-1914)," T. E. Levi (ed.), *The Archaeology of Society in the Holy Land*, Leicester: Leicester University Press, 1995, pp. 524-541.

Kark, Ruth, "Post Civil War American Millenarian Utopian Commune Linking Chicago, Nas, Sweden, and Jerusalem," *Communal Societies* 15 (1995), pp. 75-113.

Kark, Ruth and Grossman, David, "The Communal (*musha'*) Village of the Middle East and North Africa," Walter Leimgruber, Roser Majoral and Chul-Woo Lee (eds.), *Policies and Strategies in Marginal Regions*, Aldergate: Ashgate, 2003, pp. 223-236.

Kark, Ruth and Oren-Nordheim, Michal, *Jerusalem and its Environs, Quarters, Neighborhoods, Villages 1800-1948*, Jerusalem: Hebrew University Magnes Press. and Detroit: Wayne State University Press, 2001.

Kark, Ruth and Shiloni, Tsvi, "The Resettlement of Gezer," Ely Schiller (ed.), *Zev Vilnay's Jubilee Volume*, Jerusalem: Ariel, 1984, pp. 331-342 (Hebrew).

Karmon, Yehuda, *The Northern Huleh Valley, Its Natural and Cultural Landscape*, Jerusalem: Magnes Press, 1956 (Hebrew).

Karmon, Yehuda, "Physiographic Conditions in the Sharon Plain and their Impact on its Settlement," *Studies in the Geography of Israel* 1 (1959) pp. 111-133 (Hebrew).

Karmon, Yehuda and Shmueli, Avshalom, *Hebron, The Image of a Mountain Town*, Tel Aviv: Gomeh, 1970 (Hebrew).

Karpat, Kemal H., "Ottoman Population Records and the Census of 1881/1893," *International Journal of Middle Eastern Studies* 9 (1978), pp. 237-274.

Karpat, Kemal H., *Ottoman Population 1830-1914: Demographic and Social Characteristics*, Madison: University of Wisconsin Press, 1985.

Kedem, Menachem, "The Endeavors of George Gawler to Establish Jewish Colonies in Eretz Israel," *Cathedra* 33 (1984), pp. 93-106 (Hebrew).

Kimmerling, Baruch, *Zionism and Economy*, Cambridge, MA.: Shenkman, 1983.

Klat, Paul J., "Musha Holdings and Land Fragmentation in Syria," *Middle East Economic Papers* (1957), pp. 12-23.

Klein, F. A., "Land Habits and Customs of the Fallahin of Palestine," *Palestine Exploration Fund Quarterly Statement* (1883), pp. 41-48.

Kressel, Gideon M., *Privacy vs Tribalism, Dynamics of a Bedouin Community in the Process of Urbanization*, Tel Aviv: *Hakibbutz Hameuchad*, 1976 (Hebrew).

Kressel, Gideon M., "The Growth of Bedouin Population in Palestine since the 19th Century: Sociological Aspects of Bedouin Immigration and Fecundity," Paper presented at a colloquium on Palestine 1840-1948: Population and Immigration, University of Haifa, 9-11.6.1986.

Kressel, Gideon M. and Ben-David, Joseph, "The Bedouin Marketplace – Corner Stone for the Founding of Beer-Sheva: Bedouin Traditions About the Development of the Negev Capital in the Ottoman Period," *Nomadic Peoples* 36/37 (1996), pp. 119-144.

Kushnir, David, 'The Last Generation of Ottoman Rule in Palestine, 1864-1914," Moshe Lissak and Gabriel Cohen (eds.), *The History of Jewish Community in Eretz-Israel since 1882, The History of Jewish Settlement in Eretz-Israel since the First Aliyah*, I, *The Ottoman Period*, Jerusalem: Israel Academy for Sciences and Humanities and Bialik Institute, 1989/90, pp. 1-34 (Hebrew).

Kushnir, David, "The Administrative Apparatus of the Districts of Palestine According to the Ottoman Yearbooks, 1864-1914," *Cathedra* 88 (1998), pp. 57-72 (Hebrew with English abstract).

Landau, Jacob M., "Eretz Israel in the Era of 'Abdul Hamid," Jerusalem: Carta, 1979.

Latron, André, *La vie rurale en Syrie et Liban: Etudes d'économie sociale*, Beirouth: L'Institute Francais de Damas, 1936.

Lee, Everett, "A Theory of Migration," *Demography* 3 (1966), pp. 47-57.

Lewis, Norman N., *Nomads and Settlers in Syria and Jordan*, Cambridge: Cambridge University Press, 1987.

Longrigg, Stephen H., *Syria and Lebanon under French Mandate*, London: Oxford University Press, 1958.

Manna', 'Adel, "Eighteenth and Nineteenth Century Rebellions in Palestine," *Journal of Palestine Studies* 24 (1994), pp. 51-66.

Manning, Samuel, *Those Holy Fields* (originally published in 1874, Reprinted by Ely Schiller) Jerusalem: Ariel Publishing House, 1976.

Ma'oz, Moshe, *Ottoman Reforms in Syria and Palestine*, Oxford: Clarendon Press, 1968.

Marsot, Afaf L. A., "Muhammad Ali and Palmerston," Derek Hopgood (ed.), *Studies in Arab History: The Antonius Lectures 1978-87*, London: Macmillan and Oxford: St. Anthony's College, 1990, pp. 61-73.

Marsot, Afaf L. A., *Egypt in the Reign of Muhammad Ali*, Cambridge: Cambridge University Press, 1984.

Marx, Emanuel, *Bedouins of the Negev*, Manchester: Manchester University Press, 1967.

McCarthy, Justin, Age, Family and Migration in Nineteenth Century Black Sea Provinces of the Ottoman Empire, *Journal of Middle East Studies* 10 (1979), pp. 309-323.

McCarthy, Justin, "Population of the Ottoman Fertile Crescent," Paper presented at a colloquium on the Economic History of the Middle East 1800-1914: A Comparative Approach, University of Haifa, 14-19.12.1980.

McCarthy, Justin, "The Population of Ottoman Syria and Iraq 1878-1914," *Asian and African Studies* 15 (1981), pp. 3-44.

McCarthy, Justin, *The Arab World, Turkey and the Balkans (1878-1914): A Handbook of Historical Statistics*, Boston: Hall, 1982.

McCarthy, Justin, *The Population of Palestine*, New York: Columbia University Press, 1990.

McCarthy, Justin, "Palestine Population during the Ottoman and the British Mandate Periods" (Internet, September 2001). http://www.palestineremembered.com/Acre/Palestine-Remembered/Story.

Meir, Avinoam, "Demographic Transition among the Negev Bedouin in Israel and its Planning Implications," *Socio-Economic Planning Sciences,* 18 (1984), pp. 399-409.

Meir, Avinoam, *As Nomadism Ends: The Israeli Bedouin of the Negev*, Boulder, CO: Westview, 1997.

Mendelsohn Rood, Judith, "The I'ana Tax, Conscription and the Urban-Rural Alliance against Muhammad Ali in 1834; The Case of Jerusalem," Daniel Panzac (ed.), *Economic and Social History of the Ottoman Empire and Turkey (1326-1960): Proceedings of the Sixth International Conference Held in Aix-en-Provence, 1-4.7.1992, Paris: Peeters, pp. 415-425.

Mülinen, E. von, "Beiträge zur Kenntnis des Karmels," *Zeitschrift des Deutschen Palästina-Vereins* 30 (1907), pp. 117-207; 31 (1908) (entire volume).

Muslih, Muhammad Y., *The Origin of Palestinian Nationalism*, The Institute of Palestine Studies Series, New York: Columbia University Press, 1988.

Nadan, Amos, "Misunderstanding of an Efficient Peasant Institution: Land Settlement and Musha' Tenure in Mandate Palestine, 1921-47," *Journal of Economic and Social History of the Orient* 46 (2003), pp. 320-354.

Nadan, Amos, *The Palestinian Peasant under the Mandate: A Story of Colonial Bungling*, Cambridge, MA: Harvard University Press, 2006.

Nasr, Vali Rez, "Islamic Economics: Novel Perspectives," *Middle Eastern Studies* 25 (1989), pp. 480-53.

Neophitos of Cyprus, "Extracts from Annals of Palestine 1821-1841," translated by S. N. Spyridon, *Journal of the Palestine Oriental Society* 18, (1938), pp. 63-132 (reprinted by Ely Schiller, Jerusalem: Ariel Publishing House 1979).

Netting, Robert, *Smallholders, Householders*, Stanford, CA: Stanford University Press, 1993.

a-Nimr, Ihsan, *The History of Jabal Nablus and Balqaa*, IV vols. Nablus: Matba'at Jam'iyat 'Amal al-Matbi'i al-Ta'awniyat Bi-Nablus, 1975 (Arabic).

Nir, Dov, *The Beth-She'an Valley, The Region and Its Challenges on the Fringe of the Desert*, 3rd ed., Yitzchak Kavkafi (ed.), Tel Aviv: Hakibbutz Hameuchad, 1989 (Hebrew).

Notestein, Frank Wallace, *Some Aspects of Population Change in Developing Countries*, New York: The American Assembly, Columbia University, 1965.

Ofer, Pinchas, "Consolidation of the Mandatory System and Laying the Foundations of a Jewish National Home 1922-1931," Moshe Lissak and Gabriel Cohen (eds.), *The History of Jewish Community in Eretz-Israel since 1882, The Period of the British Mandate I,* Jerusalem: Israel Academy for Sciences and Humanities and Bialik Institute, 1993, pp. 223-328 (Hebrew).

Okyar, Osman, "Economic Growth, Land, Technological Change and Investment in the Ottoman Empire," Paper presented at a colloquium on the Economic History of the Middle East 1800-1914: A Comparative Approach, University of Haifa, 14-19.12.1980.

Oliphant, Laurence, *Haifa or Life in Modern Palestine*, New York: Harper, 1887.

Pagis, Jonathan (ed.), *Ottoman Population Censuses in Palestine, 1875-1918,* Jerusalem: State Archives, 1997 (Hebrew).

Pamuk, Sevket, *The Ottoman Empire and European Capitalism: Trade, Investment and Production*, Cambridge: Cambridge University Press, 1987.

Panzac, Daniel, *La peste dans l'empire ottoman 1700-1850*, Leuven: Peeters, 1985.

Panzac, Daniel (ed.), *Economic and Social History of the Ottoman-Empire and Turkey (1326-1960)*: Proceedings of the Sixth International Conference Held in Aix-en-Provence, 1-4.7.1992, Paris: Peeters.

Parfitt, Tudor, *The Jews in Palestine 1800-1882*, Woodbridge: Boydell Press, 1987.

Parkes, James, *A History of Palestine from 135 A.D. to Modern Times*, London: Gollancz, 1949.

Patai, Raphael, Musha' Tenure and Cooperation in Palestine, *American Anthropologist* 51 (1949), pp. 436-445.

Patai, Raphael, *The Arab Mind*, New York: Charles Scribner's Sons, 1973.

Perroux, F., "Note sur la notion de 'pôle de croissance,'" *Economie Appliquée* 8, 1955.

Peters, Joan, *From Time Immemorial: The Origin of the Arab-Jewish Conflict over Palestine*, New York: Harper & Row, 1984.

Philipp, Thomas, "The Rise and Fall of Acre: Population and Economy between 1700 and 1856," Paper presented at a colloquium on Palestine 1840-1948: Population and Immigration, University of Haifa, 9-11.6.1986.

Pitrie, Flinders, *The Revival of Palestine*, [n.p., n.d]

Poliak, Avraham Nahum, *Feudalism in Egypt, Syria, Palestine and the Lebanon, 1250-1900*, London: Royal Asian Society, 1939.

Porath, Yehoshua, *From Disturbances to Rebellion, The Arab National Movement in Palestine, 1929-1939*, Tel Aviv: Am Oved: 1978 (Hebrew).

Porath, Yehoshua, *New York Review of Books*, March 27, 1986.

Porath, Yehoshua, Letters, *Commentry*, October, 1986, p. 5.

Porter, Philip W., "The Concept of Environmental Potential as Exemplified by Tropical African Research," Wilbur Zelinsky, Leszek A. Kosinski, and R. Mansell Prothero (eds.), *Geography in a Crowding World*, New York: Oxford University Press, 1970, pp. 187-219.

Post, George E., "Land Tenure, Agriculture, Physical, Mental and Moral Characteristics," *Palestine Exploration Fund Quarterly Statement* (1891), pp. 99-147.

Rafeq, Abdul-Karim, "Land Tenure Problems and Their Social Impact in Syria around the Middle of the Nineteenth Century," Tarif Khalidi (ed.), *Land Tenure and Social Transformation in the Middle East*, Beirut: American University of Beirut, 1984, pp. 371-396.

Reichman, Shalom, *From Foothold to Settled Territory: The Jewish Settlement, 1918-1948, A Geographical Interpretation and Documentation*, Jerusalem: Yad Izhak Ben Zvi, 1979 (Hebrew).

Reichman, Shalom, Katz, Yossi, and Paz, Yair, "The Absorptive Capacity of Palestine, 1882-1948: A Geographic Appraisal," *Eretz-Israel* 22 (1991), pp. 206-220 (Hebrew with English abstract).

Reuveny, Ya'akov, *The Administration of Palestine under the British Mandate, An Institutional Analysis,* Ramat Gan: Bar-Ilan University, 1993 (Hebrew).

Robinson, Edward and Smith, Eli, *Biblical Researches in Palestine Mount Sinai and Arabia Petraea: A Journal of Travels in the Year 1838*, III vols., Boston: Brewster, 1841.

Robinson, Edward and Smith, Eli, *Later Biblical Researches in Palestine and in the Adjacent Regions: A Journal of Travels in the Year 1852*, London: Murray, 1856

Rogan, Eugene, Ottomans, Merchants and Tribes in the Syrian Frontier (1867-1900), Daniel Panzac (ed.), *Economic and Social History of the Ottoman-Empire and Turkey (1326-1960)*: Proceedings of the Sixth International Conference Held in Aix-en-Provence, 1-4.7.1992, Paris: Peeters, pp. 251-262.

Rokach, Y., *The Orchards Speak*, Ramat Gan: Masada, 1970 (Hebrew).

Ron, Zvi, "Agricultural Terraces in the Judean Hills," *Israel Exploration Journal* 6 (1966), pp. 33-49, 111-122.

Ron, Zvi, Y. D., "Development and Management of Irrigation Systems in Mountain Regions of the Holy Land," *Transactions: Institute of British Geographers*, New.Series, 10 (1985) pp. 149-169.

Rosenan, N., "One Hundred Years of Rainfall in Jerusalem: A Homotopic Series of Annual Amounts," *Israel Exploration Journal* 5 (1955), pp. 137-155.

Ruppin, Arthur, "Syrien als Wirtschafsgebeit," Berlin: Kolonial Wirtschaftliches Komitee, 1917.

Ruppin, Arthur, *The Jews in the Modern World*, London: Macmillan, 1934.

Ruppin, Arthur, *Thirty Years of Building in Eretz-Israel*, Jerusalem: Schocken, 1936/37 (Hebrew).

Rustum, Asad J., *The Royal Archives of Egypt and the Causes of the Egyptian Expedition to Syria*, Beirut: American Press, 1936.

Sabri, M., *L'empire egyptien sous Mohamed-Ali et la question d'Orient 1811-1849*, Paris: Lib. Orientaliste Paul Geuthner, 1930.

Saleh, Shakib, *History of the Druzes*, Ramat Gan: Bar-Ilan University Press, 1989 (Hebrew).

Salibi, Kamal Suleiman, *The Modern History of Lebanon*, New York: Praeger, 1965.

Sar Shalom, Rahamim, *Gateway to the Hebrew Calendar*, Natanya: Pub. by author, 1983/84 (Hebrew).

Schatkowski-Schilcher, Linda, "Violence in Rural Syria in the 1880s and 1890s: Some Centralization, Rural Integration and the World Market," Farhad Kazemi and John Waterbury (eds.), *Peasants and Politics in the Middle East*, Miami, FL: International University Press, 1991.

Schick, Conrad, "Zur einwohnerzahl des bezirks Jerusalem," *Zeitschrift des Deutschen Palästina Vereins* 19 (1896), pp. 120-127.

Schilcher, Linda, "The Grain Economy of Late Ottoman Syria and the Issue of Large-Scale Commercialization," Caglar Keyder and Faruk Tabak (eds.), *Landholding and Commercial Agriculture in the Middle East*, Albany: State University of New York Press, 1991, pp. 173-195.

Schmelz, Uziel O., *Modern Jerusalem's Demographic Evolution*, Jerusalem: The Jerusalem Institute for Israel Studies, 1987.

Schmelz, Uziel O., Review of *The Population of Palestine* by Justin McCarthy, *Middle Eastern Studies* 28 (1992), pp. 803-807.

Schölch, Alexander, "European Penetration and the Economic Development of Palestine 1856-82," R. Owen (ed.), *Studies in the Economic and Social History of Palestine in the Nineteenth and Twentieth Centuries*, Carbondale: Illinois University Press, 1982, pp. 10-87.

Schölch, Alexander, "The Demographic Development of Palestine 1850-1882," *International Journal of Middle East Studies* 17 (1985), pp. 485-505.

Schölch, Alexander, *Palestine in Transformation 1856-1882: Studies in Social, Economic and Political Development,* trans. W. C. Young and M. C. Gerrity, Washington, DC: Institute for Palestine Studies, 1993.

Schultz, Theodore W., *Transforming Traditional Agriculture*, New Haven, CT: Yale University Press, 1964.

Schumacher, Gottlieb, "Population List of the Liva of Acca," *Palestine Exploration Fund Quarterly Statement* (1887), pp. 169-181.

Schumacher, Gottlieb, "Researches in the Plain North of Caesarea," *Palestine Exploration Fund Quarterly Statement* (1887), pp. 83-84.

Schur, Nathan, "The Numerical Relationship between the Number of Households and the Total Population in the Cities of Eretz-Israel in the Ottoman Period," *Cathedra* 17 (1980), pp. 102-106 (Hebrew).

Schur, Nathan, *History of Safed*, Tel Aviv: Am Oved, 1983 (Hebrew).

Schur, Nathan, "The Change that Occurred in the Size of Households in Eretz Israel during the Ottoman Period and its Significance," *Israel People and Land, Israel Museum Yearbook* n.s. 22 (1986/87), pp. 251-252 (Hebrew with English abstract).

Schwöbel, V., "Die Verkehrswege und Ansiedlungen Galiläas in ihrer Abhängigkeit von den natürlichen Bedingungen," *Zeitschrift des Deutschen Paläestina-Vereins* 27 (1904), pp. 1-149.

Shechter, Yitzhak, "Land Registration in Eretz-Israel in the Second Half of the 19th Century, *Cathedra* 45 (1987), pp. 147-160 (Hebrew with English abstract).

Shiller, Ely, "The Earthquake in Safad in the Year 1837," *Ariel* 157-158 (2002), pp. 106-112 (Hebrew).

Socin, Albert, "Alphabetisches verzeichniss von ortschaften des Paschalik Jerusalem," *Zeitscrift des Deutschen Paläestina-Vereins* 2 (1879), pp. 135-163.

Soffer, Arnon, "A Note on the Demography of Arab Settlements on the Coastal Plain of Palestine," Paper presented at a colloquium on Palestine 1840-1948: Population and Immigration, University of Haifa, 9-11.6.1986.

Stein, Kenneth W., "Laws Protecting the Rights of Sharecroppers and How They Were Bypassed in Mandatorial Palestine," *The New East* 29 (1979/80), pp. 66-88 (Hebrew with English abstract).

Stein, Kenneth W., *The Land Question in Palestine 1917-1939*, Chapel Hill: University of North Carolina Press, 1984.

Stein, Kenneth, W., "The Political Implication of Palestine's Rural Economy," *Cathedra* 41 (1986), pp. 133-154 (Hebrew with English abstract).

Stein, Kenneth, W., "Rural Change and Peasant Destitution: Contributing Causes to the Arab Revolt in Palestine 1936-1939," Farhad Kazemi and John Waterbury (eds.), *Peasants and Politics in the Middle East*, Miami: Florida International University Press, 1991, pp. 143-170.

Stepansky, Yosef, "Safad and its Environs in Ancient Times," *Ariel* 157-58 (2002), pp. 51-58 (Hebrew).

"Survey of Social and Economic Conditions in Arab Villages," *General Monthly of Current Statistics* (1944), pp. 426-447.

Tabak, Faruk, "Agrarian Fluctuations and Modes of Labor Control in the Western Arc of the Fertile Crescent c. 1700-1800," Caglar Keyder and Faruk Tabak (eds.), *Landholding and Commercial Agriculture in the Middle East*, Albany: State University of New York Press, 1991, pp. 135-154.

Thalmann, Naftali, "The Character and Development of the Farm Economy in the Templer Colonies in Palestine 1869-1930," unpublished Ph.D. dissertation, The Hebrew University of Jerusalem, 1991 (Hebrew with English abstract).

Thomson, W. V., *The Land and the Book*, London: Nelson, 1894.

Tolkovski, Shmuel, *Citrus Fruits*, Jerusalem: Bialik Institute, 1965/66 (Hebrew).

Tristram, Henry Baker, *The Land of Israel, A Journal of Travels in Palestine Undertaken with Special Reference to its Physical Character, Diary 1863-1864*, London: Society for Promoting Christian Knowledge,1866.

Twain, Mark (Samuel L. Clemens), *The Innocents Abroad or: The New Pilgrims' Progress*, New York: Heritage Press, 1962 (originally published 1869).

Vilan, Avraham, "The Demographic Development of the Arabs in Eretz-Israel (1919-1946) Migration or Population Growth?" unpublished Master's thesis, Tel Aviv University, 2006 (Hebrew with English abstract).

Volney, M. C-F., *Travels through Syria and Egypt in the Years 1783-1785*, II vols., London: Robinson, 1787.

Weitz, Yosef, *Hasharon,* Tel Aviv: Omanut, 1939 (Hebrew).

Weullersse, Jacques, *Paysans de Syrie et du Proche-Orient*, Paris: Gallimard, 1946.

Wilson, Charles W., *The Land of Judea & The Jerusalem Environs* (originally published in 1880 under the title *Picturesque Palestine Sinai and Egypt*), Jerusalem: Ariel Publishing House, 1976.

Ya'ari, Avraham, *Memories of Eretz-Israel*, II vols., Jerusalem: Zionist Organization, 1946/47 (Hebrew).

Ya'ari, Avraham, *Letters from Eretz-Israel*, Ramat Gan: Massada, 1971 (Hebrew).

Ya'ari, Avraham and Harizman, M., *Jubilee Volume in Honor of Petach Tikva's Foundation*, Tel Aviv: Jubilee Volume Committee, 1928/29 (Hebrew).

Yapp, Malcome E., *The Making of the Modern Near East, 1792-1923*, London: Longman, 1987.

Yazbak, Mahmud, *Haifa in the Nineteenth Century: History of the City and the Society*, Haifa: The Jewish-Arab Center, University of Haifa, 1998 (Hebrew).

Zimmerman, Erich W., *World Resources and Industries*, revised edition, New York: Harper, 1951.

Zipf, George Kingsley, *Human Behavior and the Principle of Least Effort*, Reading, MA: Addison-Wesley, 1949.

Public Documents and Official Reports

Nineteenth Century and Mandate Period Reports

Bowring, John, Report on the Commercial Statistics of Syria, London: H.M.S.O., 1840.

French, Louis, Report on Agricultural Development and Land Settlement in Palestine, II vols., London: H.M.S.O., 1931-1932.

Government of Palestine, Report and General Abstracts of the Census of 1922, taken on the 23rd of October, 1922, Jerusalem: H.M.P.O., 1923.

Government of Palestine, *Census of Palestine*, Jerusalem, H.M.P.O., 1932.

Great Britain, Colonial Office, Palestine, Statement of Policy by his Majesty's Government in the United Kingdom, presented by the Secretary for the Colony, (Passfield Report), London: H.M.S.O., October 1930.

Hyamson, Albert M. (ed.), The British Consulate in Jerusalem in Relation to the Jews of Palestine, 1838-1914, Part I: 1838-1861; Part II: 1862-1914, London: Edward Goldston, 1941.

Johnson, William J. and Crosbie, R. E. H. Report of the Committee to Examine into the Economic Condition of Agriculturalists and the Fiscal Measures of Government in Relation Thereto, 1930 (Published pamphlet. The original document, File C.O. 733/185/77072 (see below, Great Britain, Colonial Office), is cited in this book

Palestine, Index to Villages & Settlements, Jerusalem: Survey Department, 1946 (Map Scale 1:250,000).

Palestine, Report on Palestine Administration for 1922, London: H.M.S.O., 1923.

Palestine, Village Statistics, 1945, Jerusalem: Government Printer, 1946.

Palestine Royal Commission, Report (Peel Report), London: H.M.S.O., 1937 (Cmd. 5479).

Simpson, John Hope, Report on Immigration, Land Settlement and Development, London: H.M.S.O., 1930.

Archival Files of the British Foreign Office (Microfilm)

FO 195/808 - Great Britain, Foreign Office.

FO 406/3, FO 406/5, FO 406/6 - Great Britain, Foreign Office, correspondence relative to the Levant 1839-1841.

Collections of British Documents

BD/5, Gillard, D. (ed.), Near and Middle East 1856-1914, The Ottoman Empire in the Aftermath of the Treaty of Berlin 1878-1883.

BD/7, Gillard, D. (ed.), The Near and Middle East 1856-1914, The Ottoman Empire, Finance and Trade 1869-1879.

BD/20, Gillard, D. (ed.), The Near and Middle East 1856-1914, The Ottoman Empire: Under the Young Turks 1908-1914.

Files of the Great Britain, Colonial Office of Palestine for the years 1926-1934

C.O. 733/185/77072/I-IV (It is referred to as "Johnson and Crosbie": see above).

C.O. 733/192/77304.

C.O. 773/207/87275.

C.O. 773/224/97270.

C.O. 773/244/17470.

C.O. 773/267/37560.

United States of America Consular Files from Jerusalem 1856-1906
RG 59 T-471 = United States of America, Department of State, U.S. Consuls'
    Dispatches from Jerusalem, Palestine, National Archives 1856-1906, Mi-
    crofilm
RG 59 T-471, 9 rolls, Washington, D.C.: G.P.O.
United States of America, Commercial Documents and Publications
United States of America, Department of State, Bureau of Statistics, Annual
    Report on the Commercial Relations between the United States and Foreign
    Nations for the year [listed below] ending September 30, Washington, D.
    C.: G. P.O.
CR, 1878; CR, 1880; CR, 1884; CR, 1889; CR, 1902.

Papers Relating to the Foreign Relations of the United States

FR, 1.12.1879 Transmitted to Congress with the Annual Message of the Presi-
    dent, Washington, D. C.: G. P. O., 1.12.1879.

Files of the Central Zionist Archives

Files of Avraham Granot, A202/146A.
Jewish Agency for Palestine, Memorandum submitted to the Palestine Royal
    Commission, London: Jewish Agency for Palestine, 1936.

Israel State Archives

Files of the German Consul in Jerusalem DKJ, A.III.
Nüfus Book, (Vital Registration Records) Daftar 352.

Various Ottoman Documents

Salnames (Provincial Yearbook) Vilayet Suriye according to H 1288; 1298,
    1300. Salnames Aliyah Othmaniya (National Yearbook) H 1312; 1314;
    1317; 1324; 1326

Name Index

Subject Index

Printed in Great Britain
by Amazon

41247988R00139